Multistate Corporate Tax Course

2012 EDITION

JOHN C. HEALY, MST, CPA
MICHAEL S. SCHADEWALD, PhD, CPA

CCH
a Wolters Kluwer business

Contributors

Authors ....John C. Healy, MST, CPA
Michael S. Schadewald, PhD, CPA
Technical Review.. Sharon Brooks, CPA
Production Coordinator ....Sharon Sofinski
Production .... Lynn J. Brown
Layout & Design... Laila Gaidulis

This publication is designed to provide accurate and authoritative information in regard to the subject matter covered. It is sold with the understanding that the publisher is not engaged in rendering legal, accounting, or other professional service. If legal advice or other expert assistance is required, the services of a competent professional person should be sought.

ISBN 978-0-8080-2709-6

© 2011 CCH. All Rights Reserved.
4025 W. Peterson Ave.
Chicago, IL 60646-6085
1 800 344 3734
www.CCHGroup.com

Printed in the United States of America

MULTISTATE CORPORATE TAX COURSE (2012 EDITION)

Introduction

The state tax laws are always changing. The complex interrelationship of phased-in and delayed new law effective dates, changing state revenue department rules, and an ever-changing mix of taxpayer wins and losses in the courts creates the need for the tax practitioner to constantly stay on top of the new rules and reassess tax strategies at the start of every year. The rules this year are different from the rules last year, and the rules next year promise to be different from those governing this year. This is a fact of life for the modern-day state tax practitioner.

CCH's *Multistate Corporate Tax Course (2012 Edition)* is a helpful resource that provides explanations of significant laws, regulations, decisions and issues that affect multistate tax practitioners. Readers get guidance, insights and analysis on important provisions and their impact on multistate tax compliance and tax planning. This Course is the top quality tax review and analysis that every state tax practitioner needs to keep a step ahead.

The topics covered in the Course include:
- Principles of Multistate Corporate Income Taxation
- State Treatment of Net Operating Losses (NOLs)
- Nexus Standards for Foreign (Non-U.S.) Corporations
- Common State Modifications to Federal Tax Base
- Nexus
- Construction Contractors and Manufacturers
- Sales and Use Tax Treatment of Services
- Electronic Sales Tax Issues

Throughout the Course you will find comments that are vital to understanding a particular strategy or idea, Examples to illustrate the topics covered, and Study Questions to help you test your knowledge. Answers to the Study Questions, with feedback on both correct and incorrect responses are provided in a special section beginning on page 195.

To assist you in your later reference and research, a detailed topical index has been included for this Course beginning on page 215.

This Course is divided into two Modules. Take your time and review each Course Module. When you feel confident that you thoroughly understand the material, turn to the CPE Quizzer. Complete one or both Module Quizzers for Continuing Professional Education credit. You can complete and return the Quizzers to CCH for grading at an additional charge. If you receive a grade of 70 percent or higher on the Quizzers, you will receive CPE credit for the Modules graded. Further information is provided in the CPE Quizzer instructions on page 227.

September 2011

COURSE OBJECTIVES

This Course was prepared to provide the participant with an overview of multistate tax issues. Upon Course completion, you will be able to:

- Explain how state taxable income is generally calculated
- Describe the different types of apportionment formulas
- Describe the impact of state NOL appportionment methods on state NOL deductions
- Identify the limitations that states may place on NOL deductions
- Recognize that a corporation may have nexus for state purposes without having nexus for federal purposes
- Identify the protections afforded by Public Law 86-272
- Differentiate between the transactional and functional tests for determining whether an item of income is business or nonbusiness
- Define which activities of a multistate corporation may create nexus
- Determine how a construction contractor's varying roles can affect its sales and use tax liability
- Identify the sales and use tax exemptions for manufacturing equipment and the requirements for eligibility
- Describe the issues involved in determining the sale and use tax treatment of professional, advertising, architectural, printing, and carrier services
- Explain the sales and use tax issues involved with electronic data transmission and telecommunications services
- Describe the state taxability of canned and custom software

CCH'S PLEDGE TO QUALITY

Thank you for choosing this CCH Continuing Education product. We will continue to produce high quality products that challenge your intellect and give you the best option for your Continuing Education requirements. Should you have a concern about this or any other CCH CPE product, please call our Customer Service Department at 1-800-248-3248.

NEW ONLINE GRADING gives you immediate 24/7 grading with instant results and no Express Grading Fee.

The **CCH Testing Center** website gives you and others in your firm easy, free access to CCH print Courses and allows you to complete your CPE Quizzers online for immediate results. Plus, the **My Courses** feature provides convenient storage for your CPE Course Certificates and completed Quizzers.

Go to **www.CCHGroup.com/TestingCenter** to complete your Quizzer online.

One **complimentary copy** of this **Course** is provided with certain CCH publications. Additional copies may be ordered for $39.00 each by calling 1-800-248-3248 (ask for product **0-4459-500**). Grading fees are additional.

MULTISTATE CORPORATE TAX COURSE (2012 EDITION)

Contents

Principles of Multistate Corporate Income Taxation

This chapter discusses the basic principles involved in multistate corporate income taxation, including nexus, apportionment, combined unitary reporting, and tax-planning strategies.

LEARNING OBJECTIVES

Upon completion of this chapter, the reader should be able to:

- Identify which activities of a multistate corporation can create nexus
- Explain how state taxable income is generally calculated
- Describe the different types of apportionment formulas
- Contrast the difference between state consolidated returns and combined unitary reporting, and how states stand on this issue
- Describe several basic multistate tax-planning strategies
- Explain the cost-of-performance rule and market-based approach for sourcing sales
- Describe the different ways in which nexus can be created
- Identify which states currently impose unconventional business taxes

INTRODUCTION

Forty-five states and the District of Columbia impose some type of income-based tax on corporations. Nevada, Ohio, South Dakota, Washington, and Wyoming do not levy a corporate income tax. However, Ohio does impose a gross receipts tax called the *commercial activity tax*, and Washington imposes a gross receipts tax called the *business and occupation tax*. Texas imposes a tax on gross margin, called the *margin tax*, and Michigan imposes both a modified gross receipts tax and a business income tax.

The corporate income taxes of California, Florida, New York, and a number of other states are formally franchise taxes imposed on, for example, the privilege of doing business in the state. Nevertheless, because the value of the franchise is measured by the income derived from that privilege, the tax is computed in essentially the same manner as a direct income tax.

This course on multistate corporate income taxation is organized into two sections, as follows:

- Basic Principles
  - Nexus
  - Computation of State Taxable Income
  - Distinction Between Business and Nonbusiness Income
  - Apportionment Formulas
  - Sales Factor
  - Property Factor
  - Payroll Factor
  - Consolidated Returns and Combined Unitary Reporting
  - Concept of a Unitary Business
  - Basic Multistate Tax Planning Strategies
- Advanced Concepts
  - Nexus
  - Specialized Industry Apportionment Formulas
  - Sourcing Sales of Services
  - Non-Income Taxes—Michigan, Ohio, Texas, and Washington
  - Mechanisms Used by States to Limit Income Shifting
  - Pass-Through Entities

BASIC PRINCIPLES

Nexus

Constitutional nexus. A threshold issue for any corporation operating in more than one state is determining the states in which it must file returns and pay income tax. A state has jurisdiction to tax a corporation organized in another state only if the out-of-state corporation's contacts with the state are sufficient to create nexus. Historically, states have asserted that virtually any type of in-state business activity creates nexus for an out-of-state corporation. This approach reflects the reality that it is politically more appealing to collect taxes from out-of-state corporations than to raise taxes on in-state business interests. The desire of state lawmakers and tax officials to, in effect, export the local tax burden is counterbalanced by the Due Process Clause and Commerce Clause of the U.S. Constitution, both of which limit a state's ability to impose a tax obligation on an out-of-state corporation.

The landmark case on constitutional nexus is ***Quill Corp. v. North Dakota*** [504 US 298 (1992)]. Quill was a mail-order vendor of office supplies that solicited sales through catalogs mailed to potential customers in North Dakota and made deliveries through common carriers. Quill was incorporated in Delaware and had facilities in California, Georgia, and Illinois. Quill had no office, warehouse, retail outlet, or other facility in

North Dakota nor were any Quill employees or representatives physically present in North Dakota. During the years in question, Quill made sales to roughly 3,000 North Dakota customers and was the sixth largest office supply vendor in the state.

Under North Dakota law, Quill was required to collect North Dakota use tax on its mail-order sales to North Dakota residents. Quill challenged the constitutionality of this tax obligation. The Supreme Court held that Quill's economic presence in North Dakota was sufficient to satisfy the Due Process Clause's "minimal connection" requirement. On the other hand, the Court ruled that an economic presence was not, by itself, sufficient to satisfy the Commerce Clause's "substantial nexus" requirement. Consistent with its ruling 25 years earlier in *National Bellas Hess, Inc. v. Department of Revenue* [386 US 753 (1967)], the Court ruled that a substantial nexus exists only if a corporation has a nontrivial physical presence in a state. In other words, the Court ruled that a physical presence is an essential prerequisite to establishing constitutional nexus, at least for sales and use tax purposes.

The Court did not address the issue of whether the physical presence test also applied for income tax purposes, which has resulted in a significant amount of controversy and litigation. (See discussion below under the heading "Economic nexus.")

Public Law 86-272. Congress enacted Public Law 86-272 in 1959 to provide multistate corporations with a limited safe harbor from the imposition of state income taxes. Specifically, Public Law 86-272 prohibits a state from imposing a "net income tax" on a corporation organized in another state if the corporation's only in-state activity is (1) solicitation of orders by company representatives, (2) for sales of tangible personal property, (3) which orders are sent outside the state for approval or rejection, and (4) if approved, are filled by shipment or delivery from a point outside the state.

Although Public Law 86-272 can provide significant protections for a multistate business, it has several important limitations. First, it applies only to taxes imposed on net income and provides no protection against the imposition of a sales and use tax collection obligation, property taxes, gross receipts taxes (e.g., Ohio commercial activity tax, or Washington business and occupation tax), or corporate franchise taxes on net worth or capital.

Second, Public Law 86-272 protects only sales of tangible personal property. It does not protect activities such as leasing tangible personal property, selling services, selling or leasing real estate, or selling or licensing intangibles.

Third, for businesses that send employees into other states to sell tangible personal property, Public Law 86-272 applies only if those employees limit their in-state activities to the solicitation of orders that are sent outside the state for approval and, if approved, are filled by a shipment or delivery from a point outside the state.

> **EXAMPLE**
>
> If a salesperson exercises an authority to approve orders within a state, the company does not qualify for protection under Public Law 86-272. Likewise, Public Law 86-272 does not protect the presence of a salesperson who performs nonsolicitation activities, such as repairs, customer training, or technical assistance, within a state.

Although Public Law 86-272 does not define the phrase *solicitation of orders*, the meaning of the phrase was addressed by the U.S. Supreme Court in ***Wisconsin Department of Revenue v. William Wrigley, Jr., Co.*** [505 US 214 (1992)]. In this case, the Court defined *solicitation of orders* as encompassing "requests for purchases" as well as "those activities that are entirely ancillary to requests for purchases—those that serve no independent business function apart from their connection to the soliciting of orders." Examples of activities that might serve an independent business function, apart from the solicitation of orders, include:

- Installation and start-up
- Customer training
- Engineering and design assistance
- Technical assistance
- Maintenance and repair
- Credit and collection

STUDY QUESTIONS

> **1.** Which of the following states does **not** impose a corporate income tax?
>
> **a.** Alabama
> **b.** California
> **c.** Florida
> **d.** South Dakota
>
> **2.** Which of the following is **not** true of Public Law 86-272?
>
> **a.** It applies only to a net income tax.
> **b.** It protects only sales of intangible personal property.
> **c.** For businesses that send employees into other states to sell tangible personal property, Public Law 86-272 applies only if those employees limit their in-state activities to the solicitation of orders that are approved out-of-state and are filled by shipment or delivery from a point outside the state.

Computation of State Taxable Income

Most states that impose a corporate income tax use either the corporation's federal taxable income before the net operating loss and special deductions (federal Form 1120, Line 28) or the corporation's net federal taxable income (federal Form 1120, Line 30) as the starting place for computing state taxable income. The states that do not tie the computation of state taxable income directly to a corporation's federal tax return typically adopt the majority of the federal provisions governing items of gross income and deduction in defining the state tax base.

A corporation's state income tax liability generally is computed using the following steps:

1. Begin with the amount of federal taxable income, which is the amount on Line 28 or Line 30 of the federal corporate income tax return, Form 1120. Add to (or subtract from) that amount the state addition and subtraction modifications. The resulting amount is the state tax base.
2. If applicable, subtract from (or add to) the state tax base the total net allocable nonbusiness income (loss). The resulting amount is the total apportionable business income (loss).
3. Multiply the total apportionable business income (loss) by the state's apportionment percentage. The resulting amount is the business income (loss) apportioned to the state.
4. Add to (or subtract from) the business income apportioned to the state the total net allocable nonbusiness income (loss), if applicable, that is allocated to the state. The resulting amount is the state taxable income (loss).
5. Multiply the state taxable income by the state tax rate to determine the state tax liability before credits.
6. Subtract the state's tax credits from the state tax liability to arrive at the net income tax liability for the state.

The use of the federal tax base as the starting point for computing state taxable income is referred to as "piggybacking." Conformity with federal provisions simplifies tax compliance for multistate corporations, but complete conformity with the federal tax laws would effectively cede control over state tax policy to the federal government. States also must be wary of the effects of federal tax law changes on state tax revenues. Therefore, although federal taxable income generally is used as the starting point in computing state taxable income, numerous state modifications are required to reflect differences in federal and state policy objectives, as well to eliminate income that a state is constitutionally prohibited from taxing.

The modifications to federal taxable income vary significantly among the states. Common addition modifications include the following:

- Interest income received on state and municipal debt obligations
- State income taxes
- Federal net operating loss carryover deductions
- Federal dividends-received deductions
- Royalties and interest expense paid to related parties
- Expenses related to state tax credits
- Federal domestic production activities deduction under Internal Revenue Code ("the Code") Sec. 199
- Expenses related to income that is exempt for state tax purposes
- Federal bonus depreciation under Code Sec. 168(k)
- Federal Code Sec. 179 asset expensing

Common subtraction modifications include the following:

- Interest income received on federal debt obligations
- State net operating loss carryover deductions
- State dividends-received deductions
- Expenses related to federal tax credits
- Federal Subpart F income with respect to foreign subsidiaries
- Federal Code Sec. 78 gross-up income

Distinction Between Business and Nonbusiness Income

In 1957, a group of state tax officials promulgated the Uniform Division of Income for Tax Purposes Act (UDITPA) to provide uniformity among the states with respect to the taxation of multistate corporations. UDITPA has been adopted, at least in part, by many states. In an attempt to distinguish income derived from a corporation's regular trade or business from income derived from any activities that are unrelated to that trade or business, UDITPA makes a distinction between business income and nonbusiness income. Under the UDITPA approach, a taxpayer apportions a percentage of its business income to each state in which it has nexus, but specifically allocates the entire amount of any nonbusiness income to a single state [UDITPA §§4 and 9]. Therefore, the principal consequence of classifying an item as nonbusiness income is that the income is excluded from the tax base of every nexus state except the state in which the nonbusiness income is taxable in full (e.g., the state of commercial domicile). Because the classification of an item as nonbusiness income can effectively remove the income from the tax base of one or more nexus states, the business versus nonbusiness income distinction has historically been an area of significant controversy between taxpayers and state tax authorities.

The distinction between business and nonbusiness income is related to the constitutional restrictions on the ability of a state to tax an out-of-state corporation. Based on these constitutional protections, taxpayers have challenged the ability of nexus states to tax an item of income that the taxpayer believes has no relationship to the business activity conducted in the state. As the Supreme Court stated in *Allied-Signal, Inc. v. Division of Taxation* [504 US 768 (1992)], "the principle that a State may not tax value earned outside its borders rests on the fundamental requirement of both the Due Process and Commerce Clauses that there be 'some definite link, some minimum connection, between a state and the person, property or transaction it seeks to tax.' *Miller Bros. Co. v. Maryland,* 347 US 340, 344-345 (1954)."

For example, the taxpayer in *Mobil Oil Corp. v. Commissioner of Taxes* [445 US 425 (1980)] was an integrated petroleum company that was incorporated and commercially domiciled in New York. Mobil challenged Vermont's ability to tax the dividends that it received from its foreign subsidiaries. The essence of Mobil's argument that Vermont could not constitutionally tax the foreign dividends was that the activities of the foreign subsidiaries were unrelated to Mobil's business activities in Vermont, which were limited to distributing petroleum products. Stating that "the linchpin of apportionability in the field of state income taxation is the unitary business principle," the Supreme Court ruled that Vermont could tax an apportioned percentage of the dividends Mobil received from its foreign subsidiaries, because those subsidiaries were part of the same integrated petroleum enterprise as its distribution activities in Vermont. In other words, because they were received from unitary subsidiaries, the dividends were includible in Mobil's apportionable business income. The Court also indicated that if the business activities of the foreign subsidiaries had "nothing to do with the activities of the recipient in the taxing state, due process considerations might well preclude apportionability, because there would be no underlying unitary business."

Each state is free to adopt its own definitions of business and nonbusiness income, subject to the constitutional constraints discussed above. Most states have adopted a definition of nonbusiness income that more or less conforms to the UDITPA definition of nonbusiness income, which is "all income other than business income." [UDITPA §1(e)] Thus, the key is the definition of business income. UDITPA §1(a) provides the following:

> "Business income" means income arising from transactions and activity in the regular course of the taxpayer's trade or business and includes income from tangible and intangible property if the acquisition, management, and disposition of the property constitute integral parts of the taxpayer's regular trade or business operations.

Therefore, under UDITPA, an item of income is classified as business income if it either arises from a transaction in the regular course of the taxpayer's business (transactional test), or from property that is an integral part of the taxpayer's business (functional test) [MTC Reg. IV.1.(a)]. The transactional test looks at the frequency and regularity of the income-producing transaction in relation to the taxpayer's regular trade or business. The critical issue is whether the transaction is frequent in nature, as opposed to a rare or extraordinary event. In contrast, the functional test looks at the relationship between the underlying income-producing asset and the taxpayer's regular trade or business. The critical issue is whether the asset is integral, as opposed to incidental, to the taxpayer's business operations.

When an item of income is determined to be nonbusiness income, most states allocate the income to a specific state under guidelines similar to UDITPA §§4-8 and the related Multistate Tax Commission (MTC) regulations. The basic thrust of these rules is that nonbusiness income derived from real and tangible personal property is allocable to the state in which the property is physically located, whereas nonbusiness income derived from intangible property is allocable to the state of commercial domicile (except for royalties, which are allocable to the state where the intangible asset is used). The MTC is an agency of state governments that was established in 1967 to promote fairness and uniformity in state tax laws.

STUDY QUESTIONS

3. Which of the following is an advantage of state conformity to federal tax provisions?

a. It simplifies tax compliance for multistate corporations.

b. Federal tax law changes can reduce state tax revenues.

c. Complete conformity with federal tax laws would effectively cede control over state tax policy to the federal government.

4. Which of the following is **not** a true statement regarding UDITPA?

a. UDITPA was promulgated to provide uniformity among the states with respect to the taxation of multistate corporations.

b. Under the UDITPA approach, a taxpayer apportions a percentage of its business income to each state in which it has nexus.

c. UDITPA makes no distinction between business and nonbusiness income.

Apportionment Formulas

A taxpayer's right to apportion its income is not automatic or elective; rather, it is a privilege that must be warranted by the corporation's activities. The requirements for establishing the right to apportion income vary from state to state, but generally include:

- Carrying on business in another state
- Maintaining a regular place of business in another state
- Being taxable in another state

Some states take the restrictive position that permits apportionment only if the corporation is actually filing returns and paying tax in another state.

Once a corporation has established its right to apportion income, the next step is to compute the applicable state apportionment percentages using the formulas provided by each taxing state. These formulas are usually based on the relative amounts of property, payroll, and/or sales that the corporation has in each taxing state. These formulas reflect the notion that a corporation's business activity in a state is properly measured by the amount of property, payroll, and sales in the state. These three components of an apportionment formula are referred to as "factors." For any given state, each factor equals the ratio of the corporation's property, payroll, or sales in the state to its property, payroll, or sales everywhere.

Factor weights vary from state to state. At present, about 10 states use a three-factor apportionment formula that equally weights sales, property, and payroll. Most states use a modified three-factor formula, under which the sales factor is assigned more weight than the property or payroll factors. States that super-weight the sales factor include Arizona (80 percent) and Pennsylvania (90 percent).

Many states double-weight the sales factor (i.e., 50 percent sales, 25 percent property, and 25 percent payroll). About a dozen states use a single-factor sales-only formula, including Colorado, Georgia, Illinois, Indiana (effective in 2011), Iowa, Maine, Michigan, Nebraska, New York, Oregon, Texas, and Wisconsin. Effective in 2011, California permits taxpayers *to elect* to use a sales-only formula.

Assigning more weight to the sales factor than to the property or payroll factor tends to increase the percentage of an out-of-state corporation's income that is subject to tax, because the out-of-state corporation's principal activity in the state—sales of its product—is weighted more heavily than its payroll and property activities. At the same time, assigning more weight to the sales factor tends to reduce the tax on in-state corporations that have significant amounts of property and payroll in the state (factors that are given relatively less weight in the apportionment formula) but sales nationwide.

The standard three-factor formula was designed to apportion the income of multistate manufacturing and mercantile businesses and may not fairly apportion the income of businesses in other industries. To address this issue, many states provide special rules for computing apportionment percentages for businesses in certain industries. Typically, these special rules involve the modification or exclusion of the conventional factors or the use of unique, industry-specific factors. Examples of industries for which states provide special apportionment factor rules include:

- Airlines
- Railroads
- Trucking companies

- Financial institutions
- Television and radio broadcasters
- Publishers
- Telecommunication services companies
- Mutual funds
- Pipelines
- Ship transportation companies
- Professional sports franchises

In theory, apportionment prevents double taxation of a corporation's income. However, because each state is free to choose its own apportionment formula and make its own rules for computing the factors, apportionment does not provide a uniform division of a taxpayer's income among the taxing states. There are significant differences among the states in terms of factor weights, as well as variations in the computation of the factors themselves. This diversity can result in more than 100 percent of a corporation's income being subject to state taxation. Another potentially adverse consequence of apportionment occurs when a taxpayer's operations in one state result in a loss, but the corporation's overall operations are profitable. In such cases, the apportionment process will assign a percentage of the corporation's overall profit to the state in which the loss was incurred, even though no profit was generated by the taxpayer's operations in that state.

To address these issues, UDITPA §18 and the tax laws of most states allow a corporate taxpayer to petition for relief when the application of the state's apportionment formula does not fairly represent the taxpayer's business activity in the state. In such situations, UDITPA §18 lists several possible alternatives to the standard formula, including the use of separate accounting, the exclusion of one or more factors, the inclusion of one or more additional factors, or some other method that provides a more equitable apportionment of the taxpayer's income. However, case law indicates that there is a presumption that a state's apportionment method is equitable. In other words, to receive relief from distortions caused by the state's standard formula, a corporation must prove by clear and convincing evidence that the apportionment method in question grossly distorts the amount of income actually earned in the state.

Sales Factor

Under UDITPA §15, the sales factor is a fraction whose numerator is the total sales of the taxpayer in the state during the tax period and whose denominator is the total sales of the taxpayer everywhere during the tax period. Because the sales factor is used to apportion a corporation's business income, only sales that generate apportionable business income are includible in the fraction. Nonbusiness sales are excluded from the sales factor. Under UDITPA §1(g), the term *sales* means all gross receipts of the taxpayer other than receipts related to nonbusiness income. Consistent with this expansive view of the sales factor, MTC Regulation IV.15(b) provides that the sales factor generally includes all gross receipts derived by the taxpayer from transactions and activities in the regular course of its trade or business. Examples include:

- Gross receipts from sales of inventory
- Fees from services
- Interest
- Dividends
- Rentals
- Royalties
- Other gains derived from other business assets and activities

Under UDITPA §16(a), sales of tangible personal property are assigned to the sales factor numerator of the state into which the goods are delivered or shipped. This so-called destination test reflects the original purpose of including a sales factor in the apportionment formula, which was to provide tax revenue to the states in which customers are located. UDITPA §16(b) contains two exceptions to the destination test:

1. Sales to the U.S. government are assigned to the state from which the goods are shipped rather than to the state in which the purchaser is located.
2. A "throwback rule" requires that if the seller is not taxable in the destination state (in which case there is no sales factor numerator to which to assign the sale under the destination test), the sale is thrown back into the sales factor numerator of the state from which the goods are shipped.

The rationale for throwback is to make sure that all of a company's sales are assigned to the numerator of some state's sales factor. Despite the logical basis for adopting a throwback rule, many states do not require throwback, primarily because that makes the state a more desirable place to locate a manufacturing or distribution facility from which to ship goods. The lack of a throwback rule results in "nowhere sales," which are sales that are not included in the numerator of any sales factor.

Under UDITPA §17, any sales other than sales of tangible personal property are considered in-state sales if the income-producing activity is performed in the state. This income-producing activity rule applies to fees for services, rental income, and income from intangibles (interest, dividends, royalties, and capital gains).

Under MTC Reg. IV.17(2), the term *income-producing activity* applies to each separate item of income and means the transactions and activity engaged in by the taxpayer in the regular course of its trade or business. Examples include:

- The rendering of personal services by employees or the use of tangible or intangible property by the taxpayer in performing a service
- The sale, rental, leasing, licensing, or other use of real property

- The rental, leasing, licensing, or other use of tangible personal property
- The sale, licensing, or other use of intangible personal property

If the income-producing activity is performed in two or more states, the sale is assigned to the state in which the greater proportion of the income-producing activity is performed, based on cost of performance [UDITPA §17]. Under MTC Reg. IV.17(3), the term *costs of performance* means direct costs determined in a manner consistent with generally accepted accounting principles and in accordance with accepted conditions or practices in the trade or business of the taxpayer. Direct costs include material and labor costs that have a causal relationship with the sale in question. Indirect costs, which include general and administrative expenses that are not associated with any specific sale, are not taken into account in determining the costs of performance.

Property Factor

Under UDITPA §10, the property factor is a fraction whose numerator is the average value of the taxpayer's real and tangible personal property owned or rented and used in the state during the tax year and whose denominator is the average value of all the taxpayer's real and tangible personal property owned or rented and used everywhere during the tax year. Under MTC Reg. IV.10(a), the definition of real and tangible personal property includes land, buildings, machinery, stocks of goods, equipment, and other real and tangible personal property. Intangible property, such as accounts receivable and marketable securities, generally is excluded from the property factor.

Property owned by the corporation is typically valued at its average original cost plus the cost of additions and improvements, but without any adjustments for depreciation. A few states require property to be included at its net book value or federal adjusted tax basis. Rented property is included in the property factor at a value equal to eight times the annual rental.

Only property that is used in producing apportionable business income is included in the property factor. Therefore, construction-in-progress, property that has been permanently withdrawn from service, and property that is used for producing nonbusiness income generally is excluded. However, property that is temporarily idled generally remains in the property factor.

Although the average value of the property is usually determined by averaging the beginning and ending property values, many states allow the average value to be calculated on a monthly or quarterly basis if the use of the annual computations substantially distorts the actual value of the property. This may occur if a significant amount of property is acquired or disposed of near the beginning or the end of the year.

Payroll Factor

Under UDITPA §13, the payroll factor is a fraction whose numerator is the total amount paid in the state during the tax year by the taxpayer for compensation and whose denominator is the total compensation paid everywhere during the tax year. For this purpose, compensation generally includes wages, salaries, commissions, and any other form of remuneration paid or accrued to an employee that is taxable to the employee for federal income tax purposes. Payments made to an independent contractor or to any other person who is not properly classifiable as an employee generally are excluded from the payroll factor. Compensation related to the production of nonbusiness income is also excluded from the payroll factor. In addition, in an attempt to make the state a more desirable place to locate a headquarters office, a few states exclude executive compensation from the payroll factor.

The rules for computing an employee's compensation and for assigning that compensation to a particular state parallel those used to compute the employer's federal and state unemployment taxes. Federal Form 940, *Employer's Annual Federal Unemployment Tax Return*, summarizes taxable compensation amounts on a state-by-state basis and is often used to compute state payroll factors. In computing the numerator of the payroll factor for a particular state, if an employee performs services exclusively within that state, that employee's compensation is included in the numerator for that state. If an employee performs services both within and without a state, the entire amount of the employee's compensation is still generally assigned to a single state, based on a hierarchy of factors, including (in the order in which they are applied) the employee's base of operations, where the employee is directed from, and the employee's state of residence [UDITPA §14].

STUDY QUESTIONS

---

5. Assigning more weight to the sales factor than to the property or payroll factor tends to decrease the percentage of an out-of-state corporation's income that is subject to tax. *True or False?*

6. Under UDITPA, sales of tangible personal property are generally assigned to the sales factor numerator of the state:
   a. From which the goods are shipped
   b. Into which the goods are delivered or shipped
   c. Where the company is commercially domiciled

Consolidated Returns and Combined Unitary Reporting

For financial reporting purposes, a parent corporation must issue consolidated financial statements that include all of its majority-owned subsidiaries. For federal income tax purposes, an affiliated group of corporations may elect to file a federal consolidated income tax return [Code Sec. 1501]. Thus, a federal consolidated return is not mandatory, and the members of an affiliated group have the option of filing federal returns on a separate-company basis. Filing a federal consolidated return is a popular election, primarily because it allows the group to offset the losses of one affiliate against the profits of other affiliates.

A federal *affiliated group* is defined as one or more chains of includible corporations connected through stock ownership with a common parent that is an includible corporation, provided that the common parent directly owns 80 percent or more of at least one of the other includible corporations, and stock meeting the 80 percent test in each includible corporation other than the common parent must be owned directly by one or more of the other includible corporations [Code Sec. 1504(a)]. An "includible corporation" is any corporation other than an exempt corporation, life insurance company, foreign corporation, Code Sec. 936 corporation, RIC, REIT, DISC, or S corporation [Code Sec. 1504(b)].

The states that impose corporate income taxes employ a wide variety of filing options for groups of commonly controlled corporations. This makes it difficult to generalize about state filing options. Roughly speaking, the different filing options fall into one of the following categories:

- Separate-company returns
- Consolidated returns
- Mandatory combined unitary reporting
- Discretionary combined unitary reporting

The lack of uniformity in state filing options means that tax practitioners must carefully analyze the filing options available in any given nexus state.

Separate-company returns. Three states—Delaware, Maryland, and Pennsylvania—require each member of a commonly controlled group of corporations to compute its income and file a return as if it were a separate economic entity. Under this mandatory separate-company return approach, consolidated returns and combined unitary reporting are not permitted or required under any circumstances.

The filing of separate-company returns provides taxpayers with the opportunity to create legal structures and intercompany transactions that shift income from affiliates based in high-tax states to affiliates based in low-tax states.

EXAMPLE

If a multistate corporation's only activities in a high-tax state are sales and distribution, which are often relatively low-margin activities, and if the high-tax state allows separate-company returns, the corporation may be able to insulate its higher-margin assets and activities from taxation in the high-tax state by forming a sales subsidiary that is responsible for marketing products in that state.

Disadvantages of the separate-company return approach include the inability to offset the losses of one affiliate against the profits of other affiliates and the need to develop defensible arm's-length transfer prices for intercompany transactions.

Consolidated returns. Roughly 20 states (including Alabama, Florida, Georgia, Iowa, and South Carolina) generally allow affiliated corporations to file separate-company returns but also permit or require such corporations to file a state consolidated return if certain conditions are met. The qualification requirements for including an affiliated corporation in a state consolidated return vary from state to state. In terms of stock ownership requirements, most states piggyback on the federal rule requiring 80 percent or more ownership. A number of states also require that an affiliated group file a federal consolidated return as a prerequisite to filing a state consolidated return. Examples of additional restrictions that a state may impose for including a specific affiliate in a state consolidated return include:

- Having nexus in the state
- Deriving income from sources in the state
- Not being subject to a special apportionment formula, such as those that often apply to financial institutions

The advantages of filing a consolidated return include:

- The ability to offset the losses of one affiliate against the profits of other affiliates
- Elimination of intercorporate dividends
- Deferral of gains on intercompany transactions
- The use of credits that would otherwise be denied because of a lack of income

A disadvantage of filing a consolidated return is that it can prevent a taxpayer from creating legal structures and intercompany transactions to shift income from affiliates based in high-tax states to affiliates based in low-tax states.

Combined unitary reporting. Twenty-three states require members of a unitary business group to compute their taxable income on a combined basis. These states are Alaska, Arizona, California, Colorado, Hawaii, Idaho, Illinois, Kansas, Maine, Massachusetts, Michigan, Minnesota, Montana, Nebraska, New Hampshire, New York (for related corporations that have substantial intercorporate transactions), North Dakota, Oregon, Texas, Utah, Vermont, West Virginia, and Wisconsin. The District of Columbia will require combined reporting starting in 2011.

Combined reporting is a methodology for apportioning the business income of a corporation that is a member of a commonly controlled group of corporations engaged in a unitary business. Generally speaking, the taxpayer member apportions its business income by multiplying the business income of all the members of the unitary business group by an apportion-ment percentage that is based on factors, the denominators of which include the factors everywhere of all group members, and the numerators of which include the in-state factors of only the taxpayer member.

Despite its surface-level resemblance to a consolidated return, combined unitary reporting differs from a federal consolidated return in several im-portant respects:

1. Whereas inclusion in a federal consolidated return requires 80 percent or more common ownership, inclusion in a combined unitary report generally requires more than 50 percent common ownership.
2. To be included in a combined report, an affiliate must be engaged in the same trade or business as the other group members, as exhibited by such factors as functional integration, centralized management, and economies of scale. There is no unitary business requirement for inclusion in a federal consolidated return.
3. Some states permit the inclusion of foreign corporations in a com-bined report.
4. In many states, each group member that has nexus in the state is treated as a separate taxpayer, whereas the federal consolidated regulations treat a consolidated group as a single taxable entity.

The advantages and disadvantages of consolidated returns and combined reporting are similar. A primary disadvantage of both filing options is that they can limit a taxpayer's ability to use intercompany transactions to shift income from affiliates based in high-tax states to affiliates based in low-tax states. A major advantage of both filing options is that losses of one affiliate can be offset against the profits of other affiliates.

Numerous states, including New Jersey, North Carolina, and Virginia, gen-erally allow commonly controlled corporations to file separate-company returns but also require or permit a combined unitary report if certain conditions are satisfied. A common reason for requiring a combined report is the state tax authority's determination that a combined report is necessary to clearly reflect the group's income earned in the state or to prevent the evasion of taxes.

> **EXAMPLE**
>
> New Jersey does not permit an affiliated group to elect to file a consolidated return, nor does it require a unitary group to compute its income on a com-bined basis. Thus, every corporation with nexus in New Jersey is generally considered a separate entity and must file its own return. The Director of the Division of Taxation may, however, require members of an affiliated group or a controlled group to file a consolidated return "if the taxpayer cannot demonstrate by clear and convincing evidence that a report by a taxpayer discloses the true earnings of the taxpayer on its business carried on in this State." [N.J. Rev. Stat. 54:10A-10.c.]

Concept of a Unitary Business

Combined unitary reporting requires a determination of whether two or more corporations are engaged in a *unitary business*. Unfortunately, there is no simple, objective definition of what constitutes a unitary business. In fact, over the years the courts have developed a number of different tests for determining the existence of a unitary business. As one Supreme Court Justice observed, "the unitary business concept … is not, so to speak, unitary." Because of the many judicial interpretations of a unitary business, it is not always clear which of the available tests should be applied. In addition, even if a taxpayer knows which test will be used, the subjective nature of the tests makes them difficult to apply with any certainty.

Generally, a vertically integrated business, in which each separate affiliate or division performs an interdependent step that leads to a finished product only when the steps are combined, will be treated as unitary. A horizontally integrated business, in which there are parallel operations in different geographic locations (e.g., a chain of retail stores), will also generally be considered unitary. A conglomerate may or may not be considered unitary, depending on whether there is strong centralized management, as exhibited by a centralized executive force and shared staff functions, as well as economies of scale in the form of common employee pension and benefit plans, common insurance policies, and so on.

As mentioned above, the courts have developed a number of different tests for determining the existence of a unitary business, including:

- The three-unities test
- The contribution or dependency test
- The flow-of-value test
- The factors-of-profitability test

Three-unities test. The three-unities test [***Butler Bros. v. McColgan,*** 315 US 501 (1942)] requires the presence of unity of ownership, unity of operation, and unity of use. Unity of ownership generally is satisfied when 50 percent or more of the corporation's stock is owned directly or indirectly by another corporation in the group. Unity of operation is evidenced by the performance of certain staff functions by one of the corporations on behalf of the entire group, such as centralized purchasing, advertising, accounting and legal services, and human resource functions. Unity of use is associated with common executive forces and general systems of operations and is evidenced by major policy decisions that are made by centralized management, intercompany product flow, and services that are provided by one affiliate to other group members.

Contribution or dependency test. The contribution or dependency test [***Edison Cal. Stores, Inc. v. McColgan,*** 176 P.2d 697 (Cal. 1947)] focuses on whether the enterprise's in-state business operations depend on, or contribute to, the enterprise's out-of-state business operations. Examples of factors that suggest contributions by or dependency among commonly controlled corporations include:

- Intercompany loans
- Intercompany sales of goods or services
- Exchanges of products or expertise
- Shared executive force and staff functions

Flow-of-value test. Under the flow-of-value test, "some sharing or exchange of value … beyond the mere flow of funds arising out of a passive investment" is needed to establish the existence of a unitary business." [*Container Corp. of Am. v. Franchise Tax Bd.*, 463 US 159 (1983)]

Factors-of-profitability test. The factors-of-profitability test [*Allied-Signal, Inc. v. Division of Taxation*, 504 US 768 (1992)] looks to functional integration, centralization of management, and economies of scale to determine the existence of a unitary business. Functional integration includes product flow among affiliates and centralized functions such as advertising, accounting, purchasing, manufacturing, and financing. Indicators of centralized management include:

- Interlocking boards of directors
- Interchange of personnel at upper management levels
- Required parent company approval on major policy decisions

In addition to judicial interpretations, state-specific statutes and regulations are important sources of authority regarding what constitutes a unitary business group. Like their judicial counterparts, however, they generally leave much to be desired in terms of providing detailed and objective guidance.

The MTC regulations portray the concept of a unitary business as follows:

> A unitary business is a single economic enterprise that is made up either of separate parts of a single business entity or of a commonly controlled group of business entities that are sufficiently interdependent, integrated and interrelated through their activities so as to provide a synergy and mutual benefit that produces a sharing or exchange of value among them and a significant flow of value to the separate parts [MTC Reg. IV.1.(b)].

The regulations also provide that a unitary business is characterized by significant flows of value evidenced by the following factors:

- **Functional integration**—Examples include common marketing programs, transfers or pooling of technical information or intellectual property, common distribution systems, common purchasing, and common or intercompany financing.

- **Centralization of management**—Joint participation of corporate directors and officers in the management decisions that affect the different business units
- **Economies of scale**—Centralized purchasing, centralized administrative functions, etc.

Finally, the MTC regulations identify same type of business, steps in a vertical process, and strong centralized management as indicators of a unitary business.

STUDY QUESTIONS

---

7. Which of the following states does **not** require each member of a commonly controlled group of corporations to file separate-company returns?

    a. Arizona
    b. Delaware
    c. Maryland

8. Inclusion in a state consolidated return generally requires 50 percent or more common ownership. **True or False?**

Basic Multistate Tax Planning Strategies

Multistate corporate income tax planning techniques generally involve an attempt either to reduce the total amount of the organization's taxable income subject to apportionment or to minimize the apportionment percentage in a given state. In determining which activities or entities to alter, the tax planner must carefully analyze the effects that each change has on the corporation's total state tax liability to ensure that the taxes saved in one state are not offset by tax increases in other states. Therefore, effective state tax planning requires a review of a corporation's activities in all states and an understanding of the apportionment formulas and other tax laws of the states in which the corporation does business. Moreover, any tax planning strategy must be reviewed in light of practical business considerations and the additional administrative or operational costs that might be incurred in implementing the strategy. The remainder of this section briefly discusses the following selected planning opportunities:

- Selecting the states in which to be taxed
- Establishing the right to apportion income
- Structuring planning techniques
- Using the most beneficial group filing method

Selecting the states in which to be taxed. When a corporation has only a limited connection with a state, it may be possible to discontinue that activity by using an alternative means of accomplishing the same result.

> **EXAMPLE**
>
> If maintaining a corporate office in a state creates an undesired nexus, the corporation might avoid nexus by providing the sales representatives with an office allowance rather than a formal company office.

When nexus is created by sales representatives performing repair and maintenance services in the state, one strategy would be to separately incorporate the sales division that operates in the state. Assuming the state does not require combined reporting, this would prevent the state from taxing the profits attributable to the parent corporation's out-of-state assets and activities. Such a technique will be successful only if the incorporated division is a bona fide business operation and the state does not successfully assert that the corporation continues to have nexus under the concepts of affiliate or agency nexus (discussed below). In addition, the pricing of any sales or services between the new subsidiary and the parent corporation must be at arm's length.

Although most planning techniques are designed to avoid nexus, there are situations in which a corporation can benefit from establishing nexus in a state. Creating nexus in a particular state can be beneficial if the corporation:

- Currently does not have the right to apportion its income
- Wants to avoid the application of a sales throwback rule by creating nexus in a destination state
- Wants to have a loss affiliate create nexus in a state that allows only nexus affiliates to join in filing a state consolidated return

Establishing nexus may not be difficult to accomplish because of the relatively low threshold for creating constitutional nexus and the limited nature of the protection afforded by Public Law 86-272.

Establishing the right to apportion income. A corporation that has nexus in only one state cannot apportion its income and therefore is subject to tax on 100 percent of its income in that state. By establishing the right to apportion its income, the taxpayer may be able to reduce its state income tax costs substantially, particularly if the corporation is domiciled in a high-tax state. The income that is removed from the tax base of the state of domicile may escape state taxation altogether if the state in which the corporation establishes nexus does not impose a corporate income tax or imposes a corporate income tax but has more liberal nexus rules than the state of domicile.

Another major factor in determining the tax benefit of apportioning income is whether the state from which the taxpayer is shipping goods has a sales throwback rule. Many states do not require throwback, in which case sales in states where the taxpayer does not have nexus are not assigned to the numerator of any state's sales factor (so-called *nowhere sales*).

To acquire the right to apportion its income, the corporation generally must have nexus in at least one state other than its state of domicile. Whether a corporation's activities or contacts in another state are considered adequate to justify apportionment is generally determined by reference to the tax laws of the domicile state. Typically, a corporation must carry on business in another state, maintain an office or other regular place of business in another state, or be taxable in another state in order to apportion its income. Some states take the restrictive position that apportionment is permitted only if the corporation is actually filing returns and paying tax in another state. A corporation should analyze its current activities in and contacts with other states to determine which, if any, activities or contacts could be redirected so that the corporation will be granted the right to apportion its income.

Structuring planning techniques. Numerous states allow a group of commonly controlled corporations to file returns on a separate-company basis. This can provide a taxpayer with the opportunity to create legal structures and intercompany transactions that shift income from affiliates based in certain high-tax states to affiliates based in low-or no-tax states.

> **EXAMPLE**
>
> If a high-tax state allows separate-company reporting, and a multistate corporation's only activity in that state is sales and distribution (which are often relatively low-margin activities), the corporation may be able to insulate its out-of-state assets and activities from taxation in the high-tax state by forming a sales subsidiary that is responsible for marketing its products in the state.

> **EXAMPLE**
>
> A financial institution holds a significant portfolio of marketable securities. The taxpayer may be able to realize significant tax savings by transferring the securities to an intangible property holding company domiciled in Delaware, which does not tax the income of a corporation whose only activities in the state are the maintenance and management of intangible property or the collection and distribution of income from such property.

Historically, large corporations (in particular, retailers) used Delaware trademark holding companies to avoid state income taxes. By transferring valuable trademarks and trade names to an intangible property holding company domiciled in Delaware, and then licensing the use of the intangibles back to the operating companies, a corporation could potentially avoid state taxation of the income attributable to the intangible assets. States have significantly curtailed the use of trademark holding companies by enacting combined reporting requirements, related-party expense add-back provisions, and economic nexus statutes.

Structure planning can also be used to take advantage of net operating losses in states that do not allow any form of consolidated or combined reporting. One way to use such losses is to merge an unprofitable affiliate into a profitable affiliate. Another potential strategy for better utilizing an affiliate's net operating losses is to convert the unprofitable affiliate into a single member limited liability company (LLC). A single-member LLC is generally treated as a disregarded entity for both federal and state income tax purposes, and therefore the use of a single-member LLC effectively produces the same result as a consolidated return. Care must be taken, however, when dealing with single-member LLCs because some states impose entity-level taxes on such entities.

Using the most beneficial group filing method. In states that permit an affiliated group to elect to file a consolidated return, such an election can be beneficial when one affiliate has losses that can be offset against the income generated by other affiliates. Other potential benefits of filing a consolidated return include:

- Elimination of intercorporate dividends
- Deferral of gains on intercompany transactions
- Use of credits that would otherwise be limited by the lack of income

In choosing whether to file a consolidated return, the corporation should determine whether the advantages of a consolidated return can be realized without adverse consequences.

EXAMPLE

A corporation that is eligible to file a consolidated return in a given state may choose not to do so if it has significant losses on intercompany transactions and would lose the deduction as a result of the election. On the other hand, another member of the same affiliated group may elect to file a consolidated state return in another state to defer recognition of intercompany gains.

A major disadvantage of filing a consolidated return is that it can limit a taxpayer's ability to use intercompany transactions that shift income from affiliates based in high-tax states to affiliates based in low-tax states.

> **CAUTION**
>
> Most states that permit affiliated corporations to file a consolidated return have adopted a reporting-consistency requirement similar to that imposed for federal consolidated return purposes. Thus, once an affiliated group begins filing a consolidated return, the group generally must continue to file on a consolidated basis, unless the group receives permission from state tax authorities to file separate-company returns.

STUDY QUESTIONS

9. Assume a manufacturer wants to establish nexus in a state to avoid throwback of its sales into that state. Which of the following activities would **most likely** create income tax nexus in that state?

    a. A sales representative engaging in nonsolicitation activity
    b. A sales representative soliciting orders for tangible personal property
    c. Providing a sales representative with a company car that is used only in solicitation activities

10. It is always beneficial to file a consolidated return in states that permit or require a consolidated return. **True or False?**

ADVANCED CONCEPTS

Nexus

Economic nexus. In *Quill,* the U.S. Supreme Court ruled that a corporation satisfies the Commerce Clause's "substantial nexus" requirement only if the taxpayer has a physical presence in the state. Yet, in ***Geoffrey, Inc. v. South Carolina Tax Commission*** [437 S.E.2d 13 (S.C. 1993), *cert. denied* 510 US 992, 1993], the South Carolina Supreme Court held that a trademark holding company that licensed its intangibles for use in South Carolina had nexus for income tax purposes despite the lack of any tangible property or employees in South Carolina. Geoffrey was the trademark holding company of the toy retailer, Toys "R" Us. Geoffrey was incorporated and domiciled in Delaware and had a license agreement with South Carolina retailers allowing them to use its trademarks and trade names, including the Toys "R" Us trademark. The court held that licensing intangibles for use in the state was sufficient to satisfy the minimum connection and substantial nexus requirements of the Due Process Clause and the Commerce Clause. The *Geoffrey* court did not follow the precedent established by *Quill*, because it believed that ruling applied only to the issue of nexus for sales and use tax purposes.

Since 1993, many states have adopted "economic nexus" standards that are based on the amount of income or sales derived from sources within a state.

EXAMPLE

For tax years beginning on or after January 1, 2010, the Connecticut corporate income tax applies to "[a]ny company that derives income from sources within this state, or that has a substantial economic presence within this state, evidenced by a purposeful direction of business toward this state, examined in light of the frequency, quantity and systematic nature of a company's economic contacts with this state, without regard to physical presence, and to the extent permitted by the Constitution of the United States." [Sec. 90, as adopted by S.B. 2052, Oct. 5, 2009]

Another approach to implementing the economic nexus concept is a factor presence standard, under which income tax nexus exists if in-state sales exceed a specified threshold.

EXAMPLE

For tax years beginning on or after January 1, 2011, an out-of-state corporation has income tax nexus in California if more than $500,000 of sales or 25 percent of its total sales are in California [S.B. 15, Feb. 20. 2009].

In addition, there has been a significant amount of litigation related to the *Geoffrey* court's interpretation of the Commerce Clause's substantial nexus requirement.

In *Lanco, Inc. v. Division of Taxation* [908 A.2d 176 (N.J. 2006); *cert. denied*, U.S. Sup. Ct., 06-1236, June 18, 2007], the New Jersey Supreme Court ruled that the Delaware trademark holding company of the clothing retailer Lane Bryant had income tax nexus in New Jersey, even though it had no physical presence in the state. The court concluded that "the better interpretation of *Quill* is the one adopted by those states that limit the Supreme Court's holding to sales and use taxes." The court also stated that "we do not believe that the Supreme Court intended to create a universal physical-presence requirement for state taxation under the Commerce Clause."

In *Tax Commissioner v. MBNA America Bank, N.A.* [640 S.E.2d 226 (W. Va. 2006); *cert. denied*, U.S. Sup. Ct., 06-1228, June 18, 2007], the taxpayer was a Delaware bank that issued credit cards, extended unsecured credit, and serviced the credit card accounts of customers nationwide. Although MBNA did not have a physical presence in West Virginia, during one of the tax years in question, it derived over $10 million of gross receipts from West Virginia customers. The West Virginia Supreme Court of Appeals ruled that the physical presence test "applies only to state sales and use taxes and not to state business franchise and corporation net income taxes," and that MBNA had "a significant economic presence sufficient to meet the substantial nexus" test under the Commerce Clause.

In *Capital One Bank and Capital One F.S.B. v. Commissioner of Revenue* [No. SJC-10105 (Mass. Sup. Jud. Ct., Jan. 8, 2009); *cert. denied*, U.S. Sup. Ct., No. 08-1169, June 22, 2009], the Massachusetts Supreme Judicial Court ruled that, despite the lack of any physical presence in the state, the two out-of-state credit card banks had substantial nexus in Massachusetts, because of their "purposeful, targeted marketing of their credit card business to Massachusetts customers ... and their receipt of hundreds of millions of dollars in income from millions of transactions involving Massachusetts residents and merchants." Likewise, in *Geoffrey, Inc. v. Commissioner of Revenue* [No. SJC-10106 (Mass. Sup. Jud. Ct., Jan. 8, 2009); *cert. denied*, U.S. Sup. Ct., No. 08-1207, June 22, 2009], the Massachusetts Supreme Judicial Court ruled that, despite the lack of a physical presence in the state, a Delaware trademark holding company that received royalty income from licensing trademarks to affiliated entities which used the trademarks for retail business activities in Massachusetts had income tax nexus in Massachusetts.

In *KFC Corporation v. Iowa Department of Revenue* [No. 09-1032 (Ia. Sup. Ct., Dec. 30, 2010)], the Iowa Supreme Court ruled that the Commerce Clause does not require a physical presence in order to tax the income that a Delaware corporation (KFC) earned from the use of its intangibles in Iowa. The court concluded that the trademarks and other intangibles owned by KFC and licensed for use by independent franchisees doing business in Iowa, "would be regarded as having a sufficient connection to Iowa to amount to the functional equivalent of 'physical presence' under *Quill*." The court also concluded that even if the use of the intangibles within the state does not amount to physical presence under *Quill*, the physical presence requirement should not be extended to prevent a state from imposing an income tax on revenue generated from the use of intangibles within the state.

Agency nexus. Under the *Quill* decision, a corporation generally has constitutional nexus in any state in which it has property or employees located on a regular basis. What if, rather than conducting business in a state through employees (dependent agents), a corporation conducts business through independent contractors (independent agents)? Do the in-state activities of independent agents, acting on an out-of-state corporation's behalf, create constitutional nexus?

In *Scripto, Inc. v. Carson* [362 US 207 (1960)], the U.S. Supreme Court addressed the issue of whether the Florida marketing activities of 10 independent sales representatives created Florida sales tax nexus for Scripto, a Georgia corporation that manufactured writing instruments. The Court held that for nexus purposes, the distinction between employees and independent contractors was "without constitutional significance," and that "to permit such formal 'contractual shifts' to make a constitutional difference would open the gates to a stampede of tax avoidance." The Court concluded that the critical fact was that the activities of the independent agents in Florida helped to create and maintain a commercial market for Scripto's goods. Thus, the presence of independent agents engaged in continuous local solicitation created Florida sales and use tax nexus for Scripto.

The Supreme Court reaffirmed these principles 25 years later in *Tyler Pipe Industries, Inc. v. Department of Revenue* [483 US 232 (1987)], holding that the activities of an independent contractor residing in Washington were sufficient to create constitutional nexus for the out-of-state principal for purposes of the Washington business and occupation tax (a type of gross receipts tax). As in *Scripto*, the Court held that the critical test was "whether the activities performed in this state on behalf of the taxpayer are significantly associated with the taxpayer's ability to establish and maintain a market in this state for the sales."

In addition to protecting solicitation activities of employee-salespersons, Public Law 86-272 protects certain in-state activities conducted by independent contractors. Specifically, Public Law 86-272 provides that independent contractors can engage in the following in-state activities on behalf of an out-of-state corporation without creating income tax nexus for the principal:

- Soliciting sales
- Making sales
- Maintaining an office

Thus, unlike employees, independent agents are permitted to maintain an in-state office without creating nexus for the principal.

The Supreme Court's decisions in *Scripto* and *Tyler Pipe* establish the principle that the use of independent agents to perform continuous local solicitation creates constitutional nexus for an out-of-state principal. Relying on these decisions, in Nexus Bulletin 95-1 [1995], the MTC took the position that the mail-order computer industry's practice of providing warranty services through third-party service providers creates constitutional nexus for sales and use tax purposes.

Affiliate nexus. A number of states have taken the position that the existence of common ownership between a corporation that has a physical presence in a state (e.g., an in-state brick-and-mortar retailer) and an out-of-state corporation that has no physical presence in the state but makes substantial sales in the state (e.g., an affiliated out-of-state mail-order vendor) is sufficient to create constitutional nexus for the out-of-state mail-order affiliate. As with agency nexus, most of the litigation concerns the issue of nexus for sales and use tax purposes.

For example, in *SFA Folio Collections, Inc. v. Tracy* [73 Ohio St. 3d 119, 652 N.E. 2d 693 (1995)], SFA Folio (Folio), a New York corporation, sold clothing and other merchandise by direct mail to customers in Ohio and delivered the merchandise using common carriers. Folio had no property or employees in Ohio, but Folio's parent corporation, Saks & Company, owned another subsidiary, Saks Fifth Avenue of Ohio (Saks-Ohio), which operated a retail store in Ohio.

Ohio tax authorities argued that Folio had "substantial nexus" in Ohio, because it was a member of an affiliated group that included a corporation that operated a store in Ohio and therefore was required to collect Ohio sales tax on its mail-order sales to Ohio customers. The state's position was based on a nexus-by-affiliate statute that the Ohio Legislature had enacted, as well as the argument that Saks-Ohio was an "agent" of Folio. The agency argument was based on the fact that Saks-Ohio accepted some returns of Folio sales and distributed some Folio catalogs. The Ohio Supreme Court rejected the affiliate nexus argument, reasoning that to impute nexus to Folio merely because a sister corporation had a physical presence in Ohio ran counter to federal constitutional law and Ohio corporation law. The court also rejected the agency nexus argument because Saks-Ohio accepted Folio's returns according to its own policy (not Folio's) and charged the returns to its own inventory (not Folio's).

Consistent with the Ohio Supreme Court's ruling in *SFA Folio*, other states have generally been unsuccessful in their attempts to argue that common ownership, by itself, creates nexus for an out-of-state affiliate. [See, e.g., *Current, Inc. v. State Bd. of Equalization*, 24 Cal. App. 4th 382, 29 Cal. Rptr. 2d 407 (Ct. App. 1994); *SFA Folio Collections, Inc. v. Bannon*, 217 Conn. 220, 585 A.2d 666 (1991); *Bloomingdale's By Mail, Ltd. v. Commonwealth*, 130 Pa. Commw. 190, 567 A.2d 773 (Commw. Ct. 1989).] On the other hand, if an in-state affiliate functions as an agent for the out-of-state affiliate, the Supreme Court's decisions in *Scripto* and *Tyler Pipe* provide a basis for arguing that the activities of the in-state affiliate create nexus for an out-of-state affiliate.

In *Borders Online, Inc.* [No. A105488 (Cal. Ct. of App., May 31, 2005)], the California Court of Appeals ruled that an out-of-state online retailer had a substantial nexus in California for sales and use tax purposes, because an affiliated corporation that sold similar products in brick-and-mortar stores in California performed return and exchange activities for the online retailer. The brick-and-mortar affiliate was considered to be an authorized representative of the online retailer because the online retailer posted a notice on its Web site that returns could be made to the brick-and-mortar retailer and the brick-and-mortar retailer's acceptance of returns was an integral part of the online retailer's sales operations. Therefore, under the relevant state statute, the online retailer was considered to be engaged in business in California and subject to the obligation to collect use tax on sales to California residents.

In *Barnesandnoble.com LLC v. State Bd. of Equalization* [No. CGC-06-456465 (Cal. Super. Ct., Oct. 11, 2007)], the California Superior Court ruled that an in-state brick-and-mortar affiliate's distribution of coupons that provided a discount on an online purchase did not create sales and use tax nexus for the related Internet retailer. The retail stores did not act as the Internet vendor's agent or representative. The court concluded that "[a]n essential element is that the agent (or representative) must have the authority to bind the principal." In the present case, the in-state retailer had no such authority and could do nothing but pass out the coupons created and distributed by the Internet vendor.

A number of states have enacted affiliate nexus statutes for sales and use taxes. For example, in H.B. 360 [Mar. 3, 2008], Idaho amended its definition of a "retailer engaged in business in this state" for sales and use tax collection purposes to include a retailer with substantial nexus in the state. A retailer has "substantial nexus" with Idaho if both of the following apply:

- The retailer and an in-state business maintaining one or more locations within Idaho are related parties.
- The retailer and the in-state business use an identical or substantially similar name, trade name, trademark, or goodwill to develop, promote, or maintain sales, or the in-state business provides services to, or that inure to the benefit of, the out-of-state business related to developing, promoting, or maintaining the in-state market.

The above provisions do not apply to a retailer that had less than $100,000 in sales in Idaho in the previous year.

Deliveries in company-owned trucks. A corporation generally has constitutional nexus in any state in which it has property or employees located on a regular basis. Thus, a number of state courts have held that the regular and systematic presence of company-owned delivery trucks driven by company employees is sufficient to create sales and use tax nexus [E.g., *Brown's Furniture, Inc. v. Wagner*, No. 78195 (Ill. 1996); *Town Crier, Inc. v. Zehnder*, No. 1-98-4251 (Ill. App. Ct. 2000); *John Swenson Granite Co. v. State Tax Assessor*, 685 A.2d 425 (Me. Super. Ct. 1996)].

For income tax purposes, Public Law 86-272 shields an out-of-state corporation from taxation if its only in-state activity is (1) solicitation of orders by company representatives (2) for sales of tangible personal property, (3) which orders are sent outside the state for approval or rejection, and (4) if approved, are filled by shipment or delivery from a point outside the state. Over the years, taxpayers have taken the position that the phrase *shipment or delivery* implies that a seller is protected by Public Law 86-272 regardless of whether it ships the goods into the state using a common carrier or its own delivery trucks. However, some states have taken the position that the seller's use of its own trucks to make deliveries is not protected by Public Law 86-272.

State supreme courts in Massachusetts and Virginia have ruled that deliveries in company-owned trucks constitute a protected activity under Public Law 86-272 [*National Private Truck Council v. Virginia Department of Taxation*, 253 Va. 74, 480 S.E.2d 500 (1997); and *National Private Truck Council v. Commissioner of Revenue*, 688 N.E.2d 936 (Mass. 1997), *cert. denied*]. In 2001, the MTC revised its Statement of Information Concerning Practices of Multistate Tax Commission and Signatory States Under Public Law 86-272 by removing from the list of unprotected activities the following item:

> Shipping or delivering goods into this state by means of private vehicle, rail, water, air or other carrier, irrespective of whether shipment or delivery fee or other charge is imposed, directly or indirectly, upon the purchaser.

Several state revenue departments have also indicated that deliveries using company-owned trucks are protected by Public Law 86-272 [Rev. Rul. 24-01-01, Neb. Dept. of Rev. (Feb. 22, 2001); Decision No. 2005-05-10-22, Okla. Tax Comn. (May 10, 2005); and Ala. Reg. 810-27-1-4-.19 (Feb. 28, 2006)].

De minimis rule. The existence of a *de minimis* rule in the nexus arena is supported by numerous authorities. With respect to constitutional nexus, the Supreme Court has ruled that the Commerce Clause requires a "substantial nexus" in a state [*Complete Auto Transit, Inc. v. Brady*, 430 US 274 (1977)]. In addition, in *Quill*, the taxpayer held title to a few floppy diskettes that were located in North Dakota. The Supreme Court indicated that, although title to a few floppy diskettes located in a state "might constitute some minimal nexus, in *National Geographic Society v. California Bd. of Equalization*, 430 US 551, 556 (1977), we expressly rejected a 'slightest presence' standard of constitutional nexus." [*Quill Corp. v. North Dakota*, 504 US 298 n.8 (1992)] Thus, the presence of a few floppy diskettes did not satisfy the substantial nexus requirement of the Commerce Clause. With respect to Public Law 86-272, in *Wrigley* the Supreme Court indicated that a *de minimis* level of in-state nonsolicitation activities does not cause a company to lose the protection afforded by Public Law 86-272.

State courts in Illinois and Michigan have adopted the "more than a slightest presence" test articulated in *Orvis Co., Inc. v. Tax Appeals Tribunal* and *Vermont Information Processing Inc. v. Tax Appeals Tribunal* [Nos. 138, 139 (N.Y. 1995)], in which the New York Court of Appeals concluded that although a physical presence is required to satisfy the *Quill* "substantial nexus" requirement, the in-state physical presence need not be substantial; instead, it must be "demonstrably more than a slightest presence." In *Brown's Furniture v. Wagner* [No. 78195 (Ill. 1996)], the Illinois Supreme Court concluded that "the *Orvis* court stated—correctly, we believe—the rule regarding substantial nexus." Likewise, in *MagneTek Controls, Inc. v. Michigan Department of Treasury* [No. 181612 (Mich. Ct. App. 1997)], the Michigan Court of Appeals stated that "we conclude that the court in *Orvis* correctly understood *Quill* and enunciated an appropriate test for applying *Quill*."

STUDY QUESTIONS

11. In which of the following cases did the court determine that the taxpayer had no nexus because of a lack of physical presence?

   a. *Geoffrey, Inc. v. South Carolina Tax Commission*

   b. *Lanco, Inc. v. New Jersey Division of Taxation*

   c. *West Virginia Tax Commissioner v. MBNA America Bank, N.A.*

   d. *Quill Corp. v. North Dakota*

12. Based on the court decisions discussed previously, in which of the following situations is it *most likely* that the company has income tax nexus?

   a. A related corporation has a physical presence in the state, but the company itself does not. The operations of the in-state affiliate have nothing to do with those of the taxpayer.

   b. The company does not have any service technicians based in the state. However, the company's out-of-state technicians travel to the state to provide repair services, as needed. During the current year, these technicians spend several weeks in the state making repairs.

   c. The company makes deliveries into the state using company-owned trucks. The drivers do not engage in any activities other than making deliveries, such as collecting payments or accepting returns (back-hauling).

Specialized Industry Apportionment Formulas

The UDITPA equally weighted three-factor property, payroll, and sales apportionment formula was designed to apportion the income of multistate manufacturing and mercantile businesses and may not fairly apportion the income of businesses in other industries. For example, the conventional UDITPA property and payroll factors are difficult to compute for property and payroll that is regularly in motion, such as that of interstate trucking companies, airlines, and railroads. In addition, since its adoption in 1957, the UDITPA §17 income-producing activity rule for sourcing sales of services has been controversial. Many commentators have argued that its effect is often to merely mimic the property and payroll factor, rather than measure the customer base within a state. The drafters of UDITPA foresaw the limitations of the standard UDITPA apportionment formula, and, under UDITPA §2, specifically excluded from UDITPA certain service businesses, including financial organizations (banks, trust companies, savings banks, private bankers, savings and loan associations, credit unions, investment companies, or insurance companies) and public utilities (defined as any business entity that owns or operates for public use any plant, equipment, property, franchise, or license for the transmission of communications; transportation of goods or persons; or the production, storage, transmission, sale, delivery, or furnishing of electricity, water, steam, oil, oil products, or gas).

To address these issues, many states provide special rules for computing apportionment percentages for businesses in certain industries. Typically, these special rules involve the modification or exclusion of the conventional factors or the use of unique, industry-specific factors. Examples of industries for which states provide special apportionment factor rules include:

- Airlines
- Railroads
- Trucking companies
- Financial institutions
- Television and radio broadcasters
- Publishers
- Telecommunication services companies
- Mutual funds
- Pipeline companies
- Ship transportation companies
- Professional sports franchises

In many cases, the equitable relief provisions of UDITPA §18, which numerous states have incorporated into their statutes, serve as the basis for state revenue departments to adopt specialized formulas. UDITPA §18 provides that if the standard apportionment formula does not fairly reflect a taxpayer's in-state business activity, tax authorities may require the exclusion of one or more of the factors or the inclusion of additional factors that will fairly represent the taxpayer's business activity in the state. Under §18, the MTC has promulgated special apportionment regulations covering construction contractors [MTC Reg. IV.18(d)], airlines [MTC Reg. IV.18(e)], railroads [MTC Reg. IV.18(f)], trucking companies [MTC Reg. IV.18(g)], television and radio broadcasters [MTC Reg. IV.18(h)], and publishers [MTC Reg. IV.18(j)]. The MTC has also promulgated a model statute for apportioning the income of financial institutions (Nov. 17, 1994). Additionally, the MTC has approved a proposed model regulation for the apportionment of income from telecommunications services.

Sourcing Sales of Services

UDITPA §17. UDITPA provides two different rules for determining the numerator of the sales factor. UDITPA §16 applies to sales of tangible personal property, and UDITPA §17 applies to all sales other than sales of tangible personal property. UDITPA §17 is a catchall provision, which applies to fees from services, rental income, as well as interest, dividends, royalties, and gains derived from the sale of intangible property.

Most states employ some variation of the UDITPA §17 income-producing activity rule to source sales of services. Under UDITPA §17(a), sales of services are attributed to the state in which "the income producing activity is performed."

EXAMPLE

A consulting firm receives a $100,000 fee for services performed by the taxpayer's employees at its offices in State P. Regardless of where the client is located, the $100,000 sale is attributed to State P, because that is where the underlying income-producing activity (i.e., employee services) is performed.

Under UDITPA §17(b), if the income-producing activity is performed in two or more states, the sale is attributed to the state in which a greater proportion of the income-producing activity is performed than in any other state, based on the "costs of performance." Thus, in order to source sales of services under the UDITPA income-producing activity rule, the taxpayer must first determine what activity produced the income. Once the taxpayer has identified the applicable income-producing activity, a cost-of-performance analysis is conducted. This involves determining the costs associated with the activity, as well as the states in which those costs were incurred.

The cost-of-performance rule is an all-or-nothing approach, whereby the entire sale is attributed to the single state in which the greater proportion of the costs of performance is incurred.

> **EXAMPLE**
>
> A consulting firm receives a $100,000 fee for services performed by its employees. Seventy percent of the costs of performance are incurred in State P, and 30 percent of the costs of performance are incurred in State Q. Under UDITPA §17(b), the entire $100,000 sale is attributed to State P, because that is where the greater proportion of the income-producing activity is performed, based on costs of performance. None of the $100,000 sale is attributed to State Q, despite the significant amount of costs of performance incurred in State Q.

UDITPA does not define the terms *income-producing activity* or *costs of performance*, but additional guidance is provided by the MTC regulations. Under MTC Reg. IV.17(2), the term *income-producing activity* applies to each separate item of income and means the transactions and activity engaged in by the taxpayer in the regular course of its trade or business. Examples of income-producing activity include:

- The rendering of personal services by employees or the use of tangible or intangible property by the taxpayer in performing a service
- The sale, rental, leasing, licensing, or other use of real property
- The rental, leasing, licensing, or other use of tangible personal property
- The sale, licensing, or other use of intangible personal property

The mere holding of intangible personal property is not, by itself, an income-producing activity.

Under MTC Reg. IV.17(3), the term *costs of performance* means direct costs determined in a manner consistent with generally accepted accounting principles and in accordance with accepted conditions or practices in the trade or business of the taxpayer. Direct costs include material and labor costs that have a causal relationship with the sale in question. In other words, a direct cost is a cost that was incurred for a specific purpose and is traceable to that purpose.

> **EXAMPLE**
>
> The direct costs associated with a service contract for maintaining business equipment would include both the cost of repair parts and the compensation costs of the service technicians.

Indirect costs, which include general and administrative expenses that are not associated with any specific sale, are not taken into account in determining the costs of performance. In 2007, the MTC amended this regulation to provide that a taxpayer's income-producing activity includes "transactions and activities performed on behalf of a taxpayer, such as those conducted on its behalf by an independent contractor," and that a taxpayer's cost of performance includes "payments to an agent or independent contractor for the performance of personal services and utilization of tangible and intangible property which give rise to the particular item of income."

MTC Reg. IV.17(4)(B)(c) provides a special rule for applying the UDITPA income-producing activity rule to gross receipts for the performance of "personal services," under which a lump-sum payment for personal services performed in two or more states is prorated among the states in proportion to the time spent in each state, based on the premise that the services performed in each state constitute a separate income-producing activity. The regulation does not define what constitutes "personal services."

Market-based source rules. The original purpose of the sales factor was to include in the apportionment formula a measure of the taxpayer's customer base within a given state. However, unlike the UDITPA §16 destination test for inventory sales, the UDITPA §17 income-producing activity rule for sales of services does not accurately measure a service company's customer base when the seller (service provider) performs services in one state and the purchaser (service recipient) is located in another state. When UDITPA was drafted in 1957, it was rare for a service provider and service recipient to be located in different states. Today, however, it is more common for customers to do business with out-of-state service providers. In such cases, the income-producing activity rule no longer measures the customer base within a state, but instead tends to mimic the property and payroll factors.

Due in part to this weakness of the income-producing activity rule, some states have adopted a market-based approach for sales of services, whereby receipts from services are attributed to a state based on where the service recipient is located. In addition to providing a more accurate measure of the taxpayer's customer base, this approach has the political appeal of reducing the tax burden on service providers that have in-state facilities but provide services primarily to out-of-state customers. A market-based rule for services also creates an incentive for regional and national service providers to locate their facilities within the state's borders. Because most states use the income-producing activity rule, a market-based source rule can result in nowhere income for service providers that locate their facilities within the state. Finally, the tax revenue on in-state service providers that is lost from switching from the income-producing activity rule to a market-based rule may be partially offset by increased taxes on out-of-state service providers that make sales to in-state customers.

The states that have adopted a market-based approach for sales of services include Georgia, Illinois, Iowa, Maine, Maryland, Michigan, Minnesota, Utah, and Wisconsin. Starting in 2011, California taxpayers who elect to use a sales-only apportionment formula must use a market-based sourcing rule for sales of services. California taxpayers who continue to use a double-weighted sales formula must use the costs of performance rule to source sales of services.

Non-Income Taxes: Michigan, Ohio, Texas, and Washington

Most states link their corporate tax structures to the federal net income tax model, primarily for ease of administration. However, some states base their corporate tax systems on different models, or impose specialized corporate taxes in addition to a regular corporate income tax.

Michigan business tax. Michigan imposes a 4.95 percent business income tax and a 0.80 percent modified gross receipts tax. Both taxes apply to business entities generally, including C corporations, S corporations, partnerships, limited liability companies, and sole proprietorships. A unitary business group must compute both the business income tax and the modified gross receipts tax on a combined basis. Taxpayers pay the sum of the two new taxes. There is currently an annual surcharge equal to 21.99 percent of a taxpayer's Michigan business tax.

The business income tax base is a taxpayer's federal taxable income, adjusted for numerous addition and subtraction modifications. The modified gross receipts tax base is a taxpayer's gross receipts reduced by purchases from other firms, which includes acquisitions of inventory, depreciable assets, and materials and supplies (including repair parts and fuel).

Ohio commercial activity tax. Ohio imposes a *commercial activity tax* (CAT) on a business entity's gross receipts. A flat tax of $150 is imposed on the first $1 million in taxable gross receipts. For amounts greater than $1 million, the tax rate is 0.26 percent.

The CAT applies to C corporations, S corporations, partnerships, and limited liability companies. Two or more commonly controlled corporations compute the CAT as either a consolidated elected taxpayer or as a combined taxpayer. Certain types of entities that are subject to other types of Ohio taxes are exempt from the CAT, including financial institutions, insurance companies, securities dealers, and public utilities.

Generally, items that are treated as gross receipts for federal income tax purposes are treated as gross receipts for CAT purposes. Examples include the amounts realized from the sale of goods, the performance of services, or the use of property. There are a number of exemptions. Specifically, the following gross receipts are not subject to the CAT:

- Interest (except on credit sales)
- Dividends and capital gains
- Principal payments on a loan
- Proceeds from issuing stock
- Insurance proceeds (except business interruption insurance)

- Damages from litigation
- Sales and use taxes collected from consumers
- Sales returns, allowances, and discounts
- Bad debts

A taxable gross receipt is a gross receipt sitused to Ohio. Sales of inventory are attributed to Ohio if the property is received in Ohio by the purchaser, rents and royalties are attributed to Ohio if the property is located or used in Ohio, and fees for services are attributed to Ohio in the proportion that the purchaser's benefit in Ohio bears to the purchaser's benefit everywhere. Thus, examples of taxable gross receipts include sales of property delivered to locations within Ohio, rents from property used in Ohio, and fees for services where the purchaser receives the benefit in Ohio.

Texas margin tax. Texas imposes a business margin tax. Taxable entities include C corporations, S corporations, limited liability companies, partnerships, and other legal entities. Certain entities are not subject to the margin tax, including sole proprietorships (does not include single-member LLCs), general partnerships with direct ownership entirely composed of natural persons, and certain passive entities. Taxable entities that are part of an affiliated group engaged in a unitary business must file a combined group report and compute their margin tax as if they were a single taxable entity. An "affiliated group" means a group of one or more taxable entities in which a controlling interest is owned by a common owner, either corporate or noncorporate, or by one or more of the member entities. A taxable entity's margin is the lowest of three amounts:

1. Total revenue minus cost of goods sold
2. Total revenue minus compensation
3. Seventy percent of total revenue

The tax rate is 0.5 percent for taxpayers primarily engaged in retail or wholesale trade, and 1 percent for all other businesses. A taxable entity with total revenue of $10 million or less may elect to calculate its margin tax due by multiplying total revenue times the apportionment factor times 0.575 percent.

A taxable entity's total revenues are defined by reference to the amounts reported on its federal income tax return, and include gross receipts or sales (less returns and allowances), dividends, interest, gross rents, gross royalties, capital gain net income, net gain or loss from the sale of trade or business assets (federal *Form 4797, Sales of Business Property*), and other income. The following items may be excluded from gross revenue:

- Bad debt expense
- Foreign dividends and royalties

- Net distributive income from a taxable entity treated as a partnership or S corporation for federal tax purposes
- Federal dividends received deduction
- Income from a disregarded entity for federal but not Texas margin tax purposes
- Dividends and interest from federal obligations
- Certain other specified items

A taxable entity may subtract cost of goods sold in computing its margin only if the entity owns the goods. Thus, service companies are generally not eligible to subtract cost of goods sold. In addition, numerous special rules apply in computing cost of goods sold for margin tax purposes; therefore, the deduction will generally not be the same as the amount used in computing federal taxable income.

> **EXAMPLE**
>
> A taxable entity may elect to currently expense allowable costs associated with the goods purchased or produced, in which case the entity will have no beginning or ending inventory.

If a taxable entity subtracts compensation in computing its margin, the compensation deduction will include both the compensation amounts reported on the employees' Form W-2s (maximum of $320,000 per person for 2010 tax reports) as well as deductible employee benefits, including workers' compensation, health care, and retirement benefits.

Washington business and occupation tax. The State of Washington imposes a gross receipts tax called the *business and occupation tax* (B&O tax). The B&O tax applies to C corporations, S corporations, partnerships, and sole proprietorships.

The B&O tax is imposed on a seller's gross receipts derived from business activities conducted within Washington. Taxable gross receipts generally include:
- Gross proceeds from sales of goods delivered to customers located in Washington
- Gross receipts from sales of services rendered in Washington
- The value of products manufactured in Washington

Gross proceeds from sales of goods that an in-state retailer or wholesaler delivers to customers located outside of Washington are generally not taxable. Generally, no deductions are allowed for cost of goods sold, salaries, supplies, taxes, or any other costs of doing business. However, there are a handful of exemptions, deductions, and credits. For example, there is an exemption for the sale or rental of real estate (other than lodging), and deductions for bad debts as well as sales returns, allowances, and discounts.

The B&O tax rate varies with the type of business activity. Also, it is possible for a single taxpayer to have gross receipts in two or more categories. The four primary business activity classifications and applicable tax rates are:

- Retailing (0.471 percent)
- Wholesaling (0.484 percent)
- Manufacturing (0.484 percent)
- Service and other activities (1.5 percent)

In addition to the primary categories, there are numerous specialized categories, each with an associated tax rate. Examples include travel agents and tour operators (0.275 percent), manufacturing commercial aircraft (0.2904 percent), highway contractors (0.484 percent), royalties (0.484 percent), and public or nonprofit hospitals (1.5 percent).

STUDY QUESTIONS

---

13. A corporation sells a service. Sixty percent of the income-producing activity is performed in State A, 30 percent in State B, and 10 percent in State C. Under the cost-of-performance rule in UDITPA §17(b), how is the sale allocated?

  a. 60 percent to State A, 30 percent to State B, and 10 percent to State C

  b. 34 percent to State A, 33 percent to State B, and 33 percent to State C

  c. 100 percent to State A

14. Under a market-based approach for sourcing sales of services, receipts from services are generally attributed to the state in which the benefit of the service is received. *True or False?*

Mechanisms Used by States to Limit Income Shifting

A principal planning objective is to create legal structures that minimize the state income taxes of the business enterprise as a whole. Through the use of separately incorporated affiliates and intercompany transactions (loans, licenses, inventory sales, etc.), income can be shifted from operations in high-tax states to operations in low-tax states. Such strategies are made possible by the large number of states that require or permit the filing of separate-company returns, whereby each member of an affiliated group that has nexus in a state computes its income and files a return as if it were a separate and distinct economic entity.

States employ a number of mechanisms to limit the ability of multistate businesses to use related party structures and transactions to shift income.

As discussed below, these include the theory of economic nexus, the judicial doctrines of economic substance and business purpose, combined reporting, Code Sec. 482-type reallocation provisions, and related party expense addback provisions.

Economic nexus. The highest courts in several states have ruled that an economic presence, such as the licensing of trademarks for use within the state by affiliated companies, is sufficient to create constitutional nexus for income tax purposes [*Geoffrey, Inc. v. South Carolina Tax Commission*, 437 S.E.2d 13 (S.C. 1993), *cert. denied* 510 US 992 (1993); *Lanco, Inc. v. Division of Taxation*, No. A-89-05 (N.J. Sup. Ct., Oct. 12, 2006); *cert. denied*, U.S. Sup. Ct., 06-1236 (2007); *Commissioner v. MBNA America Bank, N.A.*, No. 33049 (W.V. Sup. Ct. of App., Nov. 21, 2006); *cert. denied*, U.S. Sup. Ct., 06-1228 (2007); *Capital One Bank and Capital One F.S.B. v. Commissioner of Revenue*, No. SJC-10105 (Mass. Sup. Jud. Ct., Jan. 8, 2009); *cert. denied*, U.S. Sup. Ct., No. 08-1169 (2009); and *KFC Corporation v. Iowa Department of Revenue*, No. 09-1032 (Ia. Sup. Ct., Dec. 30, 2010)].

Economic substance and business purpose. In *Gregory v. Helvering* [293 US 465, 1935], the U.S. Supreme Court ruled that a transaction is respected only if it has economic substance and serves a business purpose other than tax avoidance. The states have invoked the judicial doctrines of economic substance and business purpose as an argument to, for example, disallow deductions for royalty payments made by an operating company to a trademark holding company.

For example, in *Syms Corp. v. Commissioner of Revenue* [No. SJC-08513 (Mass. Sup. Jud. Ct., Apr. 10, 2002)], the Massachusetts Supreme Judicial Court ruled that the transfer and licensing back of trademarks between a retailer and its trademark holding company was a sham transaction, and therefore no deduction was allowed for the royalty payments. The Massachusetts Appeals Court reached similar conclusions in *Talbots, Inc. v. Commissioner of Revenue* [Nos. C266698, C271840, and C276882 (Mass. App. Ct., Sept. 29, 2009)], and *TJX Companies, Inc. v. Commissioner of Revenue* [No. 07-P-1570 (Mass. App. Ct., Apr. 3, 2009)].

On the other hand, in *The Sherwin-Williams Co. v. Commissioner of Revenue* [No. SJC-08516 (Mass. Sup. Jud. Ct., Oct. 31, 2002)], the Massachusetts Supreme Judicial Court ruled that two trademark holding companies had economic substance and served valid business purposes. Likewise, in *HMN Financial, Inc. v. Commissioner of Revenue* [No. A09-1164 (Minn. Sup. Ct., May 20, 2010)], the Minnesota Supreme Court ruled that the Commissioner did not have the authority to disregard the taxpayer's captive REIT structure, which was motivated solely by tax avoidance, because the taxpayer complied with the relevant corporate franchise tax statutes in structuring its business and reporting its income.

Combined reporting. Requiring an out-of-state trademark holding company or financing company to file a combined report with an in-state operating company eliminates the tax benefits of intercompany royalty and interest payments. When computing the unitary group's combined income, the in-state operating company's royalty and interest expense deductions are offset by the royalty and interest income of the out-of-state holding and financing companies.

> **EXAMPLE**
>
> New Jersey does not permit an affiliated group to elect to file a consolidated return nor does it require all unitary groups to compute their tax on a combined basis. Thus, every corporation with nexus in New Jersey generally is considered a separate entity and must file its own return. The Director of the Division of Taxation may, however, require members of an affiliated group or a controlled group to file a consolidated return "if the taxpayer cannot demonstrate by clear and convincing evidence that a report by a taxpayer discloses the true earnings of the taxpayer on its business carried on in this State." [N.J. Rev. Stat. 54:10A-10.c.]

Section 482-type reallocation. Code Sec. 482 authorizes the IRS to reallocate income among commonly controlled corporations whenever necessary to prevent the evasion of taxes or to clearly reflect the income of the related entities. Congress enacted Code Sec. 482 to ensure that commonly controlled corporations report and pay tax on their actual share of income arising from intercompany transactions. Many states have enacted Section 482-type statutes, although the details of these statutes vary significantly from state to state.

> **EXAMPLE**
>
> Florida tax authorities may make adjustments to clearly reflect a taxpayer's income if an arrangement exists between related entities that causes a taxpayer's income to be "reflected improperly or inaccurately." [Fla. Stat. ch. §220.44]

Related party expense add-back provisions. Another technique that many states use to limit income shifting is to require corporations to add back any royalty or interest payments made to related parties when computing state taxable income (hereinafter referred to as "addback provisions").

Although the different state addback provisions share many common themes, there are significant differences, particularly with respect to the circumstances under which an exception applies and the related party expense need not be added back. Therefore, it is essential to thoroughly analyze each state's specific provisions to ensure compliance.

State related party expenses addback provisions are generally targeted at interest expenses and intangible expenses. Most states define *interest expense* by reference to Code Sec. 163. States generally define *intangible expenses* to include not only royalties, but also a broad range of other costs, expenses, and losses related to intangible property.

State addback provisions are designed to prevent taxpayers from using intercompany licensing and financing arrangements to avoid corporate income taxes. Under the general rules, however, state addback provisions apply automatically to all related party intangible and interest expenses, including those related party payments that are motivated by legitimate business purposes rather than tax avoidance. As a consequence, each state provides some relief in the form of exceptions from the automatic addback requirement. These exceptions are complex and vary from state to state. However, there are some common themes, including exceptions that apply when:

- The related payee's corresponding income is subject to tax in another U.S. state or a foreign country.
- The related payee pays the amount to an unrelated person.
- The addback adjustment produces an unreasonable result.
- The taxpayer and the state tax authorities agree to an alternative adjustment.

Pass-Through Entities

States generally conform to the federal tax treatment of S corporations and partnerships as pass-through entities, as well as the federal "check-the-box" classification of an LLC as a partnership or a disregarded entity. Despite this broad conformity, numerous states impose entity-level taxes on S corporations, partnerships, and LLCs. Examples include California, Illinois, Massachusetts, Michigan, Ohio, Pennsylvania, Tennessee, Texas, and Washington.

STUDY QUESTION

> **15.** Which of the following is ***not*** a mechanism used by states to limit tax base erosion?
>
> **a.** Separate-company reporting
> **b.** Combined reporting
> **c.** Economic nexus

State Treatment of Net Operating Losses

This chapter explains why differences arise between federal and state net operating loss (NOL) deductions. It also discusses the various ways in which states calculate and treat these deductions.

LEARNING OBJECTIVES

Upon completion of this chapter, the reader should be able to:

- List reasons for differences in state and federal NOL deductions
- Describe the impact of state NOL apportionment methods on state NOL deductions
- Identify the limitations that states may place on NOL deductions
- Explain how NOLs are treated for federal and state purposes when mergers and acquisitions take place

OVERVIEW

If a corporation has cyclical earnings, the effective tax rate on the corporation's net earnings over time could significantly exceed the statutory tax rate if the corporation's taxable income is determined on a strict annual basis, in which case losses from one year could not offset profits from another year. To prevent such inequities, Congress enacted Internal Revenue Code ("Code") Sec. 172, which permits taxpayers to claim a net operating loss (NOL) deduction against current year taxable income in a carryover year. Generally, for federal tax purposes, NOLs can be carried back two years and forward 20 years. Code Sec. 172(b)(3) gives taxpayers the option to forgo the two-year carryback in favor of a carryforward.

DIFFERENCES BETWEEN FEDERAL AND STATE NOLS

Most states allow NOL deductions, but the specific rules vary significantly from state to state. As a consequence, there is often a difference between the amount of the federal and state NOL deductions. These federal-state differences arise for a number of reasons, including:

- States requiring that the taxpayer have nexus in the year the NOL arises in order to carry over the loss
- No state provision for NOL carrybacks, and state carryforward periods that are shorter than the 20-year federal carryforward

- State statutory limitations on the dollar amount of the carryover allowed
- Different group filing methods for federal and state tax purposes
- The application of the state NOL deduction on a pre- versus post-apportionment basis

Depending on whether the state uses Line 28 (federal taxable income before NOL and special deductions) or Line 30 (federal taxable income) of federal Form 1120 as the starting point for computing state taxable income, the requisite adjustments to convert a federal NOL deduction to the state deduction may take the form of an addition and/or subtraction modification.

Carryover Periods

Code Sec. 172 generally permits taxpayers to carry an NOL back two years and forward 20 years, and claim as a deduction in the carryover year. Most states allow NOL deductions, but the specific rules vary from state to state. Many states do not permit a carryback, and a number of states have carryforward periods that are shorter than 20 years. These differences are due in large part to state budgetary constraints; in particular, the negative tax revenue consequences of refund claims associated with NOL carrybacks. When facing severe budgetary constraints, some states temporarily suspend the NOL carryover deduction as a revenue raising measure.

During periods of economic recession, Congress has enacted enhanced carryback periods to infuse cash in the form of tax refunds into the economy. For example, the Job Creation and Worker Assistance Act of 2002 (P.L. 107-147) extended the carryback period to five years for NOLs arising in taxable years ending in 2001 and 2002.

The American Recovery and Reinvestment Act of 2009 (P.L. 111-5, Feb. 17, 2009) allows an eligible small business to elect up to a five-year carryback for an NOL sustained in a tax year beginning or ending in 2008. To be eligible, the business must satisfy a $15 million gross receipts test. An eligible business can carry back its 2008 NOL either three, four, or five years.

The Worker, Homeownership, and Business Assistance Act of 2009 (P.L. 111-92, Nov. 6, 2009) significantly broadened the availability of the enhanced carryback. Under Public Law 111-92, any taxpayer may elect to carryback an NOL arising in either 2008 or 2009, but not both, for either three, four, or five years. If a taxpayer elects a five-year carryback, however, the amount that can be carried back to the fifth preceding tax year is limited to 50 percent of the taxpayer's taxable income in the carryback year.

For most taxpayers, the extended carryback period applies for only one tax year, 2008 or 2009. However, an eligible small business that elected an extended carryback for a 2008 NOL under prior law may also elect an extended carryback for a 2009 NOL. In addition, the 50 percent of taxable income limitation does not apply to eligible small businesses which, under prior law, elected a five-year carryback for a 2008 NOL.

For alternative minimum tax purposes, the usual rule that an NOL deduction is limited to 90 percent of alternative minimum taxable income does not apply to 2008 or 2009 NOLs that are carried back either three, four or five years.

Federal law allows a taxpayer to forgo the automatic carryback period in favor of an NOL carryforward [Code Sec. 172(b)(3)]. Most states that allow a carryback also permit the election to forgo the state carryback, provided that the taxpayer has made the same election for federal purposes. If a loss corporation is a member of a consolidated return group, different rules may apply.

EXAMPLE

If a corporation's current year loss is absorbed by the profits of other affiliates included in a federal consolidated return, it may still be possible to carry over a state-only NOL in certain separate-company return states.

Because states generally follow the federal rules for paying interest on carrybacks (i.e., no interest is paid if the refund is made within 45 days after the claim for refund is filed), amended state returns using a federal carryback should be filed as soon as possible after the federal or state return generating the loss is filed.

STUDY QUESTION

1. Which of the following is **not** a reason for federal-state differences in NOL deductions?
   a. No federal provision for NOL carrybacks
   b. State carryforward periods less than 20 years
   c. Different group filing methods for federal and state purpose

Impact of Apportionment Percentage

Some states require that the total NOL generated in a loss year be adjusted by the loss year's apportionment percentage before it is applied in a carryover year, and then the apportioned NOL is offset against the amount of apportioned income in the carryover year. This is known as a *post-apportionment* NOL deduction.

Other states require that the full amount of the loss year's NOL be offset against the carryover year's total apportionable income before applying the apportionment percentage for the carryover year to the net amount of apportionable income. This is known as a *pre-apportionment* NOL deduction.

If there is a major change in the corporation's state apportionment percentage between the loss year and the carryover year, the amount of the NOL deduction can vary significantly with the method (pre- versus post-apportionment) employed by the state.

> **EXAMPLE**
>
> In 20X1, Acme Corporation sustains a $100 NOL and has a State X apportionment percentage of 50 percent. In 20X2, Acme has taxable income before the NOL deduction of $300 and a State X apportionment percentage of 70 percent.
>
> If State X applies an NOL on a *pre-apportionment* basis, Acme's 20X2 taxable income is $140 [($300 – $100 NOL) x 70%]. On the other hand, if State X applies an NOL on a *post-apportionment* basis, Acme's 20X2 taxable income is $160 [($300 x 70%) – ($100 NOL x 50%)].

Impact of Addition and Subtraction Modifications

Regardless of whether Line 28 or Line 30 of the federal income tax return is used as the starting point in computing state taxable income, each state requires a number of addition and subtraction modifications. Generally, states require that the same modifications used in determining state taxable income be reflected in the computation of a state NOL. In addition, a corporation must generally be subject to tax and file a state tax return in the loss year in order to establish a state NOL—although there are some exceptions.

Several states have statutory or regulatory provisions mandating that the starting point before state modifications (i.e., federal taxable income) may not be smaller than zero, unless an NOL is generated in that year. Therefore, in those states, if the state-specified addition modifications *exceed* the subtraction modifications in a year in which a federal NOL deduction is being used, the taxpayer may have state taxable income—even though it has no federal taxable income for that year.

Statutory Limitations

A number of states impose flat dollar limitations on the amount of an NOL carryback deduction.

> **EXAMPLE**
>
> Utah limits carrybacks to $1 million, and Idaho limits carrybacks to $100,000.

Some states impose flat dollar or percentage limitations on NOL carryforward deductions.

In 2010, Pennsylvania limits NOL carryforward deductions to the greater of $3 million or 20 percent of taxable income.

Some states impose temporary limitations on NOL carryforward deductions in response to fiscal constraints.

From 2011 to 2013, Colorado limits its NOL carryforward deduction to $250,000 per year.

Some states permit an NOL deduction only to the extent that such a deduction is allowed in computing federal taxable income. If such a state also requires a member of a federal consolidated group to file a separate-company return for state purposes, the current year's NOLs that are absorbed by an affiliate on a federal consolidated return may *never* be available to the loss-generating corporation for state tax purposes, because the loss will never be reflected as an NOL deduction on the loss corporation's federal return.

The limitation is illustrated by the Oklahoma Supreme Court's decision in *Utica Bankshares Corp. v. Oklahoma Tax Commission* [892 P.2d 979 (Okla. 1994)]. The court held that the federal NOL can be used only to offset federal taxable income for the carryback year and not for positive modifications for years in which Oklahoma taxable income was greater than federal taxable income. In other words, the taxpayer may not claim on the state tax return an NOL deduction based on the federal NOL that is in excess of the federal NOL deduction actually allowed by the IRS for the corresponding tax years.

In *Sovran Bank/D.C. National v. District of Columbia* [731 A.2d 387 (D.C. Ct. of App. 1999)], the taxpayer successfully argued that because it was required to file a District of Columbia return on a separate-company basis, the appropriate construction of the District's NOL provision was to determine NOL carrybacks as if the taxpayer had filed a separate federal return. The District codified this decision by allowing NOLs to be computed on a separate-company basis, regardless of how the NOL is used on a federal consolidated return [D.C. Code Ann. §47-1803.3(a)(14)(E)(ii)].

STUDY QUESTION

> **2.** If a corporation's state apportionment percentage is higher in the carryforward year than the loss year, then the benefit of an NOL carryforward deduction is greater if the state uses the pre-apportionment method rather than the post-apportionment method. ***True or False?***

Different Federal and State Consolidation Rules

In the case of an affiliated group of corporations filing a federal consolidated return, the computation of a state NOL deduction may be complicated by the use of different group filing methods for state tax purposes, such as:

- Separate-company returns
- Consolidated returns
- Combined unitary reporting

In such cases, the state NOL deduction may be determined on a federal *pro forma* basis—that is, what the allowable federal NOL carryover or deduction would be if only the separate company or the companies included in the state consolidated or combined return were included in the federal return.

However, states that permit the filing of a consolidated or combined return may impose separate return limitation year (SRLY) restrictions on the use of a specific affiliate's NOLs to reduce consolidated taxable income.

In ***Golden West Financial Corp. v. Florida Department of Revenue*** [No. 1D07-0135, 975 (Fla. Dist. Ct., Feb. 19, 2008)], a Florida District Court of Appeal ruled that that a Florida regulation, which prohibited corporations that incurred losses when filing Florida returns on a separate-company basis to share those losses with members of their affiliated group when electing to file on a consolidated basis, was invalid because it impermissibly contravened the specific provisions of the enabling statutes. The Florida Department of Revenue subsequently deleted the invalid provision [Fla. Dept. of Rev., Regs. 12C-1.013, Apr. 14, 2009], and such corporations are now permitted to share Florida NOL carryovers on a consolidated return.

North Carolina's Net Economic Loss Approach

For North Carolina tax purposes, an operating loss is deductible only if it is a net economic loss, rather than a net operating loss. A *net economic loss* is the amount by which allowable deductions, other than prior years' losses, exceed income from all sources in the year—including nontaxable income.

NOLS IN MERGERS AND ACQUISITIONS

Federal Tax Treatment

When the assets of a corporation that has NOL carryovers (*loss corporation*) are acquired by another corporation, an important issue for the acquiring corporation is whether it can use the loss corporation's pre-acquisition NOLs to offset the earnings from its other business activities.

Over the years, Congress has enacted numerous restrictions to prevent profitable corporations from *trafficking in NOLs*, that is, acquiring corporations with NOL carryovers merely as a device to avoid taxes. The principal provisions governing the transfer of NOLs in such situations are Code Secs. 381 and 382.

Code Sec 381. Code Sec. 381 provides that an acquiring corporation succeeds to the NOL carryovers of a loss corporation when it acquires the assets of the loss corporation (or target) in one of the following transactions:

- Subsidiary liquidation under Code Sec. 332
- Type A reorganization (statutory merger or consolidation)
- Type C reorganization (acquisition of substantially all of the target's assets in exchange for the stock of the acquiring corporation)
- Nondivisive Type D reorganization (acquisition of substantially all of the target's assets in exchange for stock, where the acquiring corporation distributes the stock it receives)
- Type F reorganization (change of identity, form, or place of organization)
- Type G reorganization (acquisition of substantially all of the target's assets in a bankruptcy proceeding)

Code Sec. 381 does *not* apply to:

- Partial liquidations (where the target remains intact and retains its tax attributes)
- Type B reorganizations (a stock-for-stock exchange in which the target becomes a subsidiary of the acquirer and retains its tax attributes)
- Divisive Type D reorganizations (where the tax attributes remain with the target in a spin-off or split-off, or expire upon the liquidation of the transferor in a split-up)
- Type E reorganizations (recapitalizations, which involve a single corporation)
- Taxable asset acquisitions (where the tax attributes remain with the target)
- Taxable stock acquisitions where the new subsidiary is not liquidated (and the tax attributes remain with the target)

Code Sec 382. For transactions in which the acquiring corporation succeeds to the NOL carryovers of the loss corporation (e.g., a statutory merger), Code Sec. 382 may limit the acquiring corporation's use of the target's pre-acquisition NOLs. Code Sec. 382 does not disallow an NOL deduction, but rather limits the amount of the deduction to the hypothetical future income that would be generated by the loss corporation's business capital. Limiting the use of the NOLs to the amount that would have been deductible by the loss corporation reflects the policy of Code Sec. 382, which is that a change in ownership of the loss corporation's assets should not make that corporation's NOL carryovers more or less valuable.

The restrictions of Code Sec. 382 apply when there has been a substantial change in the stock ownership of the loss corporation. More specifically, Code Sec. 382 applies when the following two requirements are met:

1. There has been either a tax-free reorganization (other than a Type F, Type G, or divisive Type D), or a change in the stock ownership of persons owning five percent or more of the loss corporation's stock.
2. The percentage of stock owned by one or more five percent shareholders increases by more than 50 percentage points (by value) during a three-year testing period.

When the requisite change in stock ownership of the loss corporation has occurred, Code Sec. 382 limits the annual amount of NOL deductions available to the acquiring corporation to an amount equal to the fair market value of the loss corporation's stock before the ownership change, multiplied by the federal long-term tax-exempt rate. Thus, Code Sec. 382 limits the use of the loss corporation's pre-acquisition NOLs to the hypothetical future income of the loss corporation, determined as if its stock were sold and the proceeds were reinvested in long-term tax-exempt securities. This federal *long-term tax-exempt rate* is published monthly by the IRS, and it is computed specifically for the purpose of applying Code Sec. 382.

Code Sec. 382 also imposes a continuity of business enterprise requirement. Specifically, if the acquiring corporation does not continue the business enterprise of the loss corporation at all times during the two-year period following the stock ownership change, no amount of the loss corporation's pre-acquisition NOLs are deductible.

Other statutory restrictions. In addition to Code Sec. 382, Congress has enacted various other restrictions on the carryover of tax attributes in mergers and acquisitions, including Code Secs. 269, 383, and 384. The regulations issued under Code Sec. 1502 also restrict the use of separate return limitation year NOLs in consolidated tax returns.

Under Code Sec. 269, the IRS may disallow an NOL carryforward deduction if one corporation acquires another corporation and the principal purpose of the acquisition is to evade or avoid income tax by claiming the benefit of a deduction that would not otherwise be available. Code Sec. 269 is the IRS's broadest and oldest weapon (first enacted in 1943) against trafficking in NOLs. The primary defense against the IRS's use of Code Sec. 269 is to document a good business purpose for the acquisition.

Code Sec. 383 extends restrictions similar to those found in Code Sec. 382 to other types of carryovers, including:

- Carryovers of capital losses
- General business credits
- Minimum tax credits
- Foreign tax credits

Code Sec. 384:

- Prevents a corporation with unrealized built-in gains from acquiring a loss corporation in order to use the target's pre-acquisition NOLs to offset its built-in gains
- Provides that, during a five-year post-acquisition period, the loss corporation's pre-acquisition NOLs may not offset the recognized built-in gains of the acquiring corporation
- Prevents an acquiring corporation from offsetting its pre-acquisition NOLs against the built-in gains of the target corporation

Finally, in the case of an affiliated group of corporations filing a consolidated tax return, if a member of the affiliated group acquires the stock of another corporation, and the new affiliate joins in the filing of the consolidated return, the consolidated group's use of the acquired corporation's pre-acquisition NOLs to offset income generated by other members of the group is limited by the separate return limitation year rules of Treasury Regulation §1.1502-21.

A *separate return limitation year* (SRLY) generally is a tax year of a subsidiary during which the subsidiary was not a member of the group. Under the SRLY rules, the SRLY losses of one group member may be used to offset income of other group members only to the extent of the SRLY member's aggregate contribution to the group's consolidated taxable income.

STUDY QUESTION

> **3.** Which Internal Revenue Code Section is the IRS's oldest weapon against NOL trafficking?
>
> **a.** Code Sec. 269
> **b.** Code Sec. 382
> **c.** Code Sec. 383
> **d.** Code Sec. 384

State Tax Treatment

General rules. Most states permit NOL deductions, but the specific rules vary significantly from state to state. A number of states incorporate the federal NOL provisions into their tax laws by directly referencing the applicable federal provisions. Those states generally follow the limitations imposed by Code Secs. 381 and 382. Accordingly, if the acquiring corporation is not permitted to carry over the target corporation's pre-acquisition NOLs for federal purposes, then those pre-acquisition NOLs may not be carried over for state tax purposes.

States that use federal Form 1120, Line 30 (federal taxable income net of all deductions, including the federal NOL deduction), as the starting point in computing state taxable income automatically accord a corporation the same NOL treatment for state and federal tax purposes, unless the state requires an additional modification for the federal NOL deduction. Some of the states that use Line 30 of the federal return as the starting point in computing state taxable income have no statutory provisions governing NOL deductions. In those states, an NOL deduction is allowable for state purposes to the extent that the NOL deduction is allowed in computing federal taxable income. By default, these states adopt the provisions of Code Secs. 381 and 382.

Even if a state NOL deduction is determined based on the federal provisions or an amount reported on a federal return, the computation of the allowable state NOL deduction may be more complicated if state returns are filed on a separate-company basis or the consolidated or combined group for state tax purposes differs from the federal consolidated group.

In either case, the state NOL deduction generally is determined on a *pro forma* federal basis—that is, the allowable federal NOL deduction determined as if only the corporation filing on a separate-company basis or the group of corporations included in the state consolidated or combined group were included in the federal return.

Some states have created their own NOL provisions in lieu of adopting the federal provisions. These states generally permit an NOL to be carried forward in transactions involving tax-free reorganizations. Some of these states, however, have not adopted provisions similar to Code Secs. 381 and 382. In such states, it is possible that NOLs, which do not carry over for federal purposes, do carry over for state tax purposes.

Continuity of business enterprise requirement. Even if a state does not impose Code Sec. 382-type limitations, it may impose a *continuity of business enterprise restriction* on the use of pre-acquisition NOLs, in which case NOLs carry over only if the acquiring corporation continues the business enterprise of the loss corporation. In *BellSouth Telecommunications, Inc. v. Department of Revenue* [No. COA96-558 (N.C. Ct. App., June 3, 1997)], the North Carolina Court of Appeals ruled that a corporation could not deduct a pre-merger net economic loss of a former subsidiary, because the continuity of business enterprise requirement was not satisfied.

Taxpayer in year of NOL requirement. Another common state restriction is that a corporation may claim an NOL deduction *only* if the corporation was doing business in the state in the year the NOL was incurred.

> ### EXAMPLE
>
> If a corporation incurs an NOL in year one while doing business in State A and expands its business to State B during year two, State B may not permit the corporation to deduct the NOL carryover from year one.

The proper application of this restriction to a merger may be uncertain.

> ### EXAMPLE
>
> If a *loss corporation* is merged into a *profitable corporation* in a tax-free statutory merger, for federal tax purposes, the surviving corporation inherits the loss corporation's pre-merger NOLs.
>
> For state tax purposes, does the fact that the surviving corporation was doing business in the state before the merger influence the determination, or is whether the loss corporation was doing business in the state before the merger the only relevant factor?

In *American Home Products Corp. v. Tracy* [No. 02AP-759 (Ohio Ct. of App., Mar. 27, 2003)], the Ohio Court of Appeals ruled that a surviving corporation could *not* deduct an NOL carryforward generated by a predecessor, because neither corporation was an Ohio taxpayer in the year the loss was generated.

Restricting NOL deduction to corporation that incurred the loss. Some states restrict the carryover of a pre-acquisition NOL to the specific corporation that actually generated the loss. In such cases, if a loss corporation is merged into a profitable corporation, the loss corporation's NOLs may disappear for state tax purposes.

In *Richard's Auto City, Inc. v. Division of Taxation* [No. A-54 (N.J. Sup. Ct. June 21, 1995)], the New Jersey Supreme Court held that the Division of Taxation regulation limiting post-merger NOL carryovers to the same corporation that originally incurred the loss was valid. Thus, a corporate survivor of a merger may *not* deduct NOLs incurred by the merged corporation.

Likewise, in *Little Six Corp. v. Johnson* [No. 01-A-01-9806-CH-00285 (Tenn. Ct. App., May 28, 1999)], the Tennessee Court of Appeals held that the corporation surviving a statutory merger may *not* deduct NOLs incurred by the merged corporation.

In *Macy's East, Inc. v. Commissioner of Revenue* [No. SJC-09194 (Mass. Sup. Jud. Ct. May 27, 2004)], the Massachusetts Supreme Judicial Court ruled that the survivor of a merger may not deduct NOLs incurred by the merged corporation. Although the pre-merger NOLs carried over and were deductible by the surviving corporation for federal tax purposes, the state regulation that prohibited such carryovers was not unconstitutional.

STUDY QUESTION

> **4.** In which of the following cases was the taxpayer denied an NOL deduction because the continuity of business enterprise requirement was *not* met?
>
> **a.** *American Home Products Corp.*
> **b.** *BellSouth Telecommunications, Inc.*
> **c.** *Richard's Auto City, Inc.*

NOLS IN A FEDERAL CONSOLIDATED RETURN

Under Code Sec. 1501, an affiliated group of corporations may elect to file a federal consolidated income tax return. Under the statutory authority provided by Code Sec. 1502, the Treasury Department has issued voluminous regulations regarding how an affiliated group computes its consolidated federal income tax liability. These regulations generally adopt the single-entity approach to determining the tax of a consolidated group. Under this approach, the members of a consolidated group are treated as divisions of a single taxpayer. Thus, a major advantage of filing a federal consolidated return is that a NOL sustained by one group member can offset income earned by other group members in computing consolidated taxable income. [Treas. Reg. § 1.1502-11]

Carryover of CNOL to a Consolidated or a Separate Return Year

In computing its consolidated taxable income, a consolidated group may claim a deduction for the consolidated NOL (CNOL), which is the aggregate of the NOL carryovers to the consolidated return year, as determined under the principles of Code Sec. 172, and includes both any CNOLs of the consolidated group, as well as any NOLs of the members arising in separate return years. [Treas. Reg. § 1.1502-21(a)]

The rules governing the carryover of a CNOL to a separate return year are found in Treasury Reg. §1.1502-21(b). A CNOL that is attributable to a member may be carried back to a separate return year of that member. However, that same loss may not be carried back to an equivalent, or earlier, consolidated return year of the group. The portion of a CNOL that is attributable to a member is determined by a fraction, the numerator of which is the separate NOL of the member for the year of the loss and the denominator of which is the sum of the separate NOLs for that year of all members having such losses.

If a corporation ceases to be a member during a consolidated return year, any portion of a CNOL carryforward attributable to the departing member which is not absorbed by the consolidated group in that year may be carried forward to the departing member's first separate return year. However, that same loss may not be carried forward to an equivalent, or subsequent, consolidated return year of the group.

Limitations on NOLs from Separate Return Limitation Years

If an acquired corporation joins the acquiring corporation in the filing of a consolidated return, the use of the acquired corporation's pre-acquisition NOLs to offset income generated by other members of the consolidated group is limited by both the separate return limitation year (SRLY) rules of Treasury Reg. §1.1502-21(c), and the Code Sec. 382 limitation. A SRLY is a tax year of a subsidiary during which the subsidiary was not a member of the consolidated group.

Under Code Sec. 382, if a more than 50 percentage point change in stock ownership occurs with respect to a loss corporation, the use of the loss corporation's NOL carryforwards is limited. The Code Sec. 382 limitation for a tax year of a loss corporation after an ownership change generally equals the fair market value of the corporation's stock immediately before the ownership change multiplied by the long-term tax-exempt rate.

To simplify the calculation of the loss limitations, Treasury Reg. §1.1502-21(g) contains an *overlap rule,* under which the Code Sec. 382 limitations, rather than the SRLY limitations, apply if certain requirements are met. If, after applying the overlap rule, the SRLY limitations apply, an acquired subsidiary's SRLY losses may be deducted by the consolidated group only to the extent of that member's cumulative contribution to the group's consolidated taxable income.

NOLS IN STATE COMBINED REPORTING AND CONSOLIDATED RETURNS

States employ a variety of filing options for groups of commonly controlled corporations, including separate-company reporting, consolidated returns, and combined unitary reporting. Under separate-company reporting, each member of a commonly controlled group of corporations computes its income and files a return as if it were a separate economic entity. Some states permit or require affiliated corporations to file a state consolidated return if certain requirements are met. Combined unitary reporting is a methodology for apportioning the business income of a taxpayer member of a commonly controlled group of corporations that is engaged in a unitary business.

In contrast to the federal single-entity approach to determining the tax of a consolidated group, some states treat each member of a combined reporting group (or each affiliate in a state consolidated return) that has nexus in the state as a separate taxpayer that must pay its own tax and file its own return.

> **EXAMPLE**
>
> Under California's combined reporting regime, each "taxpayer member" of the unitary business group (i.e., a member that has income tax nexus in California) generally must separately compute its own tax. Consistent with this separate-entity approach to combined reporting, a California source NOL incurred by one member of the combined reporting group cannot be used to offset the income of other group members in a subsequent tax year.

Consistent with the federal tax regulations, some states have SRLY-type rules that restrict the use of an acquired subsidiary's pre-acquisition NOLs.

> **EXAMPLE**
>
> Oregon requires that if a consolidated Oregon return is filed, the SRLY rules found in Treasury Reg. §1.1502-1 must be followed.

Recent Developments

California. California suspended its NOL deduction for tax years beginning in 2008 to 2011. For 2010 and 2011, California does not allow an NOL deduction for taxpayers whose pre-apportionment income exceeds $300,000 (determined on an aggregate basis for members of a combined reporting group). For 2008 and 2009, California does not allow an NOL deduction for taxpayers with taxable income of $500,000 or more. The carryforward period for suspended NOLs is extended one year for an NOL incurred in 2010, two years for an NOL incurred in 2009, three years for an NOL incurred in 2008, and four years for an NOL incurred prior to 2008. On the other hand, beginning with NOLs incurred after 2012, California will allow a two-year NOL carryback. During the phase-in period, the carryback will be limited to 50 percent of an NOL incurred in 2013, and 75 percent of an NOL incurred in 2014. After 2014, the full amount of an NOL can be carried back two years. [S.B. 858, Oct. 19, 2010; and A.B. 1452, Sept. 30, 2008]

Colorado. For tax years beginning in 2011 to 2013, the NOL deduction is limited to $250,000 per year. If the limitation prevents the use of any part of an NOL carryforward in a tax year, then all NOLs carried forward to such tax year may be carried forward one additional year for each tax year the restriction applies. Additionally, any portion of an NOL carryforward that cannot be used solely due to the limitation is increased by 3.25 percent per year until the loss is used. [H.B. 1199, Feb 24, 2010] Colorado does not allow NOL carrybacks.

Idaho. Effective January 1, 2010, Idaho codified the Tax Commission's practice of applying federal law to determine whether NOLs survive after a merged corporation ceases to exist. Under H.B. 381 (Feb. 23, 2010), Idaho NOLs will, pursuant to Code Secs. 381 and 382, survive a merger if all of the following are true:

- The transaction meets all federal laws, criteria, and procedures.
- The liquidated or merged entity had an Idaho business activity and incurred an Idaho NOL.
- The continuity of business requirements are satisfied.

Illinois. Illinois suspended its NOL for tax years ending in 2011 to 2014. The carryforward period for the suspended NOLs is extended by the number of years that the deduction is suspended. [S.B. 2505, Jan. 13, 2011]

Iowa. In 2009, Iowa eliminated the two-year carryback, effective for NOLs incurred in tax years beginning on or after January 1, 2009. Corporations are still permitted a 20-year carryforward period. [S.B. 483, May 22, 2009]

Maine. Maine does not allow any NOL deductions for tax years beginning in 2009, 2010, and 2011. The NOL not deducted due to this restriction may be deducted in tax years beginning after 2011, subject to certain restrictions. [L.D. 353, May 28, 2009]

Massachusetts. Effective for tax years beginning on or after January 1, 2010, Massachusetts extends the NOL carryforward period from five years to 20 years. [S.B. 2582, Aug. 5, 2010]

New Jersey. Effective for NOLs incurred in tax years ending after June 30, 2009, New Jersey extends the NOL carryforward period from seven years to 20 years. [S.B. 2130, Nov. 24, 2008]

Pennsylvania. Prior to 2007, Pennsylvania limited NOL carryforward deductions to $2 million. The cap increased to the greater of $3 million or 12.5 percent of taxable income for tax years beginning in 2007 and 2008 [H.B. 859, July 12, 2006], the greater of $3 million or 15 percent of taxable income for tax years beginning in 2009, and the greater of $3 million or 20 percent of taxable income for tax years beginning after 2009. [H.B. 1531, Oct. 9, 2009]

STUDY QUESTION

5. Which of the following states will allow an NOL carryback starting in 2013?

   a. Colorado

   b. Iowa

   c. California

Nexus Standards for Foreign (Non-U.S.) Corporations

This chapter discusses state nexus standards, and how they compare to federal nexus standards for corporations organized in foreign countries.

LEARNING OBJECTIVES

Upon completion of this chapter, the reader should be able to:

- Describe the federal nexus standard of a permanent establishment under an income tax treaty
- Explain the physical presence test for state tax nexus
- Identify the protections from state income tax nexus afforded by Public Law 86-272
- Recognize that a corporation organized in a foreign country may have nexus for state tax purposes without having nexus for federal income tax purposes

FEDERAL NEXUS STANDARDS

U.S. Trade or Business

The United States uses a two-pronged system to tax the income of a "foreign corporation," that is, a corporation which is created or organized under the laws of a foreign country or U.S. possession. [Internal Revenue Code ("Code") Sec. 7701(a)] If the foreign corporation is engaged in a trade or business within the United States, the net amount of income effectively connected with that U.S. trade or business is taxed at the regular graduated rates. [Code Sec. 882] In addition, the gross amount of a foreign corporation's U.S.-source dividend, interest, royalty, and other investment-type income is subject to a flat-rate withholding tax of 30 percent. [Code Secs. 881(a) and 1442] Income tax treaties generally reduce the withholding tax rate to 15 percent or less [IRS Pub. 515, Table 1], and a statutory exemption is provided for portfolio interest income. [Code Sec. 881(c)]

Under Code Sec. 882(a), a foreign corporation's business profits are subject to U.S. taxation if the foreign corporation is "engaged in trade or business within the United States." However, neither the Code nor the Regulations provide a comprehensive definition of the term *trade or business*. Code Sec. 864(b) provides that a U.S. trade or business includes "the performance of personal services within the United States," but does not include the trading of stocks, securities, or commodities, if such trades are either made through an independent agent or made for the taxpayer's own account (unless the taxpayer is a dealer). These exceptions do not apply if the foreign corporation has an office in the United States through which the trades are made.

Case law suggests that a foreign corporation is engaged in a U.S. trade or business if its employees are engaged in considerable, continuous, and regular business activity within the United States [e.g., *Spermacet Whaling & Shipping Co. S/A v. Commissioner*, 30 T.C. 618 (1958); and *Inverworld, Inc. v. Commissioner*, 71 TCM 3231 (1996)]. The conduct of a U.S. trade or business by a domestic subsidiary corporation is not imputed to a foreign parent corporation [e.g., *Eugene Higgins v. Commissioner*, 312 US 212 (1941)]. However, if a partnership, estate, or trust is engaged in a U.S. trade or business, then each partner or beneficiary is considered to be engaged in a U.S. trade or business. [Code Sec. 875]

Permanent Establishment

The United States has entered into bilateral income tax treaties with approximately 60 foreign countries:

Australia	Austria	Bangladesh	Barbados	Belgium
Bulgaria	Canada	China	Commonwealth of Independent States*	Cyprus
Czech Republic	Denmark	Egypt	Estonia	Finland
France	Germany	Greece	Hungary	Iceland
India	Indonesia	Ireland	Israel	Italy
Jamaica	Japan	Kazakhstan	Korea	Latvia
Lithuania	Luxembourg	Mexico	Morocco	Netherlands
New Zealand	Norway	Pakistan	Philippines	Poland
Portugal	Romania	Russia	Slovak Republic	Slovenia
South Africa	Spain	Sri Lanka	Sweden	Switzerland
Thailand	Trinidad and Tobago	Tunisia	Turkey	Ukraine
United Kingdom	Venezuela			

* The U.S.-U.S.S.R. income tax treaty applies to the countries of Armenia, Azerbaijan, Belarus, Georgia, Kyrgyzstan, Moldova, Tajikistan, Turkmenistan, and Uzbekistan.
Source: IRS Pub. No. 515, Table 3 (February 2010).

The United States Model Income Tax Convention of November 15, 2006 (hereinafter the "U.S. Model Treaty") reflects the baseline negotiating position of the United States in establishing income tax treaties with other countries. Many treaties are patterned after, or have provisions similar to, the U.S. Model Treaty. Therefore, it is used as a reference point in the following discussion of treaty provisions. It is important to remember, however, that each tax treaty is separately negotiated and therefore is unique. As a consequence, to determine the impact of treaty provisions in any specific situation, one must consult the applicable treaty.

A primary goal of income tax treaties is to mitigate international double taxation through tax reductions or exemptions on certain types of income derived by residents of one treaty country from sources within the other treaty country. Prime examples are:

- Permanent establishment protections for business profits
- Reduced withholding tax rates on dividend, interest, royalty, and other investment-type income

These tax benefits are available only to a treaty country "resident," which is generally defined as any person who, under the country's internal laws, is subject to taxation by reason of domicile, residence, citizenship, place of management, place of incorporation, or other criterion of a similar nature. A resident does not include a person who is subject to tax in the country only with respect to income derived from sources in that country or on profits attributable to a permanent establishment in that country. [Article 4 of U.S. Model Treaty]

Under a permanent establishment provision, the business profits of a foreign corporation that is a resident of the treaty country are exempt from U.S. taxation unless the foreign corporation carries on business in the United States through a permanent establishment situated therein. If a foreign corporation has a permanent establishment in the United States, the United States may tax the foreign corporation's business profits, but only to the extent those business profits are attributable to the permanent establishment. [Article 7 of U.S. Model Treaty]

A *permanent establishment* generally includes a fixed place of business, such as a place of management, a branch, an office, a factory, a workshop, or a mine, well, quarry, or other place of natural resource extraction. There are numerous exceptions, however. In particular, a permanent establishment does not include the following:

- The use of facilities solely for the purpose of storage, display, or delivery of goods or merchandise belonging to the foreign corporation
- The maintenance of a stock of goods or merchandise belonging to the foreign corporation solely for the purpose of storage, display, or delivery
- The maintenance of a stock of goods or merchandise belonging to the foreign corporation solely for the purpose of processing by another enterprise

- The maintenance of a fixed place of business solely for the purpose of purchasing goods or merchandise, or of collecting information, for the foreign corporation
- The maintenance of a fixed place of business solely for the purpose of carrying on, for the foreign corporation, any other activity of a preparatory or auxiliary character
- The maintenance of a fixed place of business solely for any combination of the activities mentioned above, provided that the overall activity of the fixed place of business resulting from this combination is of a preparatory or auxiliary character

A permanent establishment also exists if employees or other dependent agents of the foreign corporation habitually exercise in the United States an authority to conclude sales contracts in the taxpayer's name. However:

- Employees who limit their activities to auxiliary or preparatory functions, such as collecting information about potential customers, with sales concluded in the home country, will not create a permanent establishment
- Marketing products in the United States solely through independent brokers or distributors also does not create a permanent establishment
- The mere presence of a U.S. subsidiary does not create a permanent establishment for a parent company incorporated in another country. [Article 5 of U.S. Model Treaty]

Treaty permanent establishment provisions are not binding for state nexus purposes, however, because income tax treaties generally apply only to selected types of federal taxes. [Article 2 of U.S. Model Treaty] As a consequence, it is possible for a foreign corporation to have nexus for state tax purposes but not federal income tax purposes.

STUDY QUESTION

> **1.** A primary goal of income tax treaties is to:
> **a.** Increase withholding tax rates on income derived by residents of a treaty country
> **b.** Alleviate international double taxation
> **c.** Provide tax exemptions for nonresidents of a treaty country

STATE NEXUS STANDARDS

In contrast to the federal nexus standards of engaging in trade or business within the United States or carrying on business in the United States through a permanent establishment situated therein, state income tax nexus standards generally require only a physical presence within the state of a type that is not protected by Public Law 86-272. In addition, some states have adopted the theories of economic nexus, agency nexus, and affiliate nexus. For example, under the theory of economic nexus, an in-state physical presence is not an absolute prerequisite for income tax nexus. Instead, a significant economic presence, such as licensing intangibles or making substantial sales in the state, is sufficient to create state income tax nexus.

As a consequence, it is possible for a foreign (non-U.S.) corporation to have nexus for state but not federal income tax purposes.

> **EXAMPLE**
>
> If a foreign corporation leases warehouse space in a state solely for the purpose of storing and delivering its merchandise to U.S. customers, the physical presence of company-owned inventory would generally create state income tax nexus, but not necessarily federal income tax nexus, because the mere storage of inventory does not constitute a permanent establishment.

Physical Presence Test

States generally attempt to impose their taxes on out-of-state corporations to the fullest extent permissible under federal law. A state has jurisdiction to tax a corporation organized in another state only if the out-of-state corporation's contacts with the state are sufficient to create nexus. Historically, states have asserted that virtually any type of in-state business activity creates nexus for an out-of-state corporation. This approach reflects the reality that it is politically more appealing to collect taxes from out-of-state corporations than to raise taxes on in-state business interests.

The desire of state lawmakers and tax officials to, in effect, export the local tax burden is counterbalanced by the Due Process Clause and Commerce Clause of the U.S. Constitution, both of which limit a state's ability to impose a tax obligation on an out-of-state corporation. The Due Process Clause provides that no state shall "deprive any person of life, liberty or property, without due process of law," and the Commerce Clause gives Congress the exclusive authority to regulate interstate commerce.

The landmark case on constitutional nexus is ***Quill Corp. v. North Dakota*** [504 US 298 (1992)]. Quill was a mail-order vendor of office supplies that solicited sales through catalogs mailed to potential customers in North Dakota and made deliveries through common carriers. Quill was incorporated in Delaware and had facilities in California, Georgia, and Illinois. Quill had no office, warehouse, retail outlet, or other facility in North Dakota nor were any Quill employees or representatives physically present in North Dakota. During the years in question, Quill made sales to roughly 3,000 North Dakota customers and was the sixth largest office supply vendor in the state.

Under North Dakota law, Quill was required to collect North Dakota use tax on its mail-order sales to North Dakota residents. Quill challenged the constitutionality of this tax obligation. The Supreme Court held that Quill's economic presence in North Dakota was sufficient to satisfy the Due Process Clause's "minimal connection" requirement. On the other hand, the Court ruled that an economic presence was not, by itself, sufficient to satisfy the Commerce Clause's "substantial nexus" requirement. Consistent with its ruling 25 years earlier in *National Bellas Hess, Inc. v. Department of Revenue* [386 US 753 (1967)], the Court ruled that a substantial nexus exists only if a corporation has a nontrivial physical presence in a state. In other words, the Court ruled that a physical presence is an essential prerequisite to establishing constitutional nexus, at least for sales and use tax purposes.

The Court did not address the issue of whether the physical presence test also applied for income tax purposes, which has resulted in a significant amount of controversy and litigation (see discussion under the heading "Economic Nexus").

STUDY QUESTION

2. Which of the following statements is true?

a. It is possible for a foreign (non-U.S.) corporation to have nexus for state income tax purposes but not for federal income tax purposes.

b. State nexus requirements are not affected by the Due Process Clause and Commerce Clause of the U.S. Constitution.

c. In *Quill*, the Supreme Court ruled that a physical presence test applies for income tax purposes.

Public Law 86-272

Another major federal restriction on state tax jurisdiction is Public Law 86-272 [15 U.S.C. 381], which Congress enacted in 1959 to provide out-of-state corporations with a limited safe harbor from the imposition of state taxes on "net income." Specifically, Public Law 86-272 prohibits a state from imposing a tax on the net income of an out-of-state corporation if the company's only in-state activity is the solicitation of orders by company representatives for sales of tangible personal property, which orders are sent outside the state for approval or rejection, and if approved, are filled by shipment or delivery from a point outside the state.

Although Public Law 86-272 can provide significant protections for a multistate business, it has several important limitations:

1. It applies only to taxes imposed on net income and provides no protection against the imposition of a sales and use tax collection obligation, gross receipts taxes (e.g., Ohio commercial activity tax, or Washington business and occupation tax), or corporate franchise taxes on net worth or capital.

2. It protects only sales of tangible personal property. It does not protect activities such as leasing tangible personal property, selling services, selling or leasing real estate, or selling or licensing intangibles.

3. For businesses that send employees into other states to sell tangible personal property, it applies only if those employees limit their in-state activities to the solicitation of orders that are sent outside the state for approval, and if approved, are filled by a shipment or delivery from a point outside the state.

> ### EXAMPLE
>
> If an employee salesperson exercises an authority to approve orders within a state, the company does not qualify for protection under Public Law 86-272. Likewise, Public Law 86-272 does not protect the presence of a salesperson who performs nonsolicitation activities, such as repairs, customer training, or technical assistance, within a state.

Although Public Law 86-272 does not define the phrase *solicitation of orders*, the meaning of the phrase was addressed by the Supreme Court in **Wisconsin Department of Revenue v. William Wrigley, Jr., Co.** [505 US 214 (1992)]. In this case, the Court defined *solicitation of orders* as encompassing "requests for purchases" as well as "those activities that are entirely ancillary to requests for purchases—those that serve no independent business function apart from their connection to the soliciting of orders." Examples of activities that might serve an independent business function, apart from the solicitation of orders, include:

- Installation and start-up
- Customer training
- Engineering and design assistance
- Technical assistance
- Maintenance and repair
- Credit and collection activities

By its terms, Public Law 86-272 applies only to "interstate commerce." Individual states are free, however, to extend the protections of Public Law 86-272 to foreign commerce to ensure that foreign and interstate commerce are treated the same.

STUDY QUESTION

---

3. Public Law 86-272 provides protection for gross receipts taxes. *True or False?*

Economic Nexus

In *Quill,* the Supreme Court ruled that a corporation satisfies the Commerce Clause's "substantial nexus" requirement only if the taxpayer has a physical presence in the state. However, an unsettled legal issue is whether the physical presence test for constitutional nexus applies to income taxes. In *Geoffrey, Inc. v. South Carolina Tax Commission* [437 S.E.2d 13 (S.C. 1993), *cert. denied* 510 US 992 (1993)], the South Carolina Supreme Court ruled that an out-of-state corporation "need not have a tangible, physical presence in a state for income to be taxable there."

Geoffrey was the trademark holding company of the toy retailer, Toys "R" Us. Geoffrey was incorporated and domiciled in Delaware and had a license agreement with South Carolina retailers allowing them to use its trademarks and trade names, including the Toys "R" Us trademark. The court held that licensing intangibles for use in the state was sufficient to satisfy the minimum connection and substantial nexus requirements of the Due Process Clause and the Commerce Clause. The *Geoffrey* court did not follow the precedent established by *Quill,* because it believed that ruling applied only to the issue of nexus for sales and use tax purposes.

Since 1993, many states have enacted "economic nexus" standards that are based on the amount of income or sales derived from sources within a state.

EXAMPLE

For tax years beginning on or after January 1, 2010, the Connecticut corporate income tax applies to "[a]ny company that derives income from sources within this state, or that has a substantial economic presence within this state, evidenced by a purposeful direction of business toward this state, examined in light of the frequency, quantity and systematic nature of a company's economic contacts with this state, without regard to physical presence, and to the extent permitted by the Constitution of the United States." [Sec. 90, as adopted by S.B. 2052, Oct. 5, 2009]

Another approach to the economic nexus concept is a factor presence nexus standard, under which income tax nexus exists if in-state sales exceed a specified threshold.

EXAMPLE

For tax years beginning on or after January 1, 2011, an out-of-state corporation has income tax nexus in California if it has more than $500,000 of sales or 25 percent of its total sales in California. [S.B. 15, Feb. 20. 2009] Effective April 30, 2010, an out-of-state corporation has income tax nexus in Colorado if it has more than $500,000 of sales or 25 percent of its total sales in Colorado. [Colo. Dept. of Rev., Reg. 39-22-301.1, Apr. 10, 2010] Effective June 1, 2010, for purposes of taxing service activities and royalty income, an out-of-state corporation has nexus in Washington if it has more than $250,000 of receipts or at least 25 percent of its total receipts in Washington. [S.B. 6143, Feb. 20. 2009]

There has also been a significant amount of litigation related to the *Geoffrey* court's interpretation of the Commerce Clause's substantial nexus requirement.

In *Lanco, Inc. v. Division of Taxation* [908 A.2d 176 (N.J. 2006); *cert. denied*, U.S. Sup. Ct., 06-1236, June 18, 2007], the New Jersey Supreme Court ruled that the Delaware trademark holding company of the clothing retailer Lane Bryant had income tax nexus in New Jersey, even though it had no physical presence in the state. The court concluded that "the better interpretation of *Quill* is the one adopted by those states that limit the Supreme Court's holding to sales and use taxes." The court also stated that "we do not believe that the Supreme Court intended to create a universal physical-presence requirement for state taxation under the Commerce Clause."

In *Tax Commissioner v. MBNA America Bank, N.A.* [640 S.E.2d 226 (W. Va. 2006); *cert. denied*, U.S. Sup. Ct., 06-1228, June 18, 2007], the taxpayer was a Delaware bank that issued credit cards, extended unsecured credit, and serviced the credit card accounts of customers nationwide. Although MBNA did not have a physical presence in West Virginia, during one of the tax years in question, it derived over $10 million of gross receipts from West Virginia customers. The West Virginia Supreme Court of Appeals ruled that the physical presence test "applies only to state sales and use taxes and not to state business franchise and corporation net income taxes," and that MBNA had "a significant economic presence sufficient to meet the substantial nexus" test under the Commerce Clause.

In *Capital One Bank and Capital One F.S.B. v. Commissioner of Revenue* [No. SJC-10105 (Mass. Sup. Jud. Ct., Jan. 8, 2009); *cert. denied*, U.S. Sup. Ct., No. 08-1169, June 22, 2009], the Massachusetts Supreme Judicial Court ruled that, despite the lack of any physical presence in the state, the two out-of-state credit card banks had substantial nexus in Massachusetts, because of their "purposeful, targeted marketing of their credit card business to Massachusetts customers ... and their receipt of hundreds of millions of dollars in income from millions of transactions involving Massachusetts residents and merchants." See also ***Geoffrey, Inc. v. Commissioner of Revenue*** [No. SJC-10106, Mass. Sup. Jud. Ct., Jan. 8, 2009; *cert. denied*, U.S. Sup. Ct., No. 08-1207, June 22, 2009)].

In *KFC Corporation v. Iowa Department of Revenue* [No. 09-1032 (Ia. Sup. Ct., Dec. 30, 2010)], the Iowa Supreme Court ruled that the Commerce Clause does not require a physical presence in order to tax the income that a Delaware corporation (KFC) earned from the use of its intangibles in Iowa. The court concluded that the trademarks and other intangibles owned by KFC and licensed for use by independent franchisees doing business in Iowa "would be regarded as having a sufficient connection to Iowa to amount to the functional equivalent of 'physical presence' under *Quill*." The court also concluded that even if the use of the intangibles within the state does not amount to physical presence under *Quill*, the physical presence requirement should not be extended to prevent a state from imposing an income tax on revenue generated from the use of intangibles within the state.

STUDY QUESTION

---

4. Which of the following statements is true?
   a. No state court has ruled that an economic presence can be sufficient to create income tax nexus.
   b. Under a factor presence nexus standard, income tax nexus generally exists if in-state sales exceed a specified threshold.
   c. No state has enacted an economic nexus standard for income tax nexus.

Agency Nexus

Under the *Quill* decision, a corporation generally has constitutional nexus in any state in which it has property or employees located on a regular basis. What if, rather than conducting business in a state through employees (dependent agents), a corporation conducts business through independent contractors (independent agents)? Do the in-state activities of independent agents, acting on an out-of-state corporation's behalf, create constitutional nexus?

In *Scripto, Inc. v. Carson* [362 US 207 (1960)], the Supreme Court addressed the issue whether the Florida marketing activities of 10 independent sales representatives created Florida sales tax nexus for Scripto, a Georgia corporation that manufactured writing instruments. The Court held that for nexus purposes, the distinction between employees and independent contractors was "without constitutional significance," and that "to permit such formal 'contractual shifts' to make a constitutional difference would open the gates to a stampede of tax avoidance." The Court concluded that the critical fact was that the activities of the independent agents in Florida helped to create and maintain a commercial market for Scripto's goods. Thus, the presence of independent agents engaged in continuous local solicitation created Florida sales and use tax nexus for Scripto.

The Supreme Court reaffirmed these principles 25 years later in *Tyler Pipe Industries, Inc. v. Department of Revenue* [483 US 232 (1987)], holding that the activities of an independent contractor residing in Washington were sufficient to create constitutional nexus for the out-of-state principal for purposes of the Washington business and occupation tax (a type of gross receipts tax). As in *Scripto,* the Court held that the critical test was "whether the activities performed in this state on behalf of the taxpayer are significantly associated with the taxpayer's ability to establish and maintain a market in this state for the sales."

In addition to protecting solicitation activities of employee-salespersons, Public Law 86-272 protects certain in-state activities conducted by independent contractors. Specifically, Public Law 86-272 provides that independent contractors can engage in the following in-state activities on behalf of an out-of-state corporation without creating income tax nexus for the principal:

- Soliciting sales
- Making sales
- Maintaining an office

Thus, unlike employees, independent agents are permitted to maintain an in-state office without creating nexus for the principal.

The Supreme Court's decisions in *Scripto* and *Tyler Pipe* establish the principle that the use of independent agents to perform continuous local solicitation creates constitutional nexus for an out-of-state principal. Relying on these decisions, in Nexus Bulletin 95-1 [1995], the Multistate Tax Commission (MTC) took the position that the mail-order computer industry's practice of providing warranty services through third-party service providers creates constitutional nexus for sales and use tax purposes.

Affiliate Nexus

A number of states have taken the position that the existence of common ownership between a corporation that has a physical presence in a state (e.g., an in-state brick-and-mortar retailer) and an out-of-state corporation that has no physical presence in the state but makes substantial sales in the state (e.g., an affiliated out-of-state mail-order or Internet vendor) is sufficient to create constitutional nexus for the out-of-state affiliate. As with agency nexus, most of the litigation concerns the issue of nexus for sales and use tax purposes. For example, in *SFA Folio Collections, Inc. v. Tracy* [73 Ohio St. 3d 119, 652 N.E. 2d 693 (1995)], SFA Folio (Folio), a New York corporation, sold clothing and other merchandise by direct mail to customers in Ohio and delivered the merchandise using common carriers. Folio had no property or employees in Ohio, but Folio's parent corporation, Saks & Company, owned another subsidiary, Saks Fifth Avenue of Ohio (Saks-Ohio), which operated a retail store in Ohio.

Ohio tax authorities argued that Folio had "substantial nexus" in Ohio, because it was a member of an affiliated group that included a corporation that operated a store in Ohio and therefore was required to collect Ohio sales tax on its mail-order sales to Ohio customers. The state's position was based on a nexus-by-affiliate statute that the Ohio Legislature had enacted, as well as the argument that Saks-Ohio was an "agent" of Folio. The agency argument was based on the fact that Saks-Ohio accepted some returns of Folio sales and distributed some Folio catalogs. The Ohio Supreme Court rejected the affiliate nexus argument, reasoning that to impute nexus to Folio merely because a sister corporation had a physical presence in Ohio ran counter to federal constitutional law and Ohio corporation law. The court also rejected the agency nexus argument because Saks-Ohio accepted Folio's returns according to its own policy (not Folio's) and charged the returns to its own inventory (not Folio's).

Consistent with the Ohio Supreme Court's ruling in **SFA Folio**, other states have generally been unsuccessful in their attempts to argue that common ownership, by itself, creates nexus for an out-of-state affiliate. On the other hand, if an in-state affiliate functions as an agent for the out-of-state affiliate, the Supreme Court's decisions in **Scripto** and **Tyler Pipe** provide a basis for arguing that the activities of the in-state affiliate create nexus for an out-of-state affiliate.

STUDY QUESTION

5. What nexus principle did the U.S. Supreme Court establish in **Scripto?**

   a. The distinction between employees and independent agents is without constitutional significance for purposes of determining whether an out-of-state corporation has sales and use tax nexus.

   b. Whether the activities performed by an independent agent in a state on behalf of the taxpayer are significantly associated with the taxpayer's ability to establish and maintain a market in the state is irrelevant for determining nexus.

   c. The use of independent agents to perform continuous local solicitation in a state does not create constitutional nexus for an out-of-state principal.

Common State Modifications to Federal Tax Base

This course explores the differences between the federal taxable income and state taxable income of a corporation, and it explains how these differences are incorporated into state taxable income calculations that generally use federal taxable income as the starting point.

LEARNING OBJECTIVES

Upon completion of this chapter, the reader should be able to:

- List the common addition modifications to federal taxable income that are required to arrive at state taxable income
- List the common subtraction modifications to federal taxable income that are required to calculate state taxable income
- Distinguish between the federal and state tax treatment of dividend income
- Describe the state income tax treatment of net operating losses
- Explain the state income tax treatment of tax payments
- Explain the state income tax treatment of interest from federal obligations and municipal bonds
- Describe the expenses targeted by related party addback provisions and the common exceptions to these provisions

OVERVIEW

For state corporate income tax purposes, most states piggyback on the federal system by adopting federal taxable income as the starting point for computing state taxable income.

Some states use Line 28 of federal Form 1120 (federal taxable income before the federal dividends-received and net operating loss deductions) as the starting point for computing state taxable income, whereas other states use Line 30 of federal Form 1120 (federal taxable income, net of all deductions) as the starting point.

Conformity to the federal corporate income tax base is important because it eases the administrative burden of computing state taxable income and creates a degree of uniformity in state income tax systems. Despite the broad conformity to the federal tax base, each state has its own unique list of addition and subtraction modifications to federal taxable income.

COMMON ADDITION MODIFICATIONS

Federal Bonus Depreciation

A major feature of the Job Creation and Worker Assistance Act of 2002 (P.L. 107-147) was Internal Revenue Code ("Code") Sec. 168(k) first-year bonus depreciation equal to 30 percent of the adjusted basis of qualified property acquired after September 10, 2001. Bonus depreciation is mandatory unless the taxpayer affirmatively elects out. A taxpayer reduces the adjusted basis of the property by the amount of bonus depreciation and then computes regular MACRS deductions based on the remaining basis.

Property eligible for Code Sec. 168(k) bonus depreciation generally includes:

- New MACRS property with a recovery period of 20 years or less, which includes most tangible personal property other than buildings
- New computer software as defined in Code Sec. 167(f)(1) (i.e., off-the-shelf software with a three-year depreciation period)
- New water utility property depreciated under MACRS
- Qualified leasehold improvement property depreciated under MACRS

Acquisition-related intangibles that are amortized over 15 years under Code Sec. 197 do not qualify for the bonus depreciation. There is no limit on the total amount of a taxpayer's bonus deprecation deduction, and bonus depreciation is deductible for both regular and alternative minimum tax purposes.

The Jobs and Growth Tax Relief Reconciliation Act of 2003 (P.L. 108-27) increased the bonus depreciation allowance from 30 percent to 50 percent for property acquired after May 5, 2003, and placed in service on or before December 31, 2004

The Economic Stimulus Act of 2008 (P.L. 110-185) reinstated the 50 percent bonus depreciation allowance for qualifying property acquired in 2008, and the American Recovery and Reinvestment Act of 2009 (P.L. 111-5) extended the 50 percent bonus depreciation to property acquired in 2009. The Tax Relief, Unemployment Insurance Reauthorization, and Job Creation Act of 2010 (P.L. 111-312) extended bonus depreciation through 2011, and provides for 100 percent bonus depreciation for property acquired after September 8, 2010, and placed in service before January 1, 2012.

Due to budgetary constraints, many states have decoupled their tax laws from the federal bonus depreciation provisions and require that the federal deduction be added back in computing state taxable income. Some states disallow most, but not all, of the bonus depreciation.

EXAMPLE

Minnesota requires an addition modification for 80 percent of the federal bonus depreciation deduction. The addback amount is then allowed as a subtraction modification in equal parts over the subsequent five tax years.

Code Sec. 179 Asset Expensing

Under Code Sec. 179, taxpayers may elect to immediately expense a portion of the cost of depreciable tangible personal property, rather than depreciating the cost over the applicable MACRS recovery period. The adjusted basis of the property is reduced by the amount of the expense allowance. The Code Sec. 179 asset expensing deduction operates independently of, and is claimed prior to, any Code Sec. 168(k) first year bonus depreciation deduction. Thus, the ordering of deductions is as follows: Code Sec. 179 asset expensing, bonus depreciation, and then MACRS depreciation is computed on the asset's remaining basis.

Property that is eligible for Code Sec. 179 expensing includes new or used tangible Code Sec. 1245 property that is depreciable under MACRS and is acquired by purchase for use in the active conduct of a trade or business. Land and buildings generally do not qualify for asset expensing, nor does property held for the production of income. An exception applies for tax years beginning in 2010 or 2011, under which a taxpayer may elect to treat qualified real property that is depreciable and acquired by purchase as Code Sec. 179 property. Qualified real property generally consists of qualified leasehold improvements, qualified retail improvement property, and qualified restaurant improvement property (Code Sec. 179(f)).

The amount of qualifying Code Sec. 179 property that a taxpayer may elect to expense is limited, and Congress has increased the maximum Code Sec. 179 deduction numerous times during the past decade. The Jobs and Growth Tax Relief Reconciliation Act of 2003 (P.L. 108-27) increased the maximum federal deduction from $25,000 to $100,000 for tax years beginning after 2002. The Small Business and Work Opportunity Tax Act of 2007 (P.L. 110-28) increased the dollar limitation to $125,000 for tax years beginning in 2007 through 2010. The Economic Stimulus Act of 2008 (P.L. 110-185) increased the dollar limitation to $250,000 for tax years that begin in 2008. The American Recovery and Reinvestment Act of 2009 (P.L. 111-5, Feb. 17, 2009) extended the $250,000 limitation to 2009, and the 2010 Hiring Incentives to Restore Employment Act (P.L. 111-147, March 18, 2010) extended the $250,000 limitation to 2010. The Small Business Jobs Act of 2010 (P.L. 111-240, Sept. 27, 2010) increased the limitation to $500,000 for tax years beginning in 2010 and 2011.

The maximum annual Code Sec. 179 deduction is phased out, dollar-for-dollar, based on the amount by which all qualifying property placed in service during the tax year exceeds the investment limitation. As with the maximum deduction, Congress has increased the investment limitation numerous times during the past decade. Most recently, the Economic Stimulus Act of 2008, American Recovery and Reinvestment Act of 2009, and The 2010 Hiring Incentives to Restore Employment Act increased the investment limitation to $800,000 for tax years that begin in 2008 through 2010, and the Small Business Jobs Act of 2010 increased the limitation to $2,000,000 for tax years beginning in 2010 and 2011. As a consequence, up to $2,500,000 ($500,000 plus $2,000,000) of qualifying property may be placed in service during 2010 or 2011 before the deduction is fully phased out.

Tax Years Beginning In:	Maximum Annual Deduction	Investment Limitation
2001 or 2002	$24,000	$200,000
2003	$100,000	$400,000
2004	$102,000	$410,000
2005	$105,000	$420,000
2006	$108,000	$430,000
2007	$125,000	$500,000
2008 or 2009	$250,000	$800,000
2010 or 2011	$500,000	$2,000,000

Due to budgetary constraints, a number of states have decoupled their tax laws from the numerous increases in the maximum Code Sec. 179 deduction during the past decade. Such states require addition modifications for the excess of the federal Code Sec. 179 expensing amount over the state maximum.

Federal Net Operating Loss Deduction

Many states do not conform to the federal net operating loss (NOL) carryover rules and do *not* permit an NOL carryback, whereas a two-year carryback is generally permitted for federal tax purposes.

Depending on whether the state uses Line 28 or Line 30 of federal Form 1120 as the starting point for computing state taxable income, the requisite adjustments may take the form of an addition and/or subtraction modification. NOLs are discussed in more detail later in this course.

Federal Dividends-Received Deduction

As with the federal NOL deduction, many states do not conform to the federal dividends-received deduction (DRD).

> **EXAMPLE**
>
> State DRD provisions generally apply equally to dividends received from U.S. corporations and foreign country corporations, whereas the federal DRD generally applies *only* to dividends received from a U.S. corporation.

Again, depending on whether the state uses Line 28 or Line 30 of Form 1120 as the starting point for computing state taxable income, the requisites adjustment may take the form of an addition and/or subtraction modification. Dividends are discussed in more detail later in this course.

Expenses Related to Income Exempt from State Tax

Another common addition modification relates to income that is taxable for federal purposes but that is either exempt or otherwise not subject to state tax. Some states provide that where certain types of gross income are not included in the state tax base, the expenses related to generating that income must be added back in computing the state tax base.

> **EXAMPLE**
>
> Interest on obligations of the U.S. government is *exempt* from a direct state income tax.
>
> Accordingly, a number of states require that expenses related to generating such income must be added back to federal taxable income or offset against the exempt interest income before they are subtracted from federal taxable income.

The states have different definitions for the expenses that may be considered to relate directly or indirectly to nontaxable income. Such expenses may include taxes, interest, payroll, related office expenses (supplies, rent, and depreciation), transaction costs, and administrative fees related to the production of such income.

Expenses Related to State Credits

If a corporation is allowed a state tax credit for expenditures that were deducted on the corporation's federal income tax return, the taxpayer generally must add back those deductions in computing its state taxable income. The purpose of this addition modification is to prevent a double tax benefit in the form of both a credit and a deduction for the same expenditures.

Related Party Royalty and Interest Expenses

To limit the ability of corporations to erode a state's income tax base through intercompany royalty and interest payments, many states require corporations to add back deductions for royalty and interest payments made to related parties. These state addback provisions are generally subject to numerous exceptions and special rules. Related party royalty and interest expenses are discussed in more detail later in this course.

Code Sec. 199 Domestic Production Activities Deduction

Code Sec. 199 was enacted as part of the American Jobs Creation Act of 2004 (P.L. 108-357). The Code Sec. 199 deduction was phased in from 2005 to 2010, with a deduction percentage of three percent for tax years beginning in 2005 and 2006, six percent for tax years beginning in 2007, 2008, and 2009, and nine percent for tax years beginning after 2009. Under Code Sec. 199, a taxpayer may claim a deduction equal to the lesser of its *qualified production activities income* (QPAI) or taxable income (but not more than 50 percent of its W-2 wages deducted in computing QPAI) for the tax year, multiplied by the applicable statutory percentage. Taxpayers may claim a Code Sec. 199 deduction for both regular income tax and alternative minimum tax purposes

A taxpayer's QPAI equals its *domestic production gross receipts* (DPGR), reduced by the cost of goods sold and other allocable direct and indirect expenses. Under Code Sec. 199(c), DPGR includes gross receipts of the taxpayer that are derived from the following qualifying production activities:

- Lease, rental, license, sale, exchange, or other disposition of:
  - Tangible personal property, computer software, or music recordings manufactured, produced, grown, or extracted by a taxpayer in whole or significant part within the United States
  - Certain films produced by the taxpayer where at least 50 percent of the total production compensation is for services performed in the United States
- Sale, exchange, or other disposition of electricity, natural gas, or potable water produced by the taxpayer in the United States
- Construction performed in the United States
- Engineering and architectural services performed in the United States in connection with U.S. construction projects

DPGR does not include gross receipts derived from the transmission or distribution of electricity, natural gas, or potable water. DPGR also does not include gross receipts from the sale of food and beverages prepared by the taxpayer at a retail establishment. On the other hand, gross receipts derived from the sale of food or beverages at the wholesale level may qualify. DPGR also does not include gross receipts that a taxpayer derives from "property leased, licensed, or rented" for use by a related person (Code Sec. 199(c)(7)). On the other hand, a sale to a related party apparently can give rise to DPGR.

Due to budgetary constraints, many states require corporations to add back the Code Sec. 199 deduction in computing state taxable income.

Cancellation of Indebtedness Income

As a general rule, a debtor must recognize cancellation of debt (COD) income equal to the amount of any debt reduction (Treas. Reg. §1.61-12(a)). Under Code Sec. 108, however, a debtor can exclude COD income to the extent the taxpayer is insolvent or in bankruptcy.

COD income can arise when a debt is forgiven, exchanged for a new debt, repurchased by the debtor, or significantly modified. A significant modification, such as a change in interest rates or a deferral of principal or interest payments, is treated as an exchange of the old debt for a new debt.

The American Recovery and Reinvestment Tax Act of 2009 (P.L. 111-5) added a new subsection (i) to Code Sec. 108, which allows taxpayers to defer recognition of COD income on debt instruments reacquired in 2009 or 2010. The income is deferred until 2014 and then included in gross income ratably over a five-year period (i.e., 20 percent per year in each of the tax years 2014 to 2018). This deferral is available regardless of whether the taxpayer is insolvent or in bankruptcy. Congress enacted Code Sec. 108(i) to enable taxpayers to restructure their debt without triggering any current income recognition.

Due to revenue concerns, many states have chosen not to conform to new Code Sec. 108(i).

Income Taxes

State income taxes and foreign income taxes are deductible in computing federal taxable income (Code Sec. 164). Federal income taxes are not deductible, however. With respect to foreign income taxes, a corporation may claim a credit in lieu of a deduction (Code Sec. 901). Because a credit is generally more valuable, taxpayers generally elect to claim a credit for foreign income taxes.

Most states require state income taxes to be added back in computing a corporation's state taxable income. A handful of states allow a subtraction modification for federal income taxes. No state allows a credit for foreign income taxes, but some states allow a deduction for foreign income taxes if they are deducted for federal tax purposes.

Whether or not a state tax qualifies as an income tax can be uncertain. For example, the tax base for the Texas margin tax is the lowest of three amounts: total revenue minus cost of goods sold, total revenue minus compensation, or 70 percent of total revenue. The Virginia Department of Taxation ruled that, because it excludes the vast majority of business expenses normally permitted in determining net income, the Texas margin tax is not based on net income and is not added back when computing Virginia taxable income. [P.D. 08-169, Va. Dept. of Tax., Sept. 11, 2008] In contrast, South Carolina classifies the Texas margin tax as a nondeductible income tax. [Rev. Rul. No. 09-10, S.C. Dept. of Rev., July 17, 2009] The Kansas Department of Revenue ruled that if it is determined by deducting cost of goods sold or compensation from gross receipts, the Texas margin tax is a nondeductible income tax. [Opinion Letter No. O-2009-05, Kan. Dept. of Rev., March 24, 2009] Finally, the California Franchise Tax Board states that it cannot provide a definitive characterization of the Texas margin tax that applies to each and every taxpayer. [Notice 2009-06, Calif. Franch. Tax Bd., July 20, 2009]

Interest from State and Local Debt Obligations

Another common addback to federal taxable income is interest income received on debt obligations issued by state and local governments. The federal government does not tax interest paid on obligations of states or their political subdivisions (Code Sec. 103). The federal exemption for municipal interest does not apply, however, to interest paid on state and municipal bonds issued to finance certain private activities, such as industrial parks and convention centers (Code Sec. 146), federally insured loans (Code Sec. 149), and arbitrage bonds issued for the purpose of using the proceeds to purchase higher yielding investments (Code Sec. 148). No deduction is allowed for any expenses allocable to tax-exempt interest (Code Sec. 265).

Only a few states tax interest from state and municipal bonds issued by in-state governments. In contrast, most states tax interest from bonds issued by other states and political subdivisions thereof. Therefore, a common pattern is for a state to exclude interest from in-state bonds while taxing interest from bonds issued by other states. In a number of states, state and municipal bonds must be registered to be exempt from taxation.

In *Kentucky Department of Revenue v. Davis* (128 SCt 1801, 2008), the U.S. Supreme Court held that limiting a state exemption to the interest on in-state bonds does not violate the Commerce Clause because the exemption permissibly favors a traditional government function (issuing debt securities to pay for public projects), rather than favoring in-state private interests while disfavoring out-of-state private interests. Thus, this conduct does not represent the sort of "private protectionism" the Commerce Clause was designed to prevent. The Court also observed that the current tax treatment is critical to the operation of the municipal bond market.

States that tax interest from state and municipal bonds generally require an addition modification for the types of state and municipal interest that are subject to state tax. Because expenses related to such interest were not deducted in computing federal taxable income (Code Sec. 265), some states permit the taxpayer to reduce the amount of the addition modification by the amount of related expenses.

COMMON SUBTRACTION MODIFICATIONS

Interest Income from Federal Debt Obligations

The federal government taxes interest income derived from federal obligations, such as U.S. Treasury notes. Thus, a corporation's federal taxable income includes interest income derived from federal debt obligations.

State taxation of interest income derived from federal obligations is governed by the intergovernmental immunity doctrine. Observing that "the power to tax involves the power to destroy," Chief Justice John Marshall established the doctrine of federal immunity from state taxation [*McCulloch v. Maryland* (1819)]. From *McCulloch* evolved the doctrine of *intergovernmental immunity*, which holds that the U.S. system of sovereign federal-state governments implicitly prohibits the federal government from taxing state governments, and state governments from taxing the federal government.

In 31 U.S.C. §3124, Congress codified this principle with respect to interest earned on federal obligations, as follows:

(a) Stocks and obligations of the United States Government are exempt from taxation by a State or political subdivision of a State. The exemption applies to each form of taxation that would require the obligation, the interest on the obligation, or both, to be considered in computing a tax, except—

(1) A nondiscriminatory franchise tax or another nonproperty tax instead of a franchise tax imposed on a corporation; and

(2) An estate or inheritance tax . . .

Thus, states that impose a direct income tax must exempt interest earned on federal obligations from taxation. In contrast, states that impose a nondiscriminatory corporate franchise tax in lieu of imposing a direct corporate income tax are not prohibited from taxing federal interest, even though the value of the franchise is measured by net income.

A *franchise tax* is an excise tax on doing business or owning property within a state, whereas a *direct* income tax is a tax on the income derived from sources within a state's borders. Nevertheless, like a direct income tax, a corporate franchise tax is usually based on income.

As required by 31 U.S.C. §3124, a franchise tax must be *nondiscriminatory* before the state can tax federal interest. A franchise tax is nondiscriminatory if the state taxes both federal interest and interest derived from the state's own obligations. In *Memphis Bank & Trust Co. v. Garner*, the U.S. Supreme Court held that a Tennessee tax that included interest on federal obligations but excluded interest on Tennessee obligations did not qualify as a nondiscriminatory franchise tax [459 US 392 (1983)]. In essence, the Court ruled that a state cannot exempt interest from in-state obligations while taxing interest from U.S. obligations. Instead, the state must either tax or exempt both types of interest.

A state that does not tax interest derived from debt obligations issued directly by the federal government (e.g., U.S. Treasury bills and notes) may nevertheless tax interest derived from debt obligations issued by quasi-public agencies, such as Ginnie Mae or Sallie Mae, even though the U.S. government guarantees the obligation. In *Rockford Life Insurance v. Illinois Department of Revenue*, the U.S. Supreme Court ruled that 31 U.S.C. §3124 did *not* prohibit states from taxing interest derived from Ginnie Mae bonds because the private institution in question (i.e., the Government National Mortgage Association, or Ginnie Mae) issued the debt and bore the primary obligation to repay the debt [482 US 182 (1987)]. In contrast, the federal government's role as guarantor makes the federal government's obligation secondary and contingent.

Under 31 U.S.C. §3124, states that impose a direct corporate income tax must exempt interest earned on federal obligations from taxation. In contrast, states that impose a nondiscriminatory corporate franchise tax are not prohibited from taxing federal interest, even if the value of the franchise is measured by net income. A *franchise tax* is an excise tax on doing business or owning property within a state, whereas a direct income tax is a tax on the income derived from sources within a state's borders.

STUDY QUESTIONS

1. Which statement best describes state conformity to the federal Code Sec. 199 domestic production activities deduction?
   a. All states conform
   b. No state conforms
   c. Some states conform

2. Which of the following is usually *exempt* from both federal and state corporate income taxation?
   a. Interest received from a U.S. Treasury note
   b. Interest received from a bond issued by the taxing state
   c. Interest received from a bond issued by another state

3. States that impose a nondiscriminatory corporate franchise tax may **not** tax federal interest. **True or False?**

State NOL Deduction

For federal tax purposes, corporate taxpayers can generally carry an NOL back two years and forward 20 years (Code Sec. 172). Most states also allow NOL deductions, but the specific rules vary from state to state. As a consequence, there is often a difference between the amount of the federal and state NOL deductions.

Depending on whether the state uses Line 28 or Line 30 of federal Form 1120 as the starting point for computing state taxable income, the requisite adjustments may take the form of an addition and/or subtraction modification.

State Dividends-Received Deduction

Most states allow some form of DRD, but the specific ownership requirements and deduction percentages vary from state to state. In contrast to the federal DRD, state DRDs generally apply to dividends received from both domestic and foreign corporations.

As with the state NOL deduction, depending on whether the state uses Line 28 or Line 30 of federal Form 1120 as the starting point for computing state taxable income, the requisite adjustments may take the form of an addition and/or subtraction modification.

Subpart F and Code Sec. 78

As discussed in more detail below, states generally provide subtraction modifications for federal Subpart F inclusions and Code Sec. 78 gross-up income.

Expenses Related to Federal Credits

The federal government allows corporate taxpayers to claim a number of credits, such as the federal credit for research and experimentation expenditures. To the extent the taxpayer claims a credit for federal tax purposes, it generally must add back the related deductions in computing federal taxable income (Code Sec. 280C).

If a state does not provide a credit comparable to that claimed for federal purposes, the state will often provide a subtraction modification for the deductions disallowed at the federal level.

Gain or Loss on the Sale of a Depreciable Asset

To the extent a depreciable asset's adjusted basis is different for federal and state tax purposes (e.g., due to the disallowance of federal bonus depreciation or Code Sec. 179 expensing), an addition or subtraction modification is required upon the sale of the asset for the difference between the federal and state gain or loss. For example, a subtraction modification is required if the state adjusted basis is higher than the federal adjusted basis.

STUDY QUESTIONS

4. For purposes of computing the state taxable income of a corporation, which of the following is **not** a common addition modification to federal taxable income?

  a. State income taxes
  b. Interest income on federal debt obligations
  c. Federal bonus depreciation

5. Which of the following statements regarding the computation of a corporation's state taxable income is true?

  a. The requisite addition and subtraction modifications to federal taxable income are identical across all 50 states.
  b. If a depreciable asset's state adjusted basis is higher than its federal adjusted basis, an addition modification is required upon the sale of the asset.
  c. Some states require an addition modification for expenses related to an item of federal income that is exempt from state tax.

TREATMENT OF DIVIDENDS

Federal Tax Treatment

Under Code Sec. 243, a corporation generally is allowed to claim a DRD equal to 70 percent of the dividends received from a less-than-20-percent-owned domestic corporation, 80 percent of the dividends received from a 20-percent-or-more-owned nonaffiliated domestic corporation, and 100 percent of the dividends received from a corporation that is a member of an affiliated group with the recipient corporation.

The purpose of the DRD is to prevent the imposition of multiple layers of U.S. corporate-level tax on the same underlying earnings.

> **EXAMPLE**
>
> Earnings of a domestic subsidiary are taxed when earned and would be taxed a second time when distributed to the parent corporation as a dividend if not for the DRD.

A U.S. parent corporation generally may not claim a DRD with respect to dividends received from foreign (non-U.S.) corporations, because the receipt of the dividend generally is the U.S. Treasury's first opportunity to tax the underlying foreign earnings.

A federal DRD is also generally not available with respect to any Subpart F inclusions or Code Sec. 78 gross-up income attributable to foreign corporations. A deduction may be available, however, with respect to the U.S. source portion of any dividends received from a foreign corporation (Code Sec. 245).

Code Sec. 78 gross-up. A U.S. parent corporation generally must include any dividends received from foreign corporations in its federal taxable income (Code Sec. 61).

Because the amount of dividend income recognized is net of any foreign income taxes paid by the foreign subsidiary, the U.S. parent is implicitly allowed a deduction for those foreign taxes. The U.S. parent can also claim a deemed paid foreign tax credit for the foreign income taxes paid by a 10-percent-or-more-owned foreign corporation (Code Sec. 902).

To prevent a double tax benefit, the U.S. parent must gross up its dividend income by the amount of the deemed paid foreign taxes, thereby eliminating the implicit deduction (Code Sec. 78). This amount is generally referred to as the *Code Sec. 78 gross-up*.

Subpart F inclusions. As a general rule, the U.S. federal government does not tax the foreign earnings of a foreign corporation—even if that foreign corporation is a wholly owned subsidiary of a U.S. parent corporation. Instead, U.S. taxation is deferred until those foreign earnings are repatriated by the U.S. parent corporation as a dividend. This policy, which is known as *deferral*, is designed to allow U.S. companies to compete in foreign markets on a tax parity with foreign competitors.

A policy of unrestricted deferral would also allow U.S. companies to avoid U.S. taxes by shifting passive investment income and inventory trading profits to base companies organized in low-tax foreign jurisdictions. As a consequence, in 1962, Congress enacted the Subpart F provisions (Code Secs. 951–964) to combat foreign base company tax avoidance schemes. Under Subpart F, certain types of undistributed foreign earnings of a controlled foreign corporation are subject to immediate U.S. taxation at the U.S. shareholder level.

A foreign corporation is a *controlled foreign corporation* if U.S. shareholders own more than 50 percent of the stock, by vote or value, of the foreign corporation. A U.S. shareholder of a controlled foreign corporation must include in gross income an amount equal to the U.S. shareholder's pro rata share of the controlled foreign corporation's insurance and foreign base company income, as well as any earnings invested in U.S. property.

State Tax Treatment

Many states conform to the federal DRD in terms of how they treat dividends from domestic corporations. The states that do not conform to the federal DRD also generally provide a deduction for domestic dividends, but the specific rules vary from state to state. In contrast with federal law, which generally limits its DRD to dividends received from domestic corporations, most states provide a DRD or subtraction modification for dividends received from foreign corporations.

> ### EXAMPLE
>
> Consistent with how they treat domestic dividends, many states provide a 100 percent deduction for dividends received from an 80-percent-or-more-owned foreign corporation.

Some states use federal taxable income after the net operating loss deduction and DRD (i.e., Line 30 of the corporation's federal Form 1120) as the starting point for computing state taxable income. Unless the state requires an additional modification for all or a portion of the DRD reported on the federal return, the corporation is accorded the same DRD treatment for state and federal tax purposes.

> ### EXAMPLE
>
> Georgia uses federal taxable income after the DRD (Form 1120, Line 30) as the starting point for computing taxable income, and does not require an addition modification for the federal DRD.

Some of these "Line 30" states require an addback of the federal DRD, but also allow a subtraction modification for the state DRD.

States that use federal taxable income before the net operating loss deduction and DRD (i.e., Line 28 of the federal return) as the starting point for computing state taxable income generally provide a DRD in the form of a subtraction modification.

State Treatment of Foreign (Non-U.S.) Dividends

The *Kraft* decision. In *Kraft General Foods, Inc. v. Department of Revenue* [505 US 71 (1992)], the Supreme Court ruled that an Iowa law that allowed taxpayers to claim a DRD for dividends from domestic, but not foreign, subsidiary corporations was unconstitutional. During the years in question, Iowa conformed to the federal DRD. As a consequence, Iowa did not tax dividends received from domestic corporations, but did tax dividends received from foreign corporations unless the dividends represented a distribution of U.S. earnings. The Court ruled that the Iowa provision that taxed only dividends paid by foreign corporations out of their foreign earnings facially discriminated against foreign commerce, in violation of the Commerce Clause.

Fallout from *Kraft* decision. Since the *Kraft* decision, a number of state courts have also struck down DRD schemes that favored dividends received from U.S. corporations over dividends received from foreign (non-U.S.) corporations.

In *Dart Industries, Inc. v. Clark*, the Rhode Island Supreme Court ruled the Rhode Island provision that allowed a deduction for dividends from domestic but not foreign subsidiaries was *discriminatory* in violation of the Commerce Clause [657 A.2d 1062 (R.I. Sup. Ct., 1995)].

Likewise, in *D.D.I Inc. v. North Dakota*, the North Dakota Supreme Court declared unconstitutional a North Dakota statute that permitted a DRD but only to the extent the dividend payer's income was subject to North Dakota corporate income tax [657 N.W.2d 228 (N.D. Sup. Ct., 2003)].

In *Hutchinson Technology, Inc. v. Commissioner of Revenue*, the Minnesota Supreme Court ruled that a state statute that excluded dividends paid by certain foreign sales corporations from the state's DRD was discriminatory in violation of the Commerce Clause [698 N.W.2d 1 (Minn. Sup. Ct., 2005)].

In *Emerson Electric Co. v. Tracy*, the Ohio Supreme Court declared unconstitutional an Ohio statute that permitted a 100 percent deduction for dividends from domestic subsidiaries, but only an 85 percent deduction for dividends from foreign subsidiaries [735 N.E.2d 445 (Ohio Sup. Ct., 2000)].

In *Conoco Inc. v. Taxation and Revenue Department*, the New Mexico Supreme Court ruled that the New Mexico scheme under which foreign but not domestic dividends were included in the tax base facially discriminated against foreign commerce, even though the state allowed a taxpayer to include a portion of the dividend-paying foreign subsidiaries' property, payroll, and sales in the denominators of its apportionment factors—thereby reducing the state apportionment percentage [122 N.M. 736 (N.M. Sup. Ct., 1996)].

In addition, the supreme courts in several water's-edge combined reporting states have focused on footnote 23 of the *Kraft* decision and ruled that it is constitutionally acceptable to include dividends from foreign subsidiaries in the tax base, while excluding dividends from domestic subsidiaries that are included in the water's-edge combined report. In footnote 23 of its decision in *Kraft*, the Supreme Court stated:

> If one were to compare the aggregate tax imposed by Iowa on a unitary business which included a subsidiary doing business throughout the United States (including Iowa) with the aggregate tax imposed by Iowa on a unitary business which included a foreign subsidiary doing business abroad, it would be difficult to say that Iowa discriminates against the business with the foreign subsidiary. Iowa would tax an apportioned share of the domestic subsidiary's entire earnings, but would tax only the amount of the foreign subsidiary's earnings paid as a dividend to the parent.

In *Appeal of Morton Thiokol, Inc.*, the Kansas Supreme Court noted that *Kraft* did not address the taxation of foreign dividends by water's-edge combined reporting states (because Iowa is an elective consolidation state) [864 P.2d 1175 (Kan. Sup. Ct., 1993)]. It also noted that that "the aggregate tax imposed by Kansas on a unitary business with a domestic subsidiary would not be less burdensome than that imposed by Kansas on a unitary business with a foreign subsidiary because the income of the domestic subsidiary would be combined, apportioned, and taxed while only the dividend of the foreign subsidiary would be taxed."

Likewise, in *E.I. Du Pont de Nemours & Co. v. State Tax Assessor*, the Maine Supreme Judicial Court held that Maine's water's-edge combined reporting method was distinguishable from Iowa's single-entity reporting method, because the income of a domestic subsidiary is included in the Maine combined report [675 A.2d 82 (Me. Sup Ct., 1996)]. Therefore, taxing dividends paid by foreign but not domestic subsidiaries did *not* constitute the kind of facial discrimination found in the Iowa system.

Finally, in *General Electric Company, Inc. v. Department of Revenue Administration,* GE challenged the constitutionality of a New Hampshire statute that permits a U.S. parent corporation to claim a DRD for dividends received from foreign subsidiaries only to the extent the foreign subsidiary has business activity and is subject to tax in New Hampshire. None of GE's unitary foreign subsidiaries had business activities in New Hampshire [No. 2005-668 (N.H. Sup. Ct., Dec. 5, 2006)]. Thus, GE could not claim a DRD for the dividends received from those foreign subsidiaries. The New Hampshire Supreme Court ruled that the New Hampshire tax scheme did *not* discriminate against foreign commerce, because both a unitary business with foreign subsidiaries operating in New Hampshire and a unitary business with foreign subsidiaries not operating in New Hampshire are each taxed only one time. Thus, there is no differential treatment that benefits the former and burdens the latter.

Code Sec. 78 gross-up and Subpart F inclusions. The rationale for including the Code Sec. 78 gross-up amount in federal taxable income does not apply for state tax purposes because no state allows a domestic corporation to claim the equivalent of a Code Sec. 902 deemed paid foreign tax credit for the foreign income taxes paid by a foreign corporation. Consequently, nearly all states provide a subtraction modification or DRD for Code Sec. 78 gross-up income, in effect excluding the federal gross-up amount from state taxation. Most states also provide a DRD or subtraction modification for Subpart F inclusions under Code Sec. 951.

In *Amerada Hess Corp. v. North Dakota* [704 N.W.2d 8 (N.D. Sup. Ct., 2005)], the North Dakota Supreme Court ruled that Code Sec. 78 gross-up amounts did not qualify as "foreign dividends" under the applicable North Dakota tax statute and therefore did not qualify for the partial exclusion from income under North Dakota water's-edge combined unitary reporting method of determining the state corporate income tax.

Consistent with the notion that a Subpart F inclusion is a deemed dividend from a controlled foreign corporation, most states provide a DRD or subtraction modification for income under Subpart F. A few states, including California, require that the income and apportionment factors of a controlled foreign corporation be included in a water's-edge combined report to the extent of the controlled foreign corporation's Subpart F income [Calif. §25110]. California does not provide a DRD for Subpart F income.

In addition, some states provide only limited deductions for income under Subpart F.

> **EXAMPLE**
>
> An Idaho water's-edge group may claim only an 85 percent deduction [Idaho §63-3027C], and a Utah water's-edge group may claim only a 50 percent deduction [Utah §59-7-106].

STUDY QUESTION

> **6.** Which of the following federal tax provisions was enacted to *prevent* a double federal tax benefit?
>   **a.** Code Sec. 78 gross-up
>   **b.** Subpart F
>   **c.** Dividends-received deduction

NET OPERATING LOSS CARRYOVERS

To provide relief for corporations that have cyclical earnings, Congress enacted Code Sec. 172, which allows taxpayers to carry NOLs back two years and forward 20 years, and claim a deduction in the carryover year. Most states also allow NOL deductions, but the specific rules vary significantly from state to state. As a consequence, there is often a difference between the amount of the federal and state NOL deductions.

These federal-state differences arise for a number of reasons, including:

- No state provision for NOL carrybacks
- State carryforward periods that are shorter than 20 years
- The application of the state NOL deduction on a post-apportionment basis
- State addition and subtraction modifications
- Different group filing methods for federal and state tax purposes
- State statutory limitations on the dollar amount of the carryover allowed

Depending on whether the state uses Line 28 or Line 30 of federal Form 1120 as the starting point for computing state taxable income, the requisite adjustments to convert a federal NOL deduction to the state NOL deduction may take the form of an addition and/or subtraction modification.

Carryover Periods

Many states do not permit a carryback, and a number of states have carryforward periods that are shorter than 20 years. These differences are due in large part to state budgetary constraints; in particular, the negative tax revenue consequences of refund claims associated with NOL carrybacks. When facing severe budgetary constraints, some states temporarily suspend the NOL carryover deduction as a revenue raising measure.

During periods of economic recession, Congress has enacted enhanced carryback periods to infuse cash, in the form of tax refunds, into the economy.

EXAMPLE

The American Recovery and Reinvestment Act of 2009 (P.L. 111-5) allows an eligible small business to elect up to a five-year carryback for an NOL sustained in a tax year beginning or ending in 2008. The Worker, Homeownership, and Business Assistance Act of 2009 (P.L. 111-92) significantly broadened the availability of the enhanced carryback.

Impact of Apportionment Percentage

Some states require that the total NOL generated in a loss year be adjusted by the loss year's apportionment percentage before it is applied in a carryover year, and then the apportioned NOL is offset against the amount of apportioned income in the carryover year. This is known as a *post-apportionment* NOL deduction.

Other states require that the full amount of the loss year's NOL be offset against the carryover year's total apportionable income before applying the apportionment percentage for the carryover year to the net amount of apportionable income. This is known as a *pre-apportionment* NOL deduction.

If there is a major change in the corporation's state apportionment percentage between the loss year and the carryover year, the amount of the NOL deduction can vary significantly with the method (pre- versus post-apportionment) employed by the state.

EXAMPLE

Assume that in 20X1 Acme Corporation sustains a $100 NOL and has a State X apportionment percentage of 50 percent. In 20X2, Acme has taxable income before the NOL deduction of $300 and a State X apportionment percentage of 70 percent.

If State X applies an NOL on a pre-apportionment basis, Acme's 20X2 taxable income is $140 ([$300 - $100 NOL] x 70%). On the other hand, if State X applies an NOL on a post-apportionment basis, Acme's 20X2 taxable income is $160 ([$300 x 70%] - [$100 NOL x 50%]).

Impact of Addition and Subtraction Modifications

Regardless of whether Line 28 or Line 30 of the federal income tax return is used as the starting point in computing state taxable income, each state requires a number of addition and subtraction modifications. Generally, states require that the same modifications used in determining state taxable income be reflected in the computation of a state NOL. In addition, a corporation must generally be subject to tax and file a state tax return in the loss year in order to establish a state NOL—although there are some exceptions.

Several states have statutory or regulatory provisions mandating that the starting point (i.e., federal taxable income) before state modifications may *not* be smaller than zero unless an NOL is generated in that year. Therefore, in those states, if the state-specified addition modifications exceed the subtraction modifications in a year in which a federal NOL deduction is being used, the taxpayer will have state taxable income—even though it has no federal taxable income for that year.

Different Federal and State Consolidation Rules

In the case of an affiliated group of corporations filing a federal consolidated return, the computation of a state NOL deduction may be complicated by the use of different group filing methods for state tax purposes, such as:

- Separate-company returns
- Consolidated returns
- Combined unitary reporting

In such situations, the state NOL deduction may be determined on a federal *pro forma* basis—that is, what the allowable federal NOL carryover deduction would be if only the separate company or the companies included in the state consolidated or combined return were included in the federal return.

States that permit the filing of a consolidated or combined return may impose separate return limitation year (or SRLY) restrictions on the use of a specific affiliate's NOLs to reduce consolidated taxable income.

Statutory Limitations

A number of states impose flat dollar limitations on the amount of an NOL carryback deduction. For example, Utah limits carrybacks to $1 million, and Idaho limits carrybacks to $100,000.

Some states impose flat dollar or percentage limitations on NOL carryforward deductions.

> **EXAMPLE**
>
> In 2010, Pennsylvania limits NOL carryforward deductions to the greater of $3 million or 20 percent of taxable income.

Some states impose temporary limitations on NOL carryforward deductions in response to fiscal constraints.

> **EXAMPLE**
>
> From 2011 to 2013, Colorado limits its NOL carryforward deduction to $250,000 per year.

STUDY QUESTIONS

7. Which one of the following statements is **not** true?

   a. An affiliated group's state NOL carryforward always conforms to the federal consolidated NOL carryforward.

   b. States generally require that the same addition and subtraction modifications used in computing state taxable income be used in computing state NOLs.

   c. Many states have NOL carryforward periods shorter than the federal carryforward period of 20 years.

8. A difference between a corporation's federal NOL deduction and state NOL deduction may arise for *all* the following reasons **except:**

   a. State NOL deduction applied on a post-apportionment basis

   b. State statutory limitations on the amount of carryover permitted

   c. No federal provision for NOL carrybacks

RELATED PARTY EXPENSE ADDBACK PROVISIONS

Most states do not require a group of commonly controlled corporations to file a combined or consolidated income tax return. Instead, states generally permit each affiliated corporation that has nexus in the state to compute its state taxable income on a separate-company basis.

The ability to file state company returns has historically allowed affiliated corporations to avoid state income taxes through the use of intangible property holding companies and similar planning techniques.

EXAMPLE

An affiliated group could establish a trademark holding company or financing subsidiary in Delaware or Nevada, neither of which imposes income taxes on intangible property companies, and then use intercompany licensing and financing transactions to reduce the income reported by the operating affiliates.

To close this perceived loophole, many states have enacted laws that require a corporation to add back to federal taxable income any royalties or interest expense paid to related parties when computing its state taxable income (*addback provisions*).

The Multistate Tax Commission has also adopted a model statute that requires taxpayers to add back certain intangible and interest expenses in computing state taxable income [Model Statute Requiring the Add-back of Certain Intangible and Interest Expenses (Aug. 17, 2006)].

Although the different state addback provisions share many common themes, there are significant differences, particularly with respect to the circumstances under which an exception applies and the related party expense need not be added back. Therefore, it is important to thoroughly analyze each state's specific provisions to ensure compliance.

Expenses Targeted

State related party expense addback provisions are generally targeted at two broad categories of expenses:

1. **Intangible expenses.** For this purpose, "intangible expenses" generally include: (1) royalty, patent, technical, copyright, and licensing fees; (2) losses related to factoring or discounting transactions; and (3) other expenses related to the acquisition, ownership, use, or disposition of intangible property. Intangible property generally means patents, trade names, trademarks, service marks, copyrights, trade secrets, and similar types of intangible assets.
2. **Interest expense.** Most states define interest expenses by reference to Code Sec. 163.

    Related party expense addback provisions are aimed at tax planning structures where an operating company pays a royalty or other intangible expense to a related party, which then lends the funds back to the operating company. The interest paid by the operating company on the loan of funds generated by the intangible expenses is an example of an intangible-related interest expense.

Definition of "Related Member"

State addback provisions apply to expenses that are directly or indirectly paid or accrued to a related person, which most statutes refer to as a *related member*. The definition of a *related member* varies somewhat from state to state, but generally includes:

- A component member of a controlled group of corporations under Code Sec. 1563
- A member of an affiliated group of corporations under Code Sec. 1504
- A person to or from whom there is attribution of stock ownership under Code Sec. 1563(e)
- Some other type of related entity, such as an individual or other stockholder who directly, indirectly, or constructively owns 50 percent or more of the stock in the taxpayer

Exceptions

State addback provisions are designed to prevent taxpayers from using intercompany licensing and financing arrangements to avoid corporate income taxes. Under the general rules, however, state addback provisions apply automatically to all related party intangible and interest expenses—including those related party payments that are motivated by legitimate business purposes rather than tax avoidance. As a consequence, each state provides some relief in the form of exceptions from the automatic addback requirement. These exceptions are complex and vary from state to state. There are some common themes, however, including exceptions that apply when:

- The related payee's corresponding income is subject to tax in another U.S. state or a foreign country.
- The related payee pays the amount to an unrelated person.
- The addback adjustment produces an unreasonable result.
- The taxpayer and the state tax authorities agree to an alternative adjustment.

Subject-to-tax exception. Many states permit a deduction for related party intangible and interest expenses if the related payee's corresponding income is subject to tax in a U.S. state or a foreign country. In many states, the subject-to-tax exception requires that the related payee's corresponding income be subject to a certain rate of taxation.

Conduit payment exception. Another common exception is the conduit payment exception, under which a state permits a deduction for related party intangibles and interest expenses if the related payee pays the amount to an unrelated person in the same tax year, and tax avoidance was not a principal purpose of the related party payment.

In such situations, the related payee serves as a conduit for the taxpayer's payment of intangible or interest expenses to an unrelated third party. An example of a conduit payment arrangement is centralized cash management, where the excess cash generated by some operating affiliates is used to pay the expenses of other affiliates.

Unreasonable result and alternative adjustment exceptions. Many states provide an exception if the taxpayer can establish that the addback of the related party intangible or interest expense produces an unreasonable result (for example, results in double taxation), or if the taxpayer and state tax authorities agree to an alternative adjustment.

STUDY QUESTIONS

9. Which of the following is *not* generally included in the definition of a related member for purposes of state addback provisions?
   a. A member of a federal controlled group of corporations
   b. A member of a federal affiliated group of corporations
   c. An entity that owns *less than* 50 percent of the taxpayer's stock

10. States have enacted related party expense addback provisions to prevent taxpayers from benefiting from tax avoidance strategies involving the use of intangible property holding companies. *True or False?*

CPE NOTE: When you have completed your study and review of chapters 1-4, which comprise Module 1, you may wish to take the Quizzer for this Module.

For your convenience, you can also take this Quizzer online at **www.CCHGroup.com/TestingCenter**.

Nexus

This chapter discusses which activities performed by a taxpayer in a particular state will cause the taxpayer to have income tax and/or sales and use tax nexus with that state.

LEARNING OBJECTIVES

Upon completing this chapter, the student will be able to:

- Recognize the historical development of the physical presence standard and its importance in influencing today's tax policy
- Describe the concept of economic nexus
- Define which activities of a multistate corporation may create nexus
- Identify the impact of affiliates and independent agents on nexus
- Explain which activities of a multistate corporation are protected by Public Law 86-272
- State how electronic commerce affects state and local taxes

OVERVIEW

Whether a corporation is required to collect sales or use tax or pay income tax hinges on whether it has nexus with the state. Nexus is defined as some definite link, some minimum connection, between the state and the corporation it seeks to tax. Nexus embodies the spirit that a state cannot impose a tax on persons doing business or activities that occur outside the state's borders.

Different taxes may have differing threshold standards for establishing nexus. Usually those standards are the outgrowth of judicial decisions that are accepted or modified as a result of legislative activity. For this reason, state court decisions and U.S. Supreme Court decisions are significant in understanding the development of our current nexus standards. This course reviews the important cases that have been instrumental in establishing state nexus rules.

The nexus standards for establishing a sales or use tax collection responsibility have traditionally been very broad, although they have been curtailed to a certain extent by the U.S. Supreme Court in the *Quill Corp. v. North Dakota* [504 US 298 (1992)] decision. This case is discussed in depth later in the chapter.

Some taxpayers point to the decision in *Quill* to support a position not to collect use tax. Although *Quill* was decided in favor of the taxpayer, application of the decision may in many ways be limited in scope. The questions then become these:

- What activities in a state will create sufficient contact with the state to impose a use tax collection responsibility?
- Will *de minimis* activities create a sufficient connection?
- Should a taxpayer voluntarily register to collect use tax?

CONSTITUTIONAL NEXUS

Historically, states have asserted that virtually any type of in-state business activity creates nexus for an out-of-state corporation. Such behavior reflects the reality that it is politically more appealing to tax out-of-state corporations than to raise taxes on in-state business interests. The desire of state lawmakers and tax officials to, in effect, export the local tax burden has been counterbalanced by the Due Process Clause and Commerce Clause of the U.S. Constitution.

The Due Process Clause states that no state shall "deprive any person of life, liberty or property, without due process of law." The U.S. Supreme Court has interpreted this clause as prohibiting a state from taxing an out-of-state corporation unless there is a "minimal connection" between the company's interstate activities and the taxing state. [E.g., *Mobil Oil Corp. v. Commissioner of Taxes,* 445 US 425 (1980)]

The Commerce Clause expressly authorizes Congress to "regulate Commerce with foreign Nations, and among the several States." The Supreme Court has interpreted the Commerce Clause as prohibiting states from enacting laws that might unduly burden or otherwise inhibit the free flow of trade among the states. More specifically, with respect to the nexus issue, the Supreme Court has interpreted the Commerce Clause as prohibiting a state from taxing an out-of-state corporation unless that company has a "substantial nexus" with the state. [*Complete Auto Transit, Inc. v. Brady,* 430 US 274 (1977)]

In summary, a state cannot impose a tax obligation on an out-of-state corporation unless the Due Process Clause minimal connection and Commerce Clause substantial nexus requirements are satisfied. Therefore, a critical question in the nexus arena is what do minimal connection and substantial nexus mean? The controlling case in this regard is *Quill.*

PHYSICAL PRESENCE REQUIREMENT

In *Quill,* the U.S. Supreme Court upheld the bright-line physical presence test established in *National Bellas Hess, Inc. v. Illinois* [386 US 753 (1967)], an earlier mail-order/use tax collection Supreme Court case. Quill Corporation was a mail-order vendor of office supplies. Sales were solicited through catalogs mailed to potential customers in North Dakota, with deliveries made through common carriers. Quill was a Delaware corporation with offices and warehouses in California, Georgia, and Illinois. Quill had no office, warehouse, retail outlet, or other facility located in North Dakota, nor were any Quill employees or sales representatives physically present in North Dakota. Thus, with respect to North Dakota, Quill was strictly an out-of-state mail-order vendor. Nevertheless, during the tax years in question, Quill made sales to roughly 3,000 North Dakota customers, and was the sixth largest office supply vendor in the state.

North Dakota was attempting to impose on Quill an obligation to collect North Dakota use tax on sales to North Dakota customers. The North Dakota Supreme Court had ruled that Quill had constitutional nexus in North Dakota, reasoning that Quill's "economic presence" in North Dakota depended on services and benefits provided by the state, and therefore generated "a constitutionally sufficient nexus to justify imposition of the purely administrative duty of collecting and remitting the use tax."

The U.S. Supreme Court reversed the lower court's ruling, and held that, although an economic presence was sufficient to satisfy the Due Process Clause requirement of a minimal connection, it was not sufficient to satisfy the Commerce Clause requirement of substantial nexus. Consistent with its ruling 25 years earlier in *National Bellas Hess,* the Court further ruled that substantial nexus exists only if the corporation has a nontrivial physical presence in the state. Therefore, physical presence is an essential prerequisite to establishing constitutional nexus, at least for sales and use tax purposes.

It is important to highlight the fact that *Quill* is a use tax case, and that the U.S. Supreme Court did not address the issue of whether the physical presence test also applied to income taxes. Many commentators have argued that there is no reason to believe that the Commerce Clause would impose a different standard for income taxes than for sales and use taxes, and therefore the same physical presence test should apply. Nevertheless, until the Supreme Court rules on the issue, no one knows for sure.

In summary, the Supreme Court has ruled that a corporation does not have constitutional nexus in a state unless that company has a nontrivial physical presence within the state's borders. Thus, a physical presence, established through the presence of either company-owned property or company employees or other agents, is generally regarded as an essential prerequisite for establishing constitutional nexus in a state for sales and use tax purposes.

Streamlined Sales Tax (SST)

The SST became operational on October 1, 2005, for taxpayers to voluntarily register to collect tax in the member states. Although initially taking effect as a voluntary program for taxpayer participation, legislation has been introduced in Congress to make it mandatory. However, at the time of publication, participation in the SST remains voluntary. If SST becomes mandatory, it would effectively eliminate the physical presence standard as articulated in *Quill* and replace it with the broader economic nexus standard. Therefore, under an economic nexus standard, taxpayers would be required to collect sales tax on all sales, regardless of whether they are physically present in a state. In states that are not members of SST (although presumably there would not be many nonmember states if the federal government made participation in SST mandatory), it remains to be seen whether the *Quill* standard will continue to govern. This could lead to substantial confusion for taxpayers and tax jurisdictions, particularly during transition periods for states adopting the SST provisions.

PUBLIC LAW 86-272

Congress enacted Public Law 86-272 in 1959 to provide multistate corporations with a limited safe harbor from the imposition of state income taxes. Under Public Law 86-272, taxpayers may engage in certain protected activities without triggering the imposition of income tax. Specifically, Public Law 86-272 prohibits a state from imposing a "net income tax" on a corporation organized in another state if the corporation's only in-state activity is (1) solicitation of orders by company representatives, (2) for sales of tangible personal property, (3) which orders are sent outside the state for approval or rejection, and (4) if approved, are filled by shipment or delivery from a point outside the state.

This protection is limited in its application to taxes measured by net income. Taxpayers frequently misinterpret these provisions as providing some shield from the obligation to collect use tax. However, Public Law 86-272 does not apply to taxes that are measured by gross receipts or sales. Therefore, physical presence, beyond some *de minimis* level, triggers an obligation to collect sales and use tax.

EXAMPLE

If employees regularly visit an out-of-state location and solicit sales of tangible personal property that are then forwarded to the out-of-state headquarters for approval and subsequent shipment from stocks located at that out-of-state location, the seller would be required to collect use tax on the sale. The seller would be required to collect the use tax because the level of physical presence exceeds some *de minimis* amount. Absent any other considerations, however, the taxpayer would not be liable for income tax in the destination state because the requirements of Public Law 86-272 have been met.

Public Law 86-272 Limitations

Although Public Law 86-272 can provide significant protections for a multistate business, it has several important limitations.

First, it applies only to taxes imposed on net income and provides no protection against the imposition of a sales and use tax collection obligation, property taxes, gross receipts taxes (e.g., Ohio commercial activity tax, or Washington business and occupation tax), or corporate franchise taxes on net worth or capital.

> **EXAMPLE**
>
> In *Home Impressions, Inc. v. Division of Taxation* [No. 000099-2003 (N.J. Tax Ct., June 7, 2004)], the New Jersey Tax Court ruled that Public Law 86-272 does not protect a taxpayer from the imposition of a flat dollar minimum tax that is part of the state's corporate business tax regime.

Second, Public Law 86-272 protects only sales of *tangible personal property*. It does not protect activities such as leasing tangible personal property, selling services, selling or leasing real estate, or selling or licensing intangibles.

> **EXAMPLE**
>
> In re *Personal Selling Power, Inc.* [No 380557 (Cal. State Bd. of Equal., Mar. 16, 2009)], the California State Board of Equalization ruled that Public Law 86-272 did not protect a Virginia media company from income tax nexus, because the employee solicitation of sales of advertisements in a magazine involved sales of a service rather than sales of tangible personal property.

Third, for businesses that send employees into other states to sell tangible personal property, Public Law 86-272 applies only if those employees limit their in-state activities to the solicitation of orders that are sent outside the state for approval, and if approved, are filled by a shipment or delivery from a point outside the state.

> **EXAMPLE**
>
> Public Law 86-272 provides no protection if salespeople are given the authority to approve merchandise orders. Likewise, Public Law 86-272 does not protect the presence of salespeople who perform nonsolicitation activities, such as repairs, customer training, or technical assistance, within a state.

Solicitation of Orders

Although Public Law 86-272 does not define the phrase *solicitation of orders*, the meaning of the phrase was addressed by the U.S. Supreme Court in *Wisconsin Department of Revenue v. William Wrigley, Jr., Co.* [505

US 214 (1992)]. In this case, the Court defined solicitation of orders as encompassing "requests for purchases" as well as "those activities that are entirely ancillary to requests for purchases—those that serve no independent business function apart from their connection to the soliciting of orders." Examples of activities that might serve an independent business function, apart from the solicitation of orders, include:

- Installation and start-up
- Customer training
- Engineering and design assistance
- Technical assistance
- Maintenance and repair
- Credit and collection

Wrigley was a chewing gum manufacturer headquartered in Illinois. Wrigley marketed its goods in Wisconsin through employee sales representatives who were residents of Wisconsin. All Wisconsin orders were sent to Chicago for acceptance and were filled by shipment through common carrier from outside the state. Wrigley did not own or lease any offices or other facilities in Wisconsin.

In determining whether Wrigley's activities in Wisconsin exceeded the protection of Public Law 86-272, the Supreme Court was faced with two fundamental questions:

1.   What is the scope of the phrase *solicitation of orders*?
2.   Does a *de minimis* exception exist for activities other than solicitation of orders?

With respect to the first issue, Wisconsin argued that *solicitation of orders* should be narrowly construed to mean "any activity other than requesting the customer to purchase the product." Wrigley, on the other hand, argued for a much broader definition; specifically, "any activities that are ordinary and necessary business activities accompanying the solicitation process or are routinely associated with deploying a sales force to conduct the solicitation, so long as there is no office, plant, warehouse or inventory in the State."

The Supreme Court rejected both definitions as too extreme, and instead crafted its own interpretation, defining *solicitation of orders* as encompassing "requests for purchases" and "those activities that are entirely ancillary to requests for purchases—those that serve no independent business function apart from their connection to the soliciting of orders."

The Court then applied this definition to the activities of Wrigley employees within Wisconsin. It found that providing a company-owned car or stock of free samples to salespeople; in-state recruitment, training, and evaluation of sales representatives; and use of hotels and homes for sales-related meetings were entirely ancillary to solicitation because they served no purpose apart from their role in facilitating requests for purchases. In contrast, the Court found that the replacement of stale gum, the supplying of gum through agency stock checks, and the storage of gum within the state were not ancillary to Wrigley's solicitation activities.

With respect to the second issue—*de minimis* nonsolicitation activities—the Supreme Court held that a *de minimis* level of nonsolicitation activities does not cause a company to lose the protections afforded by Public Law 86-272, and that whether nonsolicitation activities are sufficiently *de minimis* to avoid the loss of tax immunity depends on whether that activity establishes a "nontrivial additional connection with the taxing state." The Court then held that, in the aggregate, Wrigley's unprotected activities (i.e., the replacement of stale gum, the supplying of gum through agency stock checks, and the storage of gum) did not meet its *de minimis* standard even though the relative magnitude of those activities was not large in comparison to Wrigley's total Wisconsin activities.

In summary, although taxpayers and the states can be expected to interpret the phrases *entirely ancillary* and *nontrivial additional connection* differently, the Supreme Court's ruling in **Wrigley** nevertheless provides a uniform standard applicable to all 50 states. Moreover, the **Wrigley** decision clearly establishes that there is a *de minimis* exception to the activities that are not protected by Public Law 86-272.

It does appear that some states will narrowly interpret the **Wrigley** definition of solicitation of orders. For example, in **Kennametal Inc. v. Massachusetts Commissioner of Revenue** [No. SJC-07448 (Mass. 1997)], the Massachusetts Supreme Judicial Court ruled that Kennametal's frequent in-plant presentations, inventory analyses for tool standardization programs, and sample testing using Kennametal's products exceeded solicitation. According to the court, those activities not only invited orders but also ingratiated customers to the company and assisted customers with making buying decisions.

Likewise, in **Amgen, Inc. v. Commissioner of Revenue** [No. SJC-07563 (Mass. 1998)], the Massachusetts Supreme Judicial Court held that the in-state activities of Amgen employees exceeded the mere solicitation of Amgen's pharmaceutical products. In particular, the employees monitored the research and clinical studies performed in Massachusetts, provided educational seminars, maintained ownership and control of the supplies used in such studies, and retained employees to review specific patient charts and answer patient-specific questions. The court ruled that these activities were not entirely ancillary to the solicitation of orders, but instead served an independent business purpose.

In **Alcoa Building Products, Inc. v. Commissioner of Revenue** [No. SJC-08939 (Mass. Sup. Jud. Ct., Oct. 21, 2003)], the Massachusetts Supreme Judicial Court held that various warranty claims activities performed by in-state sales personnel, such as initiating warranty claims, analyzing the merits of claims, and assisting customers in filing claims, exceeded mere solicitation and created income tax nexus for an out-of-state manufacturer.

Although taxpayers generally prefer to avoid nexus, a narrow interpretation of the meaning of *solicitation* can be helpful in avoiding the application of a state's sales factor throwback rule, as was illustrated in ***Colgate-Palmolive Company v. Commissioner of Revenue*** [No. C255116 (Mass. App. Tax Bd., April 3, 2003)]. On the other hand, the Texas Comptroller of Public Accounts rejected a taxpayer's argument that throwback did not apply to the company's sales to Alabama customers because while visiting family in Alabama, an employee checked the company's voice mail system and responded to work-related telephone calls. [Tex. Comp. of Pub. Accts., Hearing No. 42,586, Jan. 6, 2004]

STUDY QUESTIONS

1. Which of the following cases dealt with whether or not the taxpayer should pay state income taxes?

   a. *National Bellas Hess*
   b. *Quill Corp.*
   c. *William Wrigley, Jr.*

2. Which of the following **prohibits** a state from taxing an out-of-state corporation, unless that company has *substantial nexus* with the state?

   a. Commerce Clause
   b. Due Process Clause
   c. Public Law 86-272

3. According to the U.S. Supreme Court **Wrigley** decision, which of the following activities is **not** ancillary to solicitation of sales?

   a. Providing a company-owned car to salespeople in the state
   b. Providing a stock of free samples to salespeople in the state
   c. Storage of inventory within the state
   d. Use of hotels and homes in the state for sales-related meetings

MTC STATEMENT OF PRACTICES: PROTECTED VS. UNPROTECTED ACTIVITIES

Created in 1967, the Multistate Tax Commission (MTC) is an agency of state governments whose mission is to promote fairness and uniformity in state tax laws. The MTC adopted a policy statement in 1986 regarding the proper application of Public Law 86-272, modified the statement in 1993 and 1994 in light of the Wrigley decision, and modified it again in 2001 to remove deliveries in company-owned vehicles from the list of unprotected activities. In the MTC's Statement of Information Concerning Practices of

Multistate Tax Commission and Signatory States Under Public Law 86-272, the states indicate that "it is the policy of the state signatories hereto to impose their net income tax, subject to State and Federal legislative limitations, to the fullest extent constitutionally permissible." The statement goes on to list activities that are considered to be entirely ancillary to the solicitation of orders (protected activities) and activities that are considered to serve an independent business function (unprotected activities).

Unprotected Activities

The following in-state activities (if they are not of a *de minimis* level) are not considered either the solicitation of orders or ancillary to the solicitation of orders or otherwise protected under Public Law 86-272 and will cause otherwise protected sales to lose their protection under Public Law 86-272:

- Making repairs or providing maintenance or service to the property sold or to be sold
- Collecting current or delinquent accounts, whether directly or by third parties, through assignment, or otherwise
- Investigating creditworthiness
- Installation or supervision of installation at or after shipment or delivery
- Conducting training courses, seminars, or lectures for personnel other than personnel involved only in solicitation
- Providing any kind of technical assistance or service (including, but not limited to, engineering assistance or design service) when one of the purposes thereof is other than the facilitation of the solicitation of orders
- Investigating, handling, or otherwise assisting in resolving customer complaints, other than mediating direct customer complaints when the sole purpose of the mediation for sales personnel is to ingratiate themselves with customers
- Approving or accepting orders
- Repossessing property
- Securing deposits on sales
- Picking up or replacing damaged or returned property
- Hiring, training, or supervising personnel, other than personnel involved only in solicitation
- Using agency stock checks or any other instrument or process by which sales are made within the state by sales personnel
- Maintaining a sample or display room in excess of two weeks (14 days) at any one location within the state during the tax year
- Carrying samples for sale, exchange, or distribution in any manner for consideration or other value
- Owning, leasing, using, or maintaining any of the following facilities or property in the state:
  - Repair shop

- Parts department
- Any kind of office other than an in-home office
- Warehouse
- Meeting place for directors, officers, or employees
- Stock of goods other than samples for sales personnel or samples whose use is entirely ancillary to solicitation
- Telephone answering service that is publicly attributed to the company or to employees or agents of the company in their representative status
- Mobile stores (i.e., vehicles with drivers who are sales personnel making sales from the vehicles)
- Real property or fixtures to real property of any kind

- Consigning stock of goods or other tangible personal property to any person, including an independent contractor, for sale
- Maintenance, by any employee or other representative, of an office or place of business of any kind (other than an in-home office located within the residence of the employee or representative (1) that is not publicly attributed to the company or to the employee or representative of the company in an employee or representative capacity, and (2) as long as the use of such office is limited to soliciting and receiving orders from customers; to transmitting such orders outside the state for acceptance or rejection by the company; or to such other activities that are protected under Public Law 86-272)
- Entering into franchising or licensing agreements; selling or otherwise disposing of franchises and licenses; or selling or otherwise transferring tangible personal property pursuant to such franchise or license by the franchisor or licensor to its franchisee or licensee within the state
- Conducting any activity not listed as a protected activity (see below) that is not entirely ancillary to requests for orders, even if the activity helps to increase purchases

Protected Activities

The following in-state activities will not cause the loss of protection for otherwise protected sales:

- Solicitation of orders by any type of advertising
- Solicitation of orders by an in-state resident employee or representative of the company, as long as such person does not maintain or use any office or other place of business in the state other than an in-home office
- Carrying samples and promotional materials only for display or distribution without charge or other consideration
- Furnishing and setting up display racks and advising customers on the display of the company's products without charge or other consideration

- Providing automobiles to sales personnel for their use in conducting protected activities
- Passing on orders, inquiries, and complaints to the home office
- Missionary sales activities (i.e., the solicitation of indirect customers for the company's goods, which would include, for example, a manufacturer's solicitation of retailers to buy the manufacturer's goods from the manufacturer's wholesale customers if such solicitation activities were otherwise immune)
- Coordinating shipment or delivery without payment or other consideration and providing information relating thereto either prior or subsequent to the placement of an order
- Checking customers' inventories without charge (for reorder but not for other purposes such as quality control)
- Maintaining a sample or display room for two weeks (14 days) or less at any one location within the state during the tax year
- Recruiting, training, or evaluating sales personnel, including occasionally using homes, hotels, or similar places for meetings with sales personnel
- Mediating direct customer complaints when the purpose of the mediation is solely for sales personnel to ingratiate themselves with customers and to facilitate requests for orders
- Owning, leasing, or maintaining personal property for use in the employee's or representative's in-home office or automobile that is solely limited to conducting protected activities

It follows from the last item that use of personal property such as a cellular telephone, facsimile machine, duplicating equipment, personal computer, and computer software that is limited to carrying on protected solicitation and activity entirely ancillary to protected solicitation or permitted by the MTC's statement will not, by itself, remove the protection under the MTC's statement.

PLANNING POINTER

One of the problems encountered by companies wishing to operate within the safety zone provided by Public Law 86-272 is that many of the unprotected activities are very logical things to do, particularly in an era where customer service is receiving more attention to attract market share. For example, it makes good business sense for the salesperson to be involved in checking the creditworthiness of a customer and to take merchandise returns for a retailer rather than having the retailer return them to some remote location. However, engaging in these activities exceeds the protections of Public Law 86-272, and salespeople engaging in these activities would be creating nexus in those jurisdictions where they engaged in these activities. Therefore, companies wishing to avoid nexus must make sure their salespeople understand and respect these limitations to avoid unanticipated consequences and tax liabilities.

De Minimis Exception

The U.S. Supreme Court noted in *Quill* that the slightest presence in the state does not meet the substantial nexus requirements of the Commerce Clause, but the Court did not define how much physical presence is necessary to establish substantial nexus. A company may therefore have a physical presence in the state and not create sales tax nexus as long as the activities in the state are *de minimis* in nature. Previous court decisions indicate that the relative value of the company's in-state property, the number of in-state employees, or the relative amount of sales made in the state may not be determinative if the company is otherwise found to have activities in the state that are more than *de minimis*.

The Florida Supreme Court upheld a district court's "insufficient nexus" decision in *Share International, Inc.* [676 So.2d 1362 (Fla. 1996), *cert. denied*, No. 96-647 (U.S. Jan. 6, 1997)] Share International is in the business of manufacturing and distributing chiropractic supplies, which are sold primarily via mail order from its office in Texas. Between 1986 and 1989, Share International participated in annual seminars in Florida, each lasting three days. The company collected sales tax on items sold at each seminar, but did not collect tax on the mail-order sales.

The Florida Department of Revenue's contention that the taxpayer's presence at each seminar was enough to satisfy nexus requirements was rejected by the trial court and the district court. Relying principally on *National Geographic Society v. State Board of Equalization* [97 S. Ct. 1386 (1977)], the district court held that under the Commerce Clause, the slight presence of an out-of-state mail-order company within the state was insufficient to permit the state to enforce a use tax against the company. Instead, the district court held that the state may only enforce such a tax against an out-of-state company whose activities create a substantial nexus to the state. The Florida Supreme Court found that "[w]hile this law may require courts to fill in the gaps and give meaning to the terms 'slightest presence' and 'substantial nexus' it is apparent that those are the standards established by the U.S. Supreme Court." Accordingly, the Florida Supreme Court found no error in the district court's interpretation and application of those terms.

The Florida Supreme Court also agreed with the district court that the bright-line test adopted in *National Bellas Hess* clearly insulates from state taxation only out-of-state vendors whose sole activities in the taxing state are mail-order sales. If such a company has additional connections to the taxing state, those connections must be analyzed under the substantial nexus test.

In *Dell Catalog Sales v. Commissioner, Department of Revenue Services* (No. CV 00 05031465 July 10, 2003), the Connecticut Superior Court held that the national retailer of computer equipment did not have a sufficient physical presence in Connecticut to constitute nexus for sales and use tax purposes. Although Dell had a third party perform service work on its behalf, that level of contact was deemed to be *de minimis* because the actual number of on-site calls was minimal.

STUDY QUESTIONS

4. Which of the following activities in a state is considered "unprotected" under a policy statement adopted by the MTC?

   a. Solicitation of orders by a salesperson

   b. Order approval by a salesperson

   c. Setting up display racks for a customer without charge

5. Which of the following activities in a state is considered "protected" under a policy statement adopted by the MTC?

   a. Maintaining a display room for 10 days at one location in a state during the tax year

   b. Collecting payment for a delinquent account

   c. Repossession of property

6. A company may have a physical presence in a state and **not** create sales tax nexus, as long as the activities in the state are *de minimis* in nature. ***True or False?***

7. States generally attempt to impose their income taxes to the fullest extent permissible. ***True or False?***

ATTRIBUTIONAL NEXUS

Agency Nexus Principle

Under the *Quill* decision, a corporation generally has constitutional nexus in any state in which the corporation's property or employees are physically present on a regular and systematic basis. What if, rather than conducting business in a state through employees, a corporation conducts business through independent agents? Does the use of independent agents, rather than employees, allow the corporation to avoid constitutional nexus?

Scripto. In *Scripto, Inc. v. Carson* [362 US 207 (1960)], the U.S. Supreme Court addressed the issue of whether the Florida marketing activities of 10 independent sales representatives created sales/use tax nexus for an out-of-state manufacturer of writing instruments. The Court held that for nexus purposes, the distinction between employees and independent contractors was "without constitutional significance," and that "to permit such formal 'contractual shifts' to make a constitutional difference would open the gates to a stampede of tax avoidance." In the Court's mind, the critical fact was that the agents' activity in Florida created and maintained a commercial market for Scripto's goods. Thus, the presence of independent agents engaged in continuous local solicitation created Florida sales/use tax nexus for Scripto.

The Court reaffirmed these principles 25 years later in ***Tyler Pipe Industries, Inc. v. Washington Department of Revenue*** [483 US 232 (1987)], holding that the activities of a single independent contractor residing in Washington were sufficient to create constitutional nexus for the out-of-state principal (Tyler Pipe). As in ***Scripto***, the Court held that the critical test was "whether the activities performed in this state on behalf of the taxpayer are significantly associated with the taxpayer's ability to establish and maintain a market in this state for the sales."

Borders Online. Borders Online operated a Web site through which it sold books, CDs, etc. It was established as a separate corporate entity from the "brick and mortar" Borders, Inc. Borders bookstores routinely accepted returns from its patrons regardless of whether the item was purchased at one of its stores, through the Borders Online Web site, or from a competitor. If the item was purchased from a competitor, Borders would give the purchaser an in-store credit; however, if the returned item was purchased from Borders Online, the store would provide a cash refund, just as if it had been purchased from Borders. In ***Borders Online, LLC v. State Board of Equalization*** [29 Cal. Rptr. 3d, 176 Ct App. 2005], the California Court of Appeals ruled in favor of the State Board of Equalization, saying that by accepting Borders Online's merchandise for return, Borders acted on behalf of Borders Online as its agent or representative in California. This determination combined with Borders Online's marketing efforts in California provided Borders Online with a sufficient presence in California to require Borders Online to collect the California sales tax on its sales, even though Borders Online did not have any physical assets in California.

Public Law 86-272 and Independent Agents

In addition to protecting solicitation activities of employee-salespeople, Public Law 86-272 protects certain in-state activities conducted by an independent contractor. Specifically, Public Law 86-272 provides that independent contractors may engage in the following in-state activities on behalf of an out-of-state corporation without creating income tax nexus for the out-of-state principal:

- Soliciting sales
- Making sales
- Maintaining an office

Thus, unlike employees, independent agents can maintain in-state offices without creating *income tax* nexus for the principal. [See, e.g., ***Universal***

Instruments Corp. v. Massachusetts Comm'r of Revenue, No. 196059 (Mass. App. Tax Bd. (1998).]

> **CAUTION**
>
> Because Public Law 86-272 provides no protection for sales or use taxes, any of these activities would create sales and use tax nexus.

For this purpose, the term *independent contractors* means a commission agent, broker, or other independent contractor who is engaged in selling, or soliciting orders for the sale of, tangible personal property for more than one principal and who holds him- or herself out as such in the regular course of his or her business activities. Under the Statement of Information Concerning Practices of Multistate Tax Commission and Signatory States Under Public Law 86-272, the maintenance of a stock of goods within a state by the independent contractor under consignment or any other type of arrangement with the out-of-state principal, except for purposes of display and solicitation, is not protected by Public Law 86-272.

MTC Nexus Bulletin 95-1

If an employee salesperson's in-state activities include non-ancillary services such as installation and repair services, these activities are not protected by Public Law 86-272 and will create income tax nexus for the employer, provided that the unprotected activities are not de minimis. A number of states also take the position that such in-state services create nexus, even if they are performed by unrelated third-party repairpersons (i.e., independent agents). Unlike the use of independent agents to perform continuous local solicitation, the issue of whether the use of independent agents to perform services that are not ancillary to the solicitation has yet to be addressed by the Supreme Court. Thus, this remains an unsettled area of the law.

In Nexus Bulletin 95-1 [1995], the MTC and roughly two dozen signatory states took the position that with respect to mail-order computer vendors, the industry practice of providing in-state warranty repair services through third-party repair service providers creates constitutional nexus. As a consequence, the out-of-state mail-order vendors may have nexus for sales and use tax purposes. This position is based on the Supreme Court's decision in *Scripto* and *Tyler Pipe,* both of which dealt with the use of independent sales representatives, as opposed to independent service providers. The computer mail-order industry and many practitioners believe that there is insufficient support in these two Supreme Court decisions for the position asserted by the MTC in Nexus Bulletin 95-1. Nevertheless, since its issuance, a number of states have taken a position similar to that espoused by Nexus Bulletin 95-1.

EXAMPLE

In TSB-A-00(42)S [Oct. 13, 2000], the New York Department of Taxation and Finance ruled that an out-of-state mail-order computer vendor's use of independent contractors to perform warranty services in the state was sufficient to create sales/use tax nexus. On the other hand, a handful of states (most notably, California) have taken a position contrary to that in Nexus Bulletin 95-1. [See, e.g., *In re Gateway 2000, Inc.,* Declaratory Ruling No. 96-30-6-0033, (Iowa Dep't. of Revenue and Finance, Mar. 19, 1996).]

Other Applications of Agency Nexus Principle

State tax authorities have becoming increasingly creative in their application of the agency nexus principle. Two examples are the decisions in *Furniture-land South, Inc.* **v.** *Comptroller* [No. C-97-37872 OC (Md. Cir. Ct., Aug. 13, 1999)], and *Kmart Properties, Inc.* [No. 00-04, (N.M. Taxation and Revenue Dept., Feb. 1, 2000].

In *Furnitureland South,* the Maryland court ruled that a trucking company (Royal Transport) created use tax nexus for an unrelated out-of-state furniture retailer (Furnitureland South) because the trucking company acted as the retailer's "agent" in Maryland. Before 1991, Furnitureland had its own fleet of trucks and drivers to make deliveries. Royal Transport was established in 1991 as a for-hire motor carrier. Royal was not a subsidiary of Furnitureland. No employee, officer, director, or shareholder of Royal was at any time an employee, officer, director, or shareholder of Furnitureland, but Furnitureland did provide initial financing to Royal, sold Royal its used trailers, assigned Royal its leased equipment, remained on the assigned equipment leases as guarantor, provided start-up capital, trained Royal drivers on the delivery and assembly of furniture, and provided Royal with rent-free office space in Furnitureland's distribution center.

The Maryland court concluded that Royal created a use tax withholding obligation for Furnitureland because it acted as its "agent" for the purpose of delivering, setting up, and servicing furniture in Maryland. Royal's drivers provided important services to Maryland customers on behalf of Furnitureland. The drivers carried tools that they used to repair damaged furniture, regularly set up new furniture in customers' homes, collected C.O.D. payments for Furnitureland, carried additional items (e.g., bed slats and mirror supports) that they sold to Furnitureland's customers, and routinely picked up damaged furniture. Royal's trucks also prominently displayed the Furnitureland logo. In addition, Furnitureland prepared and scheduled each trip to be taken by a Royal driver. As it emphasized in its marketing, this personalized delivery service helped Furnitureland, "your neighborhood furniture store," become the largest furniture retailer in the world.

In *Quill*, the Supreme Court observed that *National Bellas Hess* created a safe harbor for out-of-state vendors "whose only connection with customers in the taxing State is by common carrier or the U.S. mail." The Maryland court concluded, however, that the "personalized delivery service" provided by Royal to Furnitureland customers did not fall within the common carrier safe harbor. When merchandise is shipped via common carrier (e.g., UPS), set-up and repair are not services expected by the typical consumer. Furthermore, when a package is shipped via common carrier, the shipper has little or no control over the time, manner, and means of delivery. In contrast, when Royal made deliveries for Furnitureland, Royal's drivers entered the customer's home, set up the furniture, made any necessary minor repairs, and even made sales of items not ordered. In addition, Furnitureland retained significant control over the time, manner, and means of delivery.

In *Kmart Properties, Inc.*, the taxpayer (Kmart Properties, Inc., or KPI) was a Michigan corporation that had no employees or tangible or real property located in New Mexico. KPI did, however, own highly valuable intangible property (trademarks, trade names) that it licensed for use by Kmart stores, which operated 22 retail stores in New Mexico. As the owner of the intangible property, KPI controlled the terms of the licenses it granted, including where that property could be used by Kmart. The licensing agreement had been negotiated and executed in Michigan, and KPI's management of its intellectual property occurred in Michigan. Despite the lack of tangible property or employees in New Mexico, the New Mexico Taxation and Revenue Department ruled that KPI was physically present in New Mexico by virtue of Kmart's (the parent company's) contractual obligations under the licensing agreements to establish, maintain, and enhance the market for KPI's trademarks in New Mexico in order to generate a revenue stream for KPI. The license agreement provided that Kmart would maintain the quality of products and services bearing the trademarks and trade names, comply with quality standards set by KPI for such products and services, advise KPI of new or changed products and services, and instruct Kmart not to use products or services failing to meet KPI's quality standards. In other words, Kmart was in effect an agent of KPI. Thus, the Department concluded, Kmart was in the same position as the salespeople in *Scripto* (1960) and *Tyler Pipe* (1987), both cases in which the Supreme Court had ruled that the actions of independent agents were sufficient to establish nexus for Commerce Clause purposes.

Finally, in *Jafra Cosmetics, Inc. v. Massachusetts* [No. SJC 08265 (Mass., Jan. 25, 2001)], the Massachusetts Supreme Judicial Court ruled that independent contractors (called "consultants") who sold the products of an out-of-state cosmetics company (Jafra) in Massachusetts created sales/use tax nexus for Jafra. Although the consultants were not agents of Jafra, the nature of the relationship between the consultants and Jafra was such that they did constitute representatives of Jafra and, as such, created sales/use tax nexus for Jafra under the applicable statute.

AFFILIATE NEXUS

A number of states have taken the position that the existence of common ownership between a corporation that has a physical presence in a taxing state (e.g., an in-state brick-and-mortar retailer) and an out-of-state corporation that has no physical presence in the state but makes substantial sales into the state (e.g., an out-of-state mail-order vendor) is sufficient to create constitutional nexus for the out-of-state mail-order affiliate. As with agency nexus, many of these cases concern the existence of nexus for sales and use tax purposes. For example, in *SFA Folio Collections, Inc. v. Tracy* [73 Ohio St.3d 119, 652 N.E.2d 693 (1995)], SFA Folio Collections (Folio), a New York corporation, sold clothing and other merchandise by direct mail to customers in Ohio. Thus, Folio mailed catalogs to potential Ohio customers, the customers placed orders with Folio by telephone, and Folio shipped the merchandise via common carrier. Folio had no property or employees in Ohio; however, Folio's parent corporation, Saks & Company, also owned another subsidiary, Saks Fifth Avenue of Ohio, which operated a retail store in Ohio.

Ohio tax authorities argued that Folio had "substantial nexus" in Ohio because it was a member of an affiliated group that included Saks-Ohio, a corporation that operated a store in Ohio, and therefore was required to collect Ohio sales tax on its mail-order sales to Ohio customers. The state's position was based on a nexus-by-affiliate statute that the Ohio legislature had enacted (since repealed), as well as the argument that Saks-Ohio was an "agent" of Folio. The agency argument was based on the fact that Saks-Ohio accepted some returns of Folio sales and distributed some Folio catalogs. The Ohio Supreme Court rejected the affiliate nexus argument, noting that Saks-Ohio was a separate legal entity, and stated that to impute nexus to Folio merely because a sister corporation had a physical presence in Ohio ran counter to federal constitutional law and Ohio corporation law. The court also rejected the agency nexus argument, reasoning that, although the acceptance of Folio's returns and distribution of Folio's catalogs by Saks-Ohio might provide a minimal connection under the Due Process Clause, these contacts did not create substantial nexus under the Commerce Clause because Saks-Ohio accepted Folio's returns according to its own policy (not Folio's), and charged the returns to its inventory (not Folio's). Moreover, the returns were a minimal part of the returns Saks-Ohio received.

Consistent with the Ohio Supreme Court ruling in *SFA Folio,* other states have generally been unsuccessful in their attempts to argue that common ownership, by itself, creates nexus for an out-of-state affiliate. [See, e.g., *Current, Inc. v. State Bd. of Equalization,* 24 Cal. App. 4th 382, 29 Cal.

Rptr. 2d 407 (Ct. App. 1994); *SFA Folio Collections, Inc. v. Bannon,* 217 Conn. 220, 585 A.2d 666 (1991); *Bloomingdale's By Mail, Ltd. v. Commonwealth,* 130 Pa. Commw. 190, 567 A.2d 773 (Pa. 1989); *J.C. Penney Nat'l Bank v. Johnson,* No. M1998-00497-COA-R3-CV (Tenn. Ct. App. 1999).] On the other hand, based on the U.S. Supreme Court's decisions in *Scripto* and *Tyler Pipe,* if the in-state affiliate truly acts as an agent for the out-of-state affiliate, there is a stronger argument that continuous local solicitation on the part of the in-state affiliate may create nexus for an out-of-state affiliate.

As noted previously, in *Borders Online, Inc.* [SC OHA 97-638364 56270, (Cal. State Bd. of Equal., Sept. 26, 2001)], the California SBE held that the nature of the interrelationship between Borders and Borders Online was such that it created nexus for the online entity that did not have a physical presence in California. In particular, the SBE determined that the refunding of cash for returned goods made Borders, Inc. the "authorized representative" of Borders Online. In addition, the SBE held that the refunding of cash for returns was a key element of the selling process and, in and of itself, constituted "selling" in California under California Revenue and Taxation Code §6203.

One year after its ruling in *Borders Online,* the SBE held that the online subsidiary of Barnes & Noble Booksellers, Inc. (B&N) had nexus in California because B&N distributed discount coupons that could be redeemed with its online affiliate Barnes & Noble.com (B&N.C). As in the Borders decision, the SBE determined that B&N acted as B&N.C's representative through their joint marketing effort whereby B&N.C paid to have printed coupons inserted into the shopping bags of B&N customers. The SBE rejected the taxpayer's argument that the discount coupons inserted into shoppers' bags were simply advertising akin to coupon inserts in magazines and newspapers. [*Barnes & Noble.com,* No. 89872 (Cal. State Bd. Equal., Sept. 12, 2002)]

In *Reader's Digest Association v. Franchise Tax Board* [No. C036307 (Cal. Ct. App. Dec. 31, 2001), *cert. denied,* Cal. Mar. 13, 2002], the California Court of Appeals held that an out-of-state parent corporation (Reader's Digest) had nexus for California corporate income tax purposes as a result of solicitation activities performed by its wholly owned in-state subsidiary (Reader's Digest Sales & Services, Inc.). Public Law 86-272 did not protect the in-state affiliate's California activities because the subsidiary had offices in the state and did not qualify as an "independent contractor" with respect to its out-of-state parent.

In *J.C. Penney National Bank v. Johnson* [No. M1998-00497-COA-R3-CV (Tenn. Ct. App. Dec. 17, 1999)], the state argued that J.C. Penney National Bank (JCPNB) had "substantial nexus" in Tennessee, because JCPNB had a physical presence in Tennessee by virtue of the fact the J.C. Penney Company, JCPNB's parent, owned and operated J.C. Penney retail stores in Tennessee. The court rejected the argument and ruled that JCPNB did not have substantial nexus in Tennessee, because the retail stores conducted no activities that assisted JCPNB in maintaining its credit card business in Tennessee. Customers could not apply for JCPNB credit cards at the J.C. Penney stores, nor could customers make a payment on their accounts at the stores. The solicitation of potential new credit card customers, which was the most important function in allowing JCPNB to maintain its business, took place through the U.S. mail, and that, under the holding in *Quill*, does not allow a finding of substantial nexus.

In *Dillard National Bank, N.A. v. Johnson* [No. 96-545-III (Tenn. Ch. Ct., June 22, 2004)], the Tennessee Chancery Court ruled that an out-of-state subsidiary corporation that issued proprietary credit cards for use in a chain of in-state department stores that were operated by the parent corporation had income tax nexus in Tennessee because of the activities conducted on its behalf by the department stores and the store employees. These activities included placing advertisements in the stores, soliciting and taking credit card applications from store customers, answering questions for store customers regarding their credit card accounts, and accepting credit card payments in the stores. The Tennessee Chancery Court's ruling in *Dillard National Bank* is consistent with the nexus principles articulated by the Tennessee Court of Appeals in *America Online, Inc. v. Johnson* [No. M2001-00927 -COA-R3-CV (Tenn. Ct. App., July 30, 2002)], in which the court stated that "substantial nexus may be established by activities carried on within the state by affiliates and independent contractors." In addition, the facts in *Dillard National Bank* are distinguishable from those in *J.C. Penney National Bank v. Johnson* [No. M1998-00497-COA-R3-CV (Tenn. Ct. App., Dec. 17, 1999)], in which the Tennessee Court of Appeals rejected the affiliate nexus argument because the in-state retail stores conducted no activities that assisted the affiliated out-of-state bank in maintaining its credit card business in Tennessee.

On the other hand, in *St. Tammany Parish Tax Collector v. Barnesand-noble.com* [No. 05-5695 (E.D. La., Mar. 22, 2007)], the U.S. District Court ruled that an Internet retailer of books, movies, and music with no physical presence in Louisiana did not have sales and use tax nexus merely because of its close business relationship with an affiliated brick-and-mortar retailer. The court stated that the "existence of a close corporate relationship between companies and a common corporate name does not mean that the physical presence of one is imputed to the other," and that "attributional nexus does not apply merely by virtue of the affiliation between the companies."

Likewise, in Determination No. 08-0128 [Wash. Dept. of Rev., App. Div., May 14, 2008], the Washington Department of Revenue ruled that wholesale sales of the identical brand name products by an in-state affiliate did not establish business and occupation tax nexus for a remote seller that used television infomercials to promote telephone and online sales, because the in-state affiliate's wholesale-level sales activities were not significantly related to establishing a market for the remote seller.

In ***Drugstore.com, Inc. v. Division of Taxation*** [No. 000637-2003 (N.J. Tax Ct., Feb. 11, 2008)], the New Jersey Tax Court held that the operator of a drugstore Web site had sales and use tax nexus because it had a physical presence in New Jersey. Drugstore.com contended that its only roles in the sales to New Jersey customers were the operation of the Web site and the performance of certain administrative functions for its subsidiaries. One of those subsidiaries, DS Non-Pharmaceutical Sales, Inc. (DSNP Sales) was the nominal retail vendor of the merchandise and had no physical presence in New Jersey. The other subsidiary involved in the transactions was DS Distribution, Inc., which distributed the merchandise to New Jersey customers from a New Jersey warehouse. The taxpayer contended that DSNP Sales was the actual retail vendor of the merchandise and made the sales to New Jersey customers through a drop shipment transaction. The Tax Court rejected this contention and held that Drugstore.com was the actual seller of merchandise and liable for collecting tax.

Instead of litigation, other states have simply passed legislation providing that companies are taxable in the state through affiliation. Under Alabama legislation, the presence of an in-state retailer is imputed to a related out-of-state vendor if the out-of-state vendor and in-state retailer share certain activities. [Ala. Stat §40-23-190] Effective January 1, 2002, a remote seller affiliated with an Arkansas retailer will have nexus with the state for the purposes of sales and use tax. The out-of-state or remote seller will have to collect and remit Arkansas use tax on sales into the state, if the seller is affiliated with an Arkansas retailer and "the vendor sells the same or substantially similar line of products…under the same or substantially similar business name, or the facilities or employees of the Arkansas retailer are used to advertise or promote sales by the vendor to Arkansas purchasers." [Ark. Code Ann. §26-53-124(a)(3)(B)]

Like Arkansas, Minnesota has amended its statutes to require that an affiliated remote seller of an in-state retailer must collect the state's use tax. An out-of-state retailer or remote seller is an affiliate of an in-state entity if "the entity uses its facilities or employees in this state to advertise, promote, or facilitate the establishment or maintenance of a market for sales of items by the retailer to purchasers in this state … or for the provision of services to the retailer's purchasers in this state, such as accepting returns of purchases for the retailer, providing assistance in resolving customer complaints of the retailer, or providing other services." [Minn. Stat. §297A.66(4)]

In TSB-A-03(25)S (June 11, 2003), the New York Department of Taxation and Finance indicated that the opening of a Bass Pro Outdoor World retail store in New York State would not create nexus for an out-of-state mail-order catalog company merely due to common ownership. For the catalog company to avoid nexus, the retailer should avoid performing the following functions:

- Assist customers with catalog company sales, service, or returns
- Refer customers
- Compile mailing lists
- Distribute advertising or merchandising materials (such as coupons)
- Maintain common inventory, accounting/legal staff, other advertising activity

STUDY QUESTIONS

8. Which of the following statements is true regarding MTC Nexus Bulletin 95-1?

   a. In Nexus Bulletin 95-1, the MTC takes the position that providing in-state warranty repair services through third-parties does not create nexus.

   b. Most states have taken a position *contrary* to that in Nexus Bulletin 95-1.

   c. The position taken in the bulletin is based on the Supreme Court decision in **Quill.**

   d. The position taken in the bulletin is based on the Supreme Court's decisions in **Scripto** and **Tyler Pipe.**

9. In which of the following cases was the taxpayer *not* deemed to have nexus because of the activities of an in-state affiliate?

   a. *Borders Online, Inc.*

   b. *Reader's Digest Association*

   c. *Dillard National Bank*

   d. *J.C. Penney National Bank*

10. In which of the following cases did the U.S. Supreme Court hold that, for nexus purposes, the distinction between employees and independent contractors was "without constitutional significance"?

   a. *Scripto Inc.*

   b. *Reader's Digest Association*

   c. *Kmart Properties, Inc.*

   d. *Share International, Inc.*

Affiliate Programs of Online Retailers

Going back to 1960 and *Scripto v. Carson* [362 US 207 1960], states have asserted that regular solicitation of sales by independent contractors or brokers satisfies the Due Process requirement in the Constitution that there be a definite link or minimum connection between a state and the person, property, or transaction it seeks to tax. However, with the growth of sales over the Internet, the methods used to solicit and secure sales no longer require that a physical presence exist in order to make the sale. Recently, states have begun to enact sales referral statutes that impose a collection requirement on a taxpayer if its sales attain a certain level and it compensates in-state businesses or individuals for customer referrals either through a Web site or a link on a Web site.

Typical among such statutes is a New York State statute, enacted in 2008. It reads as follows:

> A person making sales of tangible personal property or services taxable under this article ("seller") shall be presumed to be soliciting business through an independent contractor or other representative if the seller enters into an agreement with a resident of this state under which the resident, for a commission or other compensation, directly or indirectly refers potential customers, whether by a link on an Internet website or otherwise, to the seller, if the cumulative gross receipts from sales by the seller to customers in the state who are referred to the seller by all residents with this type of an agreement with the seller is in excess of ten thousand dollars during the preceding four quarterly periods...This presumption may be rebutted by proof that the resident with whom the seller has an agreement did not engage in any solicitation in the state on behalf of the seller that would satisfy the nexus requirement of the United States Constitution during the four quarterly periods in question.

In 2009, Rhode Island enacted a provision modeled on New York's so-called Amazon provision. The new law establishes a rebuttable presumption for sales and use tax purposes that a seller is soliciting business in the state through an agent if the seller enters into an agreement with a state resident under which the resident, in exchange for a commission or other consideration, refers potential customers to the seller through a Web site link or otherwise. The presumption applies if the seller's cumulative gross receipts from sales to Rhode Island customers referred by residents with such an agreement exceed $5,000 during the four preceding quarterly periods. The presumption can be rebutted by proof that the state resident did not engage in any solicitation on behalf of the seller that would satisfy the nexus requirements of the U.S. Constitution during the four quarterly periods in question.

Deliveries in Company-Owned Trucks

A corporation generally has constitutional nexus in any state in which it has property or employees located on a continuous basis. Thus, a number of state courts have held that the regular and systematic presence of company-owned delivery trucks driven by company employees is sufficient to create sales/use tax nexus. [E.g., *Brown's Furniture, Inc. v. Wagner,* No. 78195 (Ill., Apr. 18, 1996); *Town Crier, Inc. v. Zehnder,* No 1-98-4251 (Ill. App. Ct., June 30, 2000); *John Swenson Granite Co. v. State Tax Assessor,* 685 A.2d 425 (Me. Super. Ct. 1996)]. In *Miller Bros. Co. v. Maryland* [347 U.S. 340 (1954)], however, the U.S. Supreme Court ruled that "occasional delivery" of goods with no solicitation other than the "incidental effects of general advertising" was not sufficient to create nexus under the Due Process Clause.

For income tax purposes, Public Law 86-272 shields an out-of-state corporation from taxation if its only in-state activity is solicitation of orders by company representatives, for sales of tangible personal property, which orders are sent outside the state for approval or rejection, and if approved, are filled by *shipment or delivery* from a point outside the state. Over the years, taxpayers have taken the position that the phrase *shipment or delivery* implies that a seller is protected by Public Law 86-272 regardless of whether it ships the goods into the state using a common carrier or its own delivery trucks. A number of states, however, have taken the position that the in-state delivery of goods in the seller's own delivery trucks exceeds solicitation and therefore is an activity that is not protected by Public Law 86-272.

Nevertheless, the National Private Truck Council has been successful in invalidating a Virginia regulation and the Massachusetts Department of Revenue position that Public Law 86-272 immunity is lost if the taxpayer delivers its products in company-owned vehicles. [*National Private Truck Council v. Virginia Dep't of Taxation,* 253 Va. 74, 480 S.E.2d 500 (1997); *National Private Truck Council v. Commissioner of Revenue,* 688 N.E.2d 936 (Mass. 1997)] In addition, reversing a 1997 decision, the Texas Comptroller of Public Accounts has held that under Public Law 86-272, a taxpayer could claim immunity from the earned surplus portion of the Texas franchise tax even though the taxpayer delivered tangible personal property into Texas using company-owned trucks. [Hearing No. 36,590 (Comptroller of Public Accounts, Jan. 20, 2000)] Thus, there is a strong argument that the use of company-owned trucks to deliver products should not, by itself, cause a taxpayer to forfeit the protections granted by Public Law 86-272.

Although in-state delivery of a corporation's goods may be a protected activity, back-hauling activities are likely to fall outside the protected definition of delivery in Public Law 86-272. For example, in Revenue Ruling No. 97-15, the Tennessee Department of Revenue ruled that a corporation's back-hauling and collection activities create nexus for Tennessee excise (income) taxes because such activities exceed solicitation. Similarly, in TSB-A-97(8)C, the New York Department of Taxation and Finance held that, although the delivery of products to New York customers using company-owned vehicles would not subject the company to franchise (income) tax, post-delivery back-hauling activities in New York would subject the company to franchise (income) tax, unless those activities were *de minimis*. The Department held that the back-hauling activities of the company at issue unrelated to the delivery of products produced 4 percent of the company's total revenues earned in New York and therefore were not *de minimis*, thus subjecting the company to New York franchise (income) tax.

STUDY QUESTION

> **11.** Which of the following activities is protected under Public Law 86-272 according to state Supreme Courts in Massachusetts and Virginia?
>   **a.** Delivery drivers in company-owned trucks accepting returns
>   **b.** Delivery drivers in company-owned trucks collecting payments
>   **c.** Delivery drivers delivering products in company-owned trucks

LICENSING INTANGIBLES: ECONOMIC PRESENCE

Historically, under a Commerce Clause analysis, a taxpayer must have a physical presence in a state before the state may impose a tax based on net income. Yet, in ***Geoffrey, Inc. v. South Carolina Tax Commissioner*** [437 S.E.2d 13 (S.C.), *cert. denied*, 114 S. Ct. 550 (1993)], the South Carolina Supreme Court held that a trademark holding company that licensed its intangibles for use in South Carolina had nexus for income tax purposes, despite the lack of any tangible property or employees in South Carolina.

Geoffrey was incorporated and domiciled in Delaware, and had a license agreement with South Carolina retailers allowing it to use its trademarks and trade names, including the Toys "R" Us trademark, in exchange for a percentage of net sales. The court rejected Geoffrey's claim that it had not purposefully directed its activities toward South Carolina and held that, by licensing intangibles for use in the state and receiving income in exchange for their use, Geoffrey had the minimum connection and substantial nexus with South Carolina required by the Due Process Clause and the Commerce Clause. The ***Geoffrey*** court did not feel compelled to follow the precedent established by ***Quill*** because, in ***Quill***, the U.S. Supreme Court explicitly limited its ruling to the issue of nexus for sales and use tax purposes.

Since 1993, many states have formally adopted ***Geoffrey*** rules or regulations, and there has been a significant amount of litigation regarding the ***Geoffrey*** concept of nexus. For example, in ***State v. Cerro Copper Products Inc.*** [No. 94-444 (Ala. Admin. Law. Div., Dec. 11, 1995)] and ***State v. Dial Bank*** [No. 95-289 (Ala. Admin. Law. Div., Aug. 10, 1998)], the taxpayers successfully argued that they did not have nexus in Alabama because they had not created the physical presence necessary to establish nexus. In both cases, the Alabama court ruled that the ***Quill*** physical presence test applies to state tax levies other than sales and use taxes. Likewise, in ***Bandag Licensing Corp. v. Rylander*** [No. 03-99-00427-CV Tex., May 11, 2000)], the court saw no principled distinction between sales taxes and income taxes when the underlying issue remained whether the Commerce Clause permits a state to impose a tax obligation on an out-of-state corporation. The court concluded that, consistent with the ruling in ***Quill***, a state cannot constitutionally impose its corporate franchise tax on an out-of-state corporation that lacks a physical presence in the state. In addition, in ***America Online, Inc. v. Johnson*** [No. 97-3786-III (Tenn. Ch. Ct. Mar. 3, 2000)], the court ruled that Tennessee did not have the right to tax the company's Internet services because the company did not have a physical presence in the state.

In ***SYL, Inc. v. Comptroller; Crown Cork & Seal Co. (Del.), Inc. v. Comptroller*** [Nos. 76 and 80 (Md. Ct. of App., June 9, 2003)], the Maryland Court of Appeals held that the trademark holding companies in question had nexus in Maryland because they were unitary with their parent companies that were doing business in Maryland, and had no economic substance as separate entities from their parent corporations.

In ***A&F Trademark, Inc. v. Tolson*** [No. COA03-1203 (N.C. Ct. of App., Dec. 7, 2004); *appeal denied*, No. 23P05, N.C. Sup. Ct., Mar. 3, 2005; *cert. denied*, U.S. No. 04-1625, Oct. 3, 2005], the North Carolina Court of Appeals held that licensing intangibles for use in North Carolina was sufficient to establish income tax nexus for an out-of-state trademark holding company, even though the holding company had no physical presence in North Carolina.

In ***Geoffrey, Inc. v. Tax Commission*** [No. 99,938 (Okla. Ct. of Civ. App., Dec. 23, 2005)], the Oklahoma Court of Civil Appeals ruled that licensing intangibles for use in Oklahoma was sufficient to establish income tax nexus for a Delaware trademark holding company, even though the holding company had no physical presence in Oklahoma. The court concluded that the *Quill* physical presence test did not apply to taxes other than sales and use taxes.

In ***Kmart Properties, Inc.,*** the New Mexico Taxation and Revenue Department ruled that a Michigan-based intangible holding company (Kmart Properties) had nexus in New Mexico because an in-state retailer (Kmart) was an "agent" of Kmart Properties, and that, given the Supreme Court's rulings in ***Scripto*** (1960) and ***Tyler Pipe*** (1987), this agency relationship was sufficient to establish nexus for Commerce Clause purposes.

However, in ***ACME Royalty Co. and Brick Investment Co.*** (Mo. S.Ct., No. SC84225 and SC84226, Nov. 26, 2002), the Missouri Supreme Court ruled that two trademark holding companies were *not* subject to the Missouri corporate income tax, because they did not have any activity in Missouri in the form of payroll, property, or sales.

The growing trend in recent years has been to construe nexus when an out-of-state company licenses the use of its intangibles to an in-state related company. For example, recently, the U.S. Supreme Court denied requests to decide whether the Commerce Clause permits a state to impose corporate income and franchise taxes on a company with no physical presence in the taxing state. The question was raised in separate petitions in which taxpayers sought review of decisions by the highest courts of New Jersey (*Lanco*) and West Virginia (*MBNA*).

In *Lanco, Inc. v. Director of Div. of Tax'n* [188 N.J. 380, 908 A.2d 176 (2006)], the New Jersey Supreme Court held that New Jersey may apply its corporation business tax to income from the licensing of intangibles in the state, despite the taxpayer's lack of a physical presence in New Jersey. The court ruled that the *Quill* decision was not intended to create a universal physical presence requirement for state taxation under the Commerce Clause and should be limited to sales and use taxes.

In *State v. MBNA America Bank, N.A.* [220 W. Va. 163, 640 S.E.2d 226 (2006)], the West Virginia Supreme Court of Appeals held the state could impose corporate net income and business franchise taxes on a bank's gross receipts from West Virginia customers, even though the bank had no physical presence in the state. The court concluded that *Quill* is limited to sales and use taxes. Furthermore, it held that a significant economic presence test is a better indicator of whether substantial nexus exists for Commerce Clause purposes than a physical presence standard. The bank's activity in the state, including direct mail and telephone solicitations, produced significant gross receipts from West Virginia customers and, therefore, satisfied the significant economic presence test, according to the court.

Both Lanco and MBNA America Bank appealed to the United States Supreme Court. While many were hopeful that the appeal of two cases on the physical presence standard for income taxes would force the Supreme Court to finally rule on its applicability to income taxes, in both cases the Supreme Court denied certiorari. So, the controversy remains unanswered as to whether the physical presence standard of *Quill* applies to income taxes or not.

In *Praxair Technology, Inc. v. Division of Taxation* [No. 007445-05 (N.J. Tax Ct. June 18, 2007)], the New Jersey Tax Court held that, based upon *Lanco,* an intangible holding company that licensed patent/trade secret intangibles to an affiliate that used the technologies to manufacture industrial gases at facilities in New Jersey had state corporate income tax nexus, even though it lacked an in-state physical presence.

In *Capital One Bank v. Commissioner of Revenue* [Docket Nos. C262391 and C262598 (Mass. Appellate Tax Bd, June 22, 2007); Mass. Sup Judicial Court No. SJC-10105 (Sup. Judicial Court, Jan. 8, 2009)], the court held that the bank's activities established a substantial nexus with Massachusetts because the bank was soliciting and conducting significant credit card business in Massachusetts with hundreds of thousands of Massachusetts residents and generating millions of dollars of income for itself, even though the bank had no physical presence in Massachusetts.

> **PLANNING POINTER**
>
> When looking at expansion plans, taxpayers should consider the impact on nexus that their new plans may have. Many times offices or employees can be assigned to new locations without consideration of the tax impact of such changes. Acceptable alternatives that do not require additional compliance or tax expense can be developed.

> **PLANNING POINTER**
>
> Because certain solicitation activities are protected, a taxpayer may be required to collect sales and use tax but not be liable for income tax. This can be a frequent point of audit contention. The taxpayer in such circumstances should be prepared to defend its position by demonstrating that, although there is physical presence, the employees meet the tests of Public Law 86-272 in terms of their duties in the state.

> **CAUTION**
>
> Taxpayers and their advisors should continuously challenge assumptions regarding nexus and physical presence of employees. Frequently, changes are made in business operations without considering the tax effects of the changes or consulting with a tax advisor regarding the implications of the change. Because of an unlimited statute of limitations for nonfilers, taxpayers need to be particularly cautious in dealing with nexus issues.

> **CAUTION**
>
> Any company making sales into a state that imposes use tax must constantly review its activities in the context of that state's nexus standards. Once nexus is determined to exist, registration and tax collection should follow immediately if the company is to avoid an assessment of tax, penalties, and interest on audit.

To the extent that the subsidiary can operate autonomously, or as autonomously as possible, the taxpayer will have greater success in asserting these arguments.

STUDY QUESTION

12. In which of the following cases was the taxpayer determined **not** to have nexus and thereby **not** subject to income taxes in the state?

a. *Geoffrey Inc. v. South Carolina Tax Commissioner*
b. *A&F Trademark, Inc. v. Tolson*
c. *Geoffrey, Inc. v. Tax Commission*
d. *ACME Royalty Co. and Brick Investment Co.*

OTHER NEXUS ISSUES

State-Specific Statutory and Administrative Exemptions

States generally attempt to impose their income taxes to the fullest extent permissible under the U.S. Constitution and Public Law 86-272. In the name of supporting in-state business interests, however, many states provide targeted exemptions for selected activities that would otherwise create nexus.

Although the ownership of property in a state typically creates nexus, a number of states provide statutory or administrative exemptions for the ownership of raw materials or finished goods at an unrelated in-state printer, or the ownership of equipment or tooling in the state for use by an unrelated in-state manufacturer.

> **EXAMPLE**
>
> Starting in 2009, Minnesota provides an exception for ownership of property on the premises of a printer when there is a contract for printing and the printer is not a member of a Minnesota unitary business. [S.F. 832, Apr. 6, 2009]

In addition, a number of states provide exemptions for employees attending in-state trade shows or conventions.

> **EXAMPLE**
>
> An out-of-state corporation does not have nexus in California if its only contact with the state is employees who (1) enter the state to attend conventions and trade shows for a total of no more than 15 days in a given year and (2) earn no more than $100,000 from those activities. [Cal. Rev. & Tax. Code §6203(e)]

Ownership of Partnership Interest

States generally take the position that an ownership interest in a partnership doing business in the state is sufficient to create constitutional nexus for a nondomiciliary corporation. In asserting nexus, the states rely primarily on the aggregate theory of partnership, which holds that a partnership is the aggregation of its owners rather than an entity that is separate from its owners (unlike a corporation). Under this theory, the partners are viewed as direct owners of the partnership's assets. Based on the aggregate theory, most states take the position that the mere ownership of a partnership interest is sufficient to create constitutional nexus for a nondomiciliary corporation, regardless of whether the corporation is a general or limited partner.

Some states apply a different rule for limited partners. The basis for this distinction is that a limited partnership interest is a passive investment akin to shares of corporate stock.

Ownership of Leased Property

In general, the ownership of business property in a state is sufficient to create nexus. In the case of leased property, the lessee is subject to the state's jurisdiction because the property is being used in the state and sufficient nexus may also be established for the lessor because of the in-state presence of owned business property. In addition to the presence of property, factors that help to support nexus include the negotiation or execution of the lease agreement in the state or the receipt of the rental payments in the state.

In the case of leased property that is immobile (e.g., machinery and equipment affixed within a manufacturing facility), the creation of nexus generally is easier to identify because, in negotiating the agreement or in addressing the shipment or delivery of the property to the lessee, the lessor is informed of the state in which the property is expected to be located during the rental period. In contrast, when mobile property (e.g., airplanes and other transportation vehicles) is at issue, the lessor typically has no control over where the property will be used. Moreover, unless otherwise specified in the lease agreement, the lessee may be under no contractual obligation to provide the lessor with any information about where the property has been used at any time during the lease.

The lessor typically is considered to have established nexus with each state where the leased immobile property is located. For leased mobile property, many states provide that an isolated landing or trip through the state will not create nexus. The presence of leased property in the state on a regular or systematic basis, however, is typically sufficient nexus with the state to subject the lessor to the state's corporate income tax. Therefore, in negotiating lease agreements, the lessor should annually require the lessee to supply the appropriate information about the states in which the property is used during the tax period. Without that information, the lessor cannot determine the states with which nexus has been established or compute its apportionment factors in the various states.

In *TTX Co. v. Idaho State Tax Commission* [128 Idaho 483 (1996)], the Idaho Supreme Court held that an out-of-state corporation that leased railcars to railroads operating within Idaho did not have nexus in Idaho. Likewise, in *Airoldi Bros., Inc. v. Illinois Department of Revenue* [Admin. Hearing Decision No. 98-IT-0330 (Ill. Dep't of Revenue, Sept. 29, 2000)], the Illinois Department of Revenue ruled that a Wisconsin truck leasing company whose customers used its trucks in Illinois did not have income tax nexus in Illinois. In both *Comdisco, Inc. v. Indiana Department of Revenue* [No. 49T10-9903-TA-19, Ind. Tax Ct., Dec. 8, 2002)] and *Enterprise Leasing Company of Chicago v. Indiana Department of Revenue* [No. 49T10-9807-TA-74, Ind. Tax Ct., Dec. 8, 2002)], the Indiana Tax Court ruled that two out-of-state leasing companies were not subject to Indiana tax on income from equipment and autos leased to Indiana customers, because their ownership of the leased property was the companies' only contact with the state. The out-of-state leasing companies did not exercise control over the leased equipment and were not active participants in the leasing activities within the state.

On the other hand, in *Truck Renting & Leasing Association, Inc. v. Commissioner of Revenue* [No. SJC-08308 (Mass. Apr. 17, 2001)], the Massachusetts Supreme Judicial Court ruled that the imposition of the Massachusetts corporate income tax on an out-of-state corporation whose leased trucks operated in Massachusetts violated neither the Due Process Clause nor the Commerce Clause of the U.S. Constitution, even though the lessor had no physical presence in Massachusetts beyond the presence of the leased trucks. By providing registration and licensing services that allowed the lessees to operate the trucks in Massachusetts, the out-of-state lessee was purposefully availing itself of the privilege of doing business in the state, as required by the Due Process Clause. In addition, the physical presence of the taxpayer's trucks within the state on a regular and systematic basis created a substantial nexus, as required by the Commerce Clause.

In *Alabama Department of Revenue v. Union Tank Car Co.* [No. 2050652 (Ala. Ct. of Civ. App., April 13, 2007)], the taxpayer (Union Tank) was a Delaware corporation that was headquartered in Illinois. Union Tank manufactured specialty railroad cars in Illinois and Texas and leased them to customers nationwide. Some of Union Tank's leased railcars were used to transport materials through Alabama and to destinations within Alabama. None of the railcars was used strictly within Alabama. The Department contended that Union Tank was subject to Alabama income tax, because the operative statute imposes an income tax on "[e]very corporation doing business in Alabama or deriving income from sources within Alabama, including income from property located in Alabama." The Alabama Court of Civil Appeals concluded, however, that Union Tank "derived income from the lease transactions in Illinois, not from sources in Alabama." Union Tank executed its lease contracts in Illinois, the railcars were picked up in Illinois or Texas, and the lessees made lease payments to Union Tank in Illinois. The amount of the lease payments was fixed, and UTCC had no control over where the railcars were used after they had been leased.

Qualification to Do Business

A number of states have statutes or regulations that require a corporation to file an income or franchise tax return and pay tax if the corporation has the authority to do business in the state. For example, under Texas Tax Code Annotated §171.001(a)(1), the state's corporate franchise tax applies to "each corporation that does business in this state or that is chartered or authorized to do business in this state." See also, for example, Cal. Code Regs. tit. 18, §23038(a); and Mass. Regs. Code tit. 830, §63.39.1.

The constitutionality of the Texas statute was tested in ***Bandag Licensing Corp. v. Rylander.*** [No. 03-99-00427-CV (Tex. App., May 11, 2000)] Bandag was incorporated in Iowa, did not own or use any property in Texas, and did not have any employees or other agents present in Texas. Nevertheless, the Texas Comptroller of Public Accounts imposed the Texas corporate franchise tax on Bandag solely on the basis that Bandag had obtained a certificate of authority to do business in Texas. The Texas appeals court saw no principled distinction between sales and income taxes when the underlying issue was whether the Commerce Clause permits a state to impose a tax obligation on an out-of-state corporation. The court went on to conclude that, consistent with the ruling in *Quill*, a state cannot constitutionally impose its corporate franchise tax on an out-of-state corporation that lacks a physical presence in the state. In response to the *Bandag* decision, the Comptroller issued a letter ruling indicating that an out-of-state corporation's possession of a certificate of authority to do business in Texas is not, by itself, sufficient to create nexus. [Comptroller's Letter No. 200106294L (Tex. Comptroller of Public Accounts, June 15, 2001)]

A related issue is whether the authority to do business in a state constitutes a separate business activity that is not protected by Public Law 86-272. For example, in ***Commissioner of Revenue v. Kelly-Springfield Tire Co.*** [419 Mass. 262 (1994)], the taxpayer had employees who were physically present in Massachusetts on a continuous basis. The parties agreed, however, that the activities of the in-state employees were protected by Public Law 86-272. At issue was whether the taxpayer's authority to do business in Massachusetts constituted a separate business activity that was sufficient to establish income tax nexus. The Massachusetts Supreme Judicial Court ruled that the authority to do business does not deny a corporation the protections afforded by Public Law 86-272. See also ***Kelly-Springfield Tire Co. v. Bajorski*** [228 Conn. 137 (1993)].

In *LSDHC Corp. v. Tracy* [No. 98-J-896 (Ohio Bd. of Tax App., Nov. 19, 2001)], the Ohio Board of Tax Appeals ruled that registration to do business was not, by itself, sufficient to create nexus for purposes of Ohio's corporate franchise tax on net income.

On the other hand, in *Buehner Block Company, Inc. v. Wyoming Department of Revenue* [No. 05-175 (Wyo. Sup. Ct., July 27, 2006)], the Wyoming Supreme Court ruled that, despite the lack of a physical presence in the state, the taxpayer had "substantial nexus" in the state because of its "historical connection with the Wyoming taxing system, including its voluntary possession and use of a Wyoming vendor's license, in combination with common-carrier delivery of its goods into this state."

Gross Receipts Taxes

Public Law 86-272 applies only to a "net income tax." It does not protect taxpayers against the imposition of a gross receipts tax.

Ohio imposes a gross receipts tax called the "commercial activity tax" (CAT). A "person" is subject to Ohio's CAT if any of the following are true:

- The person owns or uses a part or all of its capital or property in this state.
- The person holds a certificate of compliance with the laws of Ohio authorizing the person to do business in this state.
- The person has bright-line presence in Ohio.
- The person has nexus with Ohio to an extent that the person can be required to remit the CAT under the U.S. Constitution.

The Department of Taxation takes the position that the *Quill* physical presence test does not apply to the CAT. Even if a person has nexus under the U.S. Constitution, the Department of Taxation will only enforce nexus against persons who possess bright-line presence, which is a method of determining whether nexus exists that relies entirely upon quantitative criteria. A person has "bright-line presence" in Ohio if the person is domiciled in Ohio; or during the calendar year, the person has $50,000 of property in Ohio, $50,000 of payroll in Ohio, $500,000 of taxable gross receipts in Ohio, or 25 percent of the person's total property, total payroll or total gross receipts in Ohio. [Commercial Activity Tax Information Release CT 2005-02 (Ohio Dept. of Taxn., Sept. 2005)]

The State of Washington imposes a gross receipts tax called the "business and occupation" (B&O) tax. The B&O tax is imposed on the act or privilege of engaging in business activities in Washington, and is measured by the "value of products, gross proceeds of sales, or gross income of the business." [Wash. Rev. Code §82.04.220] Therefore, Public Law 86-272 does not prohibit the imposition of the B&O tax on sales solicited by in-state employees of an out-of-state manufacturer. Effective June 1, 2010, for purposes of imposing the Washington business and occupation tax (a gross receipts tax) on service activities and royalty income, an out-of-state corporation has nexus if it has more than $50,000 of property, $50,000 of payroll, $250,000 of receipts, or at least 25 percent of its total property, payroll, or receipts in Washington. [S.B. 6143, Feb. 20. 2009]

Effective January 1, 2008, Michigan replaced its single business tax with the Michigan Business Tax (MBT), which includes both a 4.95 percent business income tax and a 0.80 percent modified gross receipts tax. Taxpayers pay the sum of the two taxes. The "modified gross receipts tax" base equals a taxpayer's gross receipts reduced by purchases of inventory, depreciable assets, materials, and supplies. A taxpayer is subject to the MBT if it "has a physical presence in this state for a period of more than one day during the tax year or if the taxpayer actively solicits sales in this state and has gross receipts of $350,000 or more sourced to this state." [Mich. Comp. Laws §208.1200(1)] According to Revenue Administrative Bulletin 2008-64 [Mich. Dept. of Treas., Oct. 21, 2008], physical presence for a portion of a day establishes physical presence for the entire day. Examples of active solicitation include:

- Sending mail order catalogs
- Sending credit applications
- Maintaining an Internet site offering online shopping, services, or subscriptions
- Soliciting through media advertising, including Internet advertisements

Public Law 86-272 protects taxpayers from the imposition of the business income tax portion of the MBT, but not the modified gross receipts tax portion.

Texas imposes a tax on a business entity's "margin," which equals the lesser of total revenue minus cost of goods sold, total revenue minus compensation, or 70 percent of total revenue. Texas has taken the position that the margin tax does not qualify as a net income tax for purposes of applying Public Law 86-272. [34 Texas Admin. Code §3.586(e)]

Telecommuters

In GIL-2009-010 [Colo. Dept. of Rev., Feb. 25, 2009], the Colorado Department of Revenue ruled that an out-of-state corporation will generally have nexus for corporate income tax purposes if it hires an employee who is a Colorado resident and works out of his home office that is located in Colorado. Most of the corporation's employees were based overseas providing analytical support to the U.S. military. The company had three administrative support employees who worked in direct support of the headquarters and were involved in recruitment, accounting, and business development activities for the company and not directly supporting a paying customer. The company was interested in hiring another administrative support employee to support the company's headquarters, and that employee would like to perform his duties out of a home he has in Colorado. He would not be working in support of a customer or directly generating revenue for the company but would be strictly supporting the company in an overhead capacity. Nevertheless, the Department concluded that a company which has an employee residing in Colorado will generally have nexus for income tax purposes, and that the company's service income would be apportioned to Colorado in proportion to the cost of the one Colorado employee to the total cost of all its employees.

Electronic Commerce

As goods that have historically been sold by brick-and-mortar retailers (books, compact discs, and clothing) are increasingly sold over the Internet, states are likely to experience an erosion of their sales and use tax base. The states' predicament is largely due to the physical presence test for nexus, as mandated by the Supreme Court in *Quill.* Because electronic commerce allows companies to exploit a commercial market without establishing a physical presence in a state, the physical presence test significantly inhibits a state's ability to impose a tax obligation on an out-of-state Internet vendor.

On the other hand, the business community has legitimate concerns about the compliance burden of collecting sales and use taxes on a nationwide basis. There are currently thousands of sales tax jurisdictions (state, county, and city), which have different tax rates, different definitions of the tax base, and different administrative procedures. In recognition of the potential negative effect that state and local taxation could have on the growth of electronic commerce, in October 1998 Congress enacted the Internet Tax Freedom Act, which imposed a three-year moratorium on any "new" state or local taxes on Internet access. Subsequent legislation in 2001, 2004, and 2007 has extended the moratorium through November 1, 2014 (H.R. 3678, Oct. 31, 2007).

From the states' perspective, one potential solution is federal legislation that allows the states to impose tax obligations on out-of-state companies that have an economic presence, but no physical presence, within a state. Another potential solution is more uniform and simplified state and local tax systems. In fact, the states have initiated a major effort to simplify and modernize sales and use tax collection and administration through the Streamlined Sales Tax Project (see www.streamlinedsalestax.org). The project was initiated in 2000 and includes representatives from state and local governments as well as the private sector. The goals of the project are to create common definitions for key items in the sales tax base, restrict the number of tax rates that a state may impose, provide for state-level administration of local sales taxes, create uniform sourcing rules for interstate sales, simplify the administration of exempt transactions, develop uniform audit procedures, and provide partial state funding of the system for collecting tax. About 20 states conform their sales and use tax laws to the provisions of the agreement.

Federal vs. State Nexus Standards

In contrast to the federal nexus standards of engaging in trade or business within the United States or carrying on business in the United States through a permanent establishment situated therein, state income tax nexus standards generally require only a physical presence within the state of a type that is not protected by Public Law 86-272. In addition, some states have adopted the theory of economic nexus, under which an in-state physical presence is not an absolute prerequisite for income tax nexus. Instead, a significant economic presence, such as licensing intangibles or deriving a substantial amount of income from sources within the state, is sufficient to create state income tax nexus.

As a consequence, it is possible for a foreign (non-U.S.) corporation to have nexus for state but not federal income tax purposes.

EXAMPLE

If a foreign corporation leases warehouse space in a state solely for the purpose of storing and delivering its merchandise to U.S. customers, the physical presence of company-owned inventory would generally create state income tax nexus but not necessarily federal income tax nexus, because the mere storage of inventory does not constitute a permanent establishment.

STUDY QUESTIONS

13. In which of the following situations would a lessor be *least* likely to have nexus with a state where the leased property is used?

   a. Negotiation of the lease agreement in the state
   b. Receipt of the rental payments in the state
   c. Lease of mobile property that made a trip through the state
   d. Lease of immobile property to be used in the state

14. In which of the following cases was Texas's decision to tax a company that had authority to do business but no physical presence in the state ruled unconstitutional?

   a. *Bandag Licensing Corp.*
   b. *Kelly-Springfield Tire Co.* (1993)
   c. *Kelly-Springfield Tire Co.* (1994)
   d. *LSDHC Corp.*

15. Which of the following statements is *not* true?

   a. Federal permanent establishment provisions are *not* binding for state nexus purposes.
   b. The Internet Tax Freedom Act allows "new" state or local taxes on Internet access.
   c. Federal legislation that allows states to tax out-of-state companies that have an economic presence but no physical presence is one potential solution to ensure the integrity of state tax bases.

NEW NOTIFICATION REQUIREMENTS

In an attempt to introduce greater compliance to use tax reporting, in 2010 the State of Colorado enacted legislation requiring that each noncollecting vendor making sales to Colorado purchasers notify them at the time of purchase that sales or use taxes are due on certain purchases from the retailer and that Colorado requires the purchaser to file a sales and use tax return. This notice must appear on each invoice issued to a Colorado purchaser. In addition, retailers that do not collect Colorado tax are required to issue an annual notification by January 31 that sales tax is due on their purchases. Non-collecting retailers are also required to file an annual statement for each purchaser with the Colorado Department of Revenue showing the total amount paid for Colorado purchases by March 1 of each year. While a Commerce Clause and/or a Due Process Clause challenge to this statutory requirement appear(s) likely, until all appeal rights have been exhausted, Colorado will be enforcing these reporting requirements, armed with newly enacted penalties to encourage compliance.

Construction Contractors and Manufacturers

This chapter discusses construction contractors and how their varying roles can affect their sales and use tax liability. It also discusses the sales and use tax treatment of manufacturers and tax exemptions that are available to them.

LEARNING OBJECTIVES

Upon completion of this course, you will be able to:

- Determine how a construction contractor's varying roles can affect its sales and use tax liability
- Identify how to distinguish between real and tangible property
- Recognize when contractors act as retailers
- Classify the implications of contractors acting as retailers for contractors and their customers.
- Determine the treatment of the construction contractor when the contractor performs a contract for a tax-exempt entity
- Utilize the treatment of contractor repair transactions
- Identify available exemptions for manufacturing equipment and the requirements for eligibility
- Apply the treatment of materials and labor used in the production process and in making repairs
- Determine the tax implications of making inventory withdrawals

TREATMENT OF CONSTRUCTION CONTRACTORS

Overview

The *sales and use tax* treatment of a construction contractor is complicated by the varying roles that a contractor may assume in fulfilling a contract or performing a job. Generally, contractors can act as either retailers or consumers, depending on the nature of the work involved in a particular project.

Contractors act as *retailers* of tangible personal property when they resell tangible personal property in its present state without transforming it into real estate. Contractors acting as retailers are required to collect tax on their sales of tangible personal property, unless selling to a tax-exempt entity, in which case they should obtain an exemption certificate.

> **EXAMPLE**
>
> **Contractor as retailer:** A plumbing contractor sells a homeowner a water heater so the homeowner can do the water heater installation himself. This would be a taxable sale of tangible personal property by the plumbing contractor and the contractor would be acting as a retailer in this instance. The plumber would therefore be required to collect sales tax on the transaction.

On other projects, contractors install or apply tangible personal property as a real property improvement and are treated as the consumers of the incorporated materials. As *consumers* of the materials incorporated into the project, contractors are subject to tax on their cost.

> **EXAMPLE**
>
> **Contractor as consumer:** A contractor purchases bricks, mortar, and lumber, which the contractor transforms into a building for one of its customers. In this case the contractor would be subject to tax on its purchases of the bricks, mortar, and lumber that is incorporated into the real estate and would either pay the tax due to its supplier if billed or self-assess the tax and report it as consumer's use tax on its sales tax return.

Contractors may also perform repairs to either real or tangible personal property with varying tax consequences, depending on the state's treatment of the labor associated with real and tangible personal property.

> **EXAMPLE**
>
> **Real estate repair:** A roofing contractor repairs a homeowner's leaking roof. The contractor would be the consumer of any supplies or materials used in making the repair to the roof since it is a repair of real estate.

> **EXAMPLE**
>
> **Tangible personal property repair:** An electrical contractor repairs a piece of production equipment for a manufacturer in a state that does not exempt manufacturing machinery and equipment. The contractor would be making a taxable repair of tangible personal property. Any materials consumed by the contractor in making the repair would be considered purchases for resale by the contractor. The contractor would be obligated to collect the tax from its customer.

In addition, contractors may perform a project management function, where they oversee the work of various other contractors in the completion of a project. As stated above, each of these activities has an impact on the sales and use tax treatment of the contractor.

> **EXAMPLE**
>
> **Contractor as project manager:** A contractor is hired to manage the construction project for a large corporation. As project manager the contractor is responsible for hiring subcontractors, coordinating completion of the project, and handling any design changes with the architects. In exchange for providing this service, the contractor is paid a fee of $1 million by the owner of the building. The $1 million fee would be considered a professional service that would generally not be subject to tax in most states.

In a few taxing jurisdictions, the type of contract (lump-sum contract or time and materials contract) can affect the tax treatment of the contractor.

In addition to imposing sales and use taxes on contractors, many states impose special excise or gross receipts taxes on contractors' sales. Therefore, contractors need to exercise caution when dealing with sales and use taxes and other local taxes to avoid incurring unnecessary or unwarranted tax liabilities that cannot be passed along to their customers.

Distinction Between Real and Tangible Property

In most jurisdictions, the key to understanding the treatment of a construction contractor is to understand the distinction that is made between *real* and *tangible personal property*. Although states can have varying criteria for making this determination, most states consider the following three factors:

1. Actual physical annexation of an item to the real property
2. Application or adaptation of an item to the purpose to which the real property is devoted
3. An intention on the part of the person making the annexation to make a permanent accession to the real property

Actual Physical Annexation of an Item to the Real Property

Generally, the tax jurisdiction evaluates the degree of attachment of an item to the real property and whether its removal would cause irreparable damage to the real estate. If the degree of annexation of an item is sufficient to cause irreparable damage to the real estate on the item's removal, the item installed or applied is more *real* property than tangible *personal* property. By contrast, if *tangible personal property* is easily removed from the real estate without damaging its function or use, that would generally be evidence that the item installed or applied retained its character as tangible personal property.

> **EXAMPLE**
>
> **Real estate:** As part of a construction project for the original construction of a building, a contractor installs drywall or sheetrock throughout a building. Once the drywall is installed, the contractor has made a permanent addition to real estate, since its removal would cause irreparable damage to the building.

> **EXAMPLE**
>
> **Tangible personal property:** As part of a remodeling project, a contractor agrees to provide certain items of furniture, such as desks, tables, and chairs, per its customer's selections. The contractor agrees to purchase the items and hold them until the project is completed, at which time the contractor will deliver them to its customer. The nature of the items purchased is tangible personal property, and the items will retain their character as tangible personal property after the contractor delivers them to the project. The items sold require no installation and can be readily moved about the facility without causing any damage to it.

Application or Adaptation of an Item to the Purpose to Which the Real Property Is Devoted

The more integrated an item is into the overall function of the real estate, the more it tends to assume the characteristics of the real estate. If the item is more independent of the real estate in function, it tends to retain its character as *tangible personal property*. For example, a large machine may be attached to a building for its safe operation, but it functions independently from the real estate. Therefore, once installed, it is *not* considered part of the real estate.

Intention on the Part of the Person Making the Annexation to Make a Permanent Accession to the Real Property

This is a more difficult factor to assess, since it deals with the presumed intent of the person making the annexation to real property. Generally, it involves applying a *prudent person* standard to the facts and circumstances to make a reasonable determination of the person's intent, based on the person's actions.

Contractors as Retailers

Contractors frequently act as *retailers* when they resell tangible personal property without installing it or by installing it in such a way that it retains its character as tangible personal property. When contactors act as retailers, they are required to collect tax from their purchasers unless exempt, just like any other retail vendor.

An example of when a contractor acts as a retailer would involve the sale of an item, such as a refrigerator, that retains its character as tangible personal property when resold. Contractors acting as retailers may purchase the item being resold as exempt for resale by providing their suppliers with a resale certificate.

> ### PLANNING POINTER
>
> Contractors operating as both *consumers* (performing real property improvements) and *retailers* (reselling tangible personal property) need to carefully segregate their purchases so that the purchases are afforded the proper sales tax treatment. Failure to do so can result in an unwanted and unnecessary tax bill.

To determine whether they are engaging in real property improvements or re-selling tangible personal property, contractors should apply the rules discussed above for distinguishing real property from tangible personal property.

Tax-Exempt Entities

Another issue that often arises involves the treatment of the construction contractor when the construction contractor is performing a contract for a tax-exempt entity or organization. If the construction contractor is performing a contract for a real property improvement in a state that considers the contractor to be the *consumer* of any tangible personal property incorporated into the real estate, the treatment of the contractor performing real property improvements for tax-exempt entities or organizations may vary.

In some jurisdictions, contractors performing real property improvements for tax-exempt entities or organizations are allowed to assume the exempt status of the tax-exempt entity or organization in making purchases of tangible personal property for incorporation into the real estate of the tax-exempt entity or organization.

In other states, the contractor is taxed as a consumer of the materials incorporated into the real estate of a tax-exempt entity or organization.

In states that allow the pass-through of the tax-exempt status, the contractor may purchase the tangible personal property incorporated into the real estate as if the tax-exempt entity or organization had purchased the materials directly and, therefore, may avoid incurring this additional cost. Most states allowing this treatment require that the contractor provide the tax-exempt entity's exemption number as part of its exemption certificate.

Repair Transactions

In many instances, the contractor acts as a *repairer* of property. When the contractor repairs real estate, in most states the contractor is treated as the consumer of materials and owes tax on the cost of materials incorporated into the project. The labor associated with the repair of real estate is typically *not* subject to tax.

The contractor acts as a *retailer* of the property when the contractor repairs tangible personal property. In such instances, the contractor's purchase of the parts consumed in performing the repairs *would* be exempt as a purchase for resale. If the state taxes labor, the contractor would charge tax on the cost of labor used to perform the repair and on the parts transferred in connection with the repair—unless the customer is exempt.

Further complexities exist in some states because certain items of real estate are deemed to retain their character as tangible personal property for repair purposes. In some jurisdictions, such quasi-tangible personal property items are referred to as *fixtures*.

For contractors working in a multistate environment, this can introduce a significant complexity into the proper taxation of repair transactions. These real estate components are typically items such as:

- Water heaters
- Water softeners
- Dishwashers
- Furnaces
- Central air conditioners

When a contractor repairs such items, even though they are real estate in nature, their repair is treated as a repair of *tangible personal property.* The contractor is therefore required to charge tax on the labor if it is taxed in the state and on the material charges for repair of the items, unless the customer is tax-exempt.

Key States

California. In California, construction contractors are generally treated as the consumers of any tangible personal property incorporated into real estate, even if the project is performed for an exempt organization.

Florida. Construction contractors are generally treated as the consumers of any tangible personal property incorporated into real estate in Florida, even if the project is performed for an exempt organization.

Illinois. Construction contractors in Illinois are generally treated as the consumers of any tangible personal property incorporated into real estate. However, pass-through of their customer's tax-exempt status is allowed if the organization has been issued a tax exemption identification number.

Texas. Construction contractors in Texas that perform new construction or residential real property improvements under lump-sum contracts are treated as consumers. Construction contractors that perform new construction and separate the charges for materials and labor are retailers and purchase materials for resale. However, they must collect tax on the charge for materials. Construction contractors that remodel or repair nonresidential real property under either lump-sum or separate contracts are retailers performing taxable services.

PLANNING POINTER

In states that will not allow the tax-exempt entity or organization to pass through its tax-exempt status to the construction contractor, it may be possible for the tax-exempt entity or organization to purchase the materials directly and then to contract with the construction contractor separately to install or apply materials purchased. Because the majority of states do not impose tax on the labor to install or apply materials sold, the tax-exempt entity would effectively avoid tax that would otherwise be incurred without careful planning.

PLANNING POINTER

Construction contractors must consider the use tax that might be due on supplies and equipment that they purchase for their own use in performing construction contracts. Many construction contractors will purchase supplies or equipment that are not consumed or incorporated into the real estate of their customer.

For example, supplies or equipment that is purchased by the contractor is generally taxable to the construction contractor in the jurisdiction where it is being stored or first-used. If the contractor has used the item in another jurisdiction and paid tax there, the contractor may be eligible for a credit for the tax paid in that jurisdiction. Generally, equipment older than one year is not subject to use tax if it is moved from jurisdiction to jurisdiction, unless it is a licensed motor vehicle.

CAUTION

Contractors engaged in multistate activities need to carefully consider the sales and use tax treatment of the state in which the contractor's customer is located. Many contractors make the mistake of assuming that all states treat contractors the same and apply the tax rules from their home state to transactions in another jurisdiction.

When bidding on a project, contractors must carefully consider the state sales and use tax treatment of their transactions to avoid over- or underbidding the project.

Contractors need to carefully evaluate the nature of their activities in a tax jurisdiction and determine whether they need to be registered as a retailer, a contractor, or both.

STUDY QUESTIONS

---

1. Contractors frequently act as _____ when they resell tangible property without installing it.

   a. Consumers
   b. Subcontractors
   c. Retailers

2. A large machine, bolted to the floor of a building that is used in manufacturing, would be considered part of the real estate once it is installed. *True or False?*

TREATMENT OF MANUFACTURERS

Materials, Machinery, and Equipment Overview

State statutes often grant sales and use tax exemptions or reduced rates for manufacturing machinery and equipment as an incentive for manufacturers to relocate to, expand in, or remain in a state. Generally, industrial machinery and equipment are exempt from tax if certain requirements are met. Some states also allow an exemption for various items of agricultural machinery and equipment.

Many sales and use tax statutes exempt sales of tangible personal property becoming an ingredient or component part of tangible personal property that is resold. A resale or manufacturer's exemption certificate typically is required to claim this exemption.

Production Machinery

Most states provide for an exemption from sales/use tax for machinery and equipment used in the manufacture or processing of tangible personal property. However, manufacturing encompasses so many diverse activities that its definition varies among states. There is no universal rule, and each state determines its own standards and statutory definitions and has its own judicial interpretations.

To qualify for the machinery and equipment exemption, a company must typically be a *manufacturer* or be *engaged in manufacturing*. Normally, a *manufacturing operation* is defined as an operation or process in which raw materials are changed, converted, or transformed into a new article with a different form, use, name, and function by a process popularly regarded as manufacturing.

EXAMPLE

Nonmanufacturing: You may be a very skilled cake baker, but unless you are mass-producing cakes, most states will not consider you eligible for the manufacturing exemption. So, while you are combining ingredients and producing something with a new name (cake) by combining those ingredients and then baking them, it is not a process that is popularly regarded as manufacturing. However, producing cakes on a large scale, packaging them, and reselling them would generally qualify as manufacturing in most states.

Most states require that machinery and equipment be *directly* used in the manufacturing operation for the exemption to apply.

What constitutes *direct use* varies among states. Some states require machinery to come into direct contact with, or be directly involved in the formation of, the item being produced to qualify for the exemption. Other states merely require that the equipment be essential to the production process.

In addition to the direct-use requirement, most states invoke a second condition, requiring that the machinery and equipment be used exclusively—solely by a manufacturer in manufacturing tangible personal property to the exclusion of all other uses (e.g., Wisconsin), primarily—more than 50 percent use in manufacturing or assembling (e.g., Illinois), or predominantly—over 50 percent of its use is directly in the production phase of the process (e.g., New York) in the production activity.

Exclusive use is generally defined as 100 percent utilization in the manufacturing process, but oftentimes allows for a *de minimis* nonmanufacturing use, generally up to 5 percent.

Primary or predominant use ordinarily means greater than 50 percent utilization in the production process.

Agricultural Machinery

Many states have special provisions exempting from sales and use tax the sale of equipment and materials to taxpayers engaged in farming, agriculture, horticulture, and floriculture. As with the exemption for manufacturing equipment, there may be direct-use and exclusive- or predominant-use requirements. Sales of feed, seed, and fertilizer are often considered exempt if they are made to persons engaged in the production of food for consumption.

Materials

Sales and use tax is imposed on the ultimate consumer of the property subject to taxation. Accordingly, sales to manufacturers and processors are generally *not* subject to sales tax if the property purchased becomes or is made a part of a product that is to be sold by the manufacturer.

In some states the material exemption is expanded to include property that is used and either consumed or destroyed in processing.

The criterion for exempting materials and supplies differs from state to state. Therefore, the statutes and regulations of each state should be carefully examined for the appropriate rules. In order for the materials and supplies that are consumed or destroyed to qualify for the exemption, most states require that the item produced be resold.

Shipping Containers and Packaging Materials

Many states provide exemptions for shipping containers and packaging materials that are used to ship products to the consumer and are sold with the products. This includes items such as:

- Wrapping material
- Bags
- Cans
- Twines
- Gummed tapes
- Boxes
- Bottles
- Drums
- Cartons

> **NOTE**
>
> Taxpayers need to exercise care in this area, since many states draw subtle distinctions between what qualifies as exempt shipping containers or packaging materials.

> **EXAMPLE**
>
> Many states distinguish between returnable and nonreturnable shipping containers and packaging materials—imposing tax on returnable shipping containers and packaging materials, such as pallets, but not on nonreturnable shipping containers and packaging materials, such as the product package or carton. Other states provide a broader exemption, allowing materials that are used to ship the product to the customer, such as shipping pallets, to be exempt.

Recognizing the crucial role that shipping containers and packaging materials play in the delivery of goods to purchasers, most states do not impose tax on all shipping containers and packaging materials.

In general, states differentiate between *taxable* and *nontaxable* shipping containers and packaging materials as follows:

- The lowest threshold for exemption requires only that the item be either a shipping container or packaging material.
- Many states impose one or two additional requirements for the item to be exempt. The shipping containers or packaging materials must be:

    1. Used to transfer the purchased product to the end user, and/or
    2. Be nonreturnable

Transfer to Purchaser

Taxpayers often misapply the treatment afforded to shipping containers and packaging materials to shipping aids used to facilitate the transfer of products to the purchaser.

In states that exempt shipping containers and packaging materials, the qualifying items must usually be incorporated into the packaging in such a manner that the item becomes a part of the product sold. This means the item must be within the product packaging or affixed to the packaging in such a way as to make it an integral part of the product.

Items in this category that would *not* qualify for the exemption include:

- Blocking, shoring, and bracing outside the product package to stabilize the load while it is in transit
- Items used to facilitate the transfer that may be returnable, such as:
  - Insulating blankets
  - Tie-downs
  - Protective pads

Even in states that provide exemptions for nonreturnable and/or returnable shipping containers or packaging materials, these items do not typically qualify for the exemption.

Repair and Maintenance

Closely related to the sales and use tax treatment of shipping containers and packaging materials is the sales and use tax treatment of the repair and maintenance of such items. Even in states that exempt certain shipping containers and packaging materials, tax may be imposed on their repair and maintenance.

PLANNING POINTER

In states that impose tax on returnable shipping containers, it may be possible to purchase the shipping containers and ship them to states that exempt returnable shipping containers. After the shipping containers have been used for a year or so, they can often be transferred to taxable states as used equipment that is not subject to tax.

> **CAUTION**
>
> Even in states that exempt returnable and nonreturnable shipping contain-ers and packaging materials, the repair and maintenance of shipping aids is usually subject to tax. Shipping aids generally include items that are used to facilitate the transfer of tangible personal property but that are not transferred to the end user or consumer, such as protective pads.

STUDY QUESTIONS

3. Which of the following statements is true?

   a. Most states exempt industrial machinery and equipment from sales tax if certain requirements are met.

   b. Most states require that industrial machinery be used directly or indirectly in the manufacturing process for an exemption to apply.

   c. Most states require that machinery and equipment be used at least 40 percent in the manufacturing process to be exempt from sales tax.

   d. Many states impose sales tax on nonreturnable shipping contain-ers but *not* on returnable shipping containers.

4. Which of the following statements is **not** true?

   a. Although most states allow a sales and use tax exemption for industrial machinery, no states allow an exemption for agricultural machinery.

   b. In states that exempt shipping containers and packaging materi-als, shipping aids used to facilitate the transfer of products to the purchaser must usually be incorporated into the packaging such that it becomes a part of the product sold in order to be exempt.

   c. Even in states that exempt certain shipping containers and packag-ing materials, tax may be imposed on their repair and maintenance.

Pollution Control Exemption Overview

In recent years, as people have become more environmentally conscious, concern has increased about potential pollution of the air, groundwater, and surface water. New laws have been enacted and enforced to punish businesses for polluting the environment, and other steps have been taken to monitor the quality of the environment. At the same time, governments have responded with requirements for businesses to curb pollution.

Exemptions have been enacted in many states to ease the cost of pur-chasing pollution abatement–related equipment, supplies, and facilities and to provide an incentive for businesses to make such purchases. While the specifics of these exemptions vary from state-to-state, pollution control exemptions generally exempt purchases of equipment used to reduce or eliminate pollution of the air, groundwater, or surface water.

In addition, states often provide an exemption for the cost of constructing and equipping a pollution control/abatement facility. Such facilities are typically used by manufacturers to treat effluents from the manufacturing process before the contaminated water is reintroduced into the environment.

EXAMPLE

Many spray-painting processes utilize a waterfall to reduce the overspray from the painting process. The contaminated water is then cleansed through a series of filters before it is discharged into the city sanitation system. This process protects the environment from harmful chemicals and additives that might otherwise be introduced into the environment if the contaminated water were not treated before it was discharged into the municipal system.

PLANNING POINTER

The manufacturing or industrial processing exemption, as it applies to machinery and equipment as well as consumable items, is usually limited to equipment used or items consumed during the manufacturing process. Thus, a determination of when a manufacturing process begins and ends must be made.

Some states also offer an exemption for the equipment used in pollution control or tangible personal property used to construct a pollution control facility and any chemicals or supplies used in the pollution control process.

As a prerequisite for exempting pollution control equipment and facilities, some states require that the equipment or facility used in pollution control be certified by the state department of natural resources or similar agency in order for it to be eligible for the exemption.

States with such requirements provide a form for taxpayers to file with the state department of natural resources or similar agency that describes the use of the equipment or facility and its intended use. Once the pollution control equipment or facility has been certified, future purchases are exempt as provided under that particular state's statutes. Taxpayers in states with these requirements must retain their certification documents for future audit use.

CAUTION

To qualify for the pollution control exemption in some states, the tax must be paid to the seller and then a claim for refund must be filed along with the state application.

Use Tax on Self-Constructed Machinery

The use tax is designed to complement the sales tax. *Sales tax* is imposed on the retail sale of tangible personal property, and *use tax* is imposed on the taxable use of an item that was not taxed in a sales tax transaction. Sales tax is collected by the seller as an agent for the tax jurisdiction. Use tax on a transaction is remitted by the purchaser when the purchaser files its sales and use tax return.

In a typical purchase, the use tax due is measured by the purchase price of the property. Therefore, the cost (or fair market value) of the item serves as the tax base. However, complications arise if the taxpayer constructs the machinery or equipment for his or her own use.

The taxpayer must determine not only whether the property is taxable but also the amount that is subject to tax. Typically, there are three possible ways of measuring taxability:

1.   Full cost
2.   Fair market value
3.   Material cost

Although the majority of states impose a use tax on self-constructed machinery, a number of states offer exemptions that could apply to equipment of such a nature. The most common exemption that would apply to self-constructed machinery is the exemption for manufacturing machinery and equipment.

The first step in determining taxability is to establish whether an exemption that would eliminate the tax on self-constructed equipment is available.

Use Tax Base

If there is no appropriate exemption, the next step is to establish a taxable measure for the item. Because the use tax complements the sales tax, some states base the use tax on the fair market value of the self-constructed asset. Other states look to the material cost of the self-constructed item, and still other states tax the total cost of the item, including the labor applied to manufacture the item.

If the machinery is unique or cannot be purchased, the valuation process can become even more complicated. In such situations, many states accept the allocated costs from the accounting records.

For machinery that is purchased and modified for another use, valuation becomes an issue if the state attempts to tax the fair market value of the machinery. Some states tax only the materials used to construct the machinery or the allocated costs per the accounting records. Most of those states include component parts used in the construction in the tax base at cost, rather than at retail value.

Labor Costs

If the taxpayer's employees are used in the construction process, allocated labor costs are generally not included in the value for use tax purposes.

Overhead Charges

Applied overhead charges are also usually excluded from the tax base. Therefore, it is generally not a good idea to rely solely on the asset or accounting records to determine the taxable value of self-constructed machinery. Some analysis of the cost elements making up the valuation can result in a significant tax savings.

Equipment and Tools

Another issue that can complicate the valuation of self-constructed machinery and equipment is the treatment of the equipment and tools that are used to manufacture the self-constructed items. In states that do not provide a manufacturing exemption, those equipment and tools are taxable.

However, in states that provide a manufacturing exemption, the equipment and tools used to self-construct production equipment may or may not be covered under the scope of the exemption.

Generally, states have adopted one of two approaches to the taxation of these items:

1. The narrow application is that the manufacturing machinery and equipment exemption includes *only* those items used directly or exclusively in the manufacturing process or those items that directly contribute to the changes in raw materials that occur as part of the manufacturing process (depending on the qualifying definition of *manufacturing* in the state statute).
2. The broad application is that the machinery and equipment exemption includes machinery or equipment that is used to manufacture production machinery or equipment that is then used in an exempt way in the manufacturing process (often referred to as the *use-on-use* exemption).

Being aware of whether a state statute allows for the narrow or broad scope of the manufacturing exemption can have a substantial impact on the tax liability associated with self-constructed assets.

PLANNING POINTER

Taxpayers that have self-constructed machinery should establish procedures to identify self-constructed assets and to analyze the costs associated with them. Self-constructed assets typically comprise both of the following:

- Items transferred from inventory, which should have been purchased without payment of tax
- Machinery component parts, which may or may not have been purchased without payment of tax

Such costs generally flow through special project accounts. Therefore, additional analysis is often required for proper reporting. Care should be exercised when assessing tax on self-constructed assets. Most accounting systems include internal labor cost as part of the asset's cost, but many states exclude that cost from their tax base.

By analyzing those accounts, taxpayers can avoid unnecessary overpayments. Having proper procedures in place to capture, review, and report those amounts is an important part of all compliance procedures to avoid additional audit assessments and penalties.

STUDY QUESTIONS

5. Which of the following statements is **not** true regarding certification for a state pollution control exemption?
   a. Some states require that pollution control equipment be certified by the state department of natural resources or similar agency for it to be eligible for an exemption.
   b. States with certification requirements provide a form for taxpayers requesting a description of the equipment.
   c. States with certification requirements provide a form for taxpayers requesting information regarding the intended use of the pollution control equipment.
   d. After certification, future pollution control purchases must also be certified.

6. Which of the following is ordinarily included in the use tax base for machinery that is purchased and modified for another use?
   a. Materials
   b. Labor
   c. Overhead

Inventory Withdrawals

Most businesses are aware that a *use tax* is due when an item is purchased from a vendor that is not registered to collect sales tax, and a subsequent taxable use is made of the item. To comply with this requirement, use tax procedures are put in place.

In most companies, the procedures involve either a systemic or manual review of the purchase order tax coding and the amount of any tax billed on the vendor's invoice. When the purchase order is taxable and the vendor fails to bill the tax, the tax is accrued and reported on the purchaser's use tax return.

Many taxpayers are not aware that a tax may be due on the taxable use of an item if it is purchased for inventory and subsequently used in a taxable manner—as a sample, in research and development, or for display.

> **EXAMPLE**
>
> When a manufacturer purchases inventory to manufacture a product, the manufacturer's intention is to resell the item purchased as an ingredient or component part of the item being manufactured. If the manufacturer makes a subsequent use of the item, either as a sample or in research and development, a tax may be due.

For most taxpayers, capturing the information to report use tax on these purchases requires a procedure that goes beyond the accounts payable procedure outlined above. That is because when the items are initially purchased and entered into the accounts payable system, the intention is that they are going to be used in manufacturing. It is a subsequent decision that removes the items from their intended use and makes them taxable. Therefore, procedures must be implemented to capture the items at their point of inventory withdrawal.

For many taxpayers, cost accumulation reports capture the inventory transfers to research and development or sales and marketing uses, such as samples or display items. Therefore, taxpayers can rely on these reports in many instances to give them the information needed for tax compliance purposes.

Frequently, items are returned to inventory and resold after a brief use in some taxable manner. While the original self-assessment for the withdrawal remains valid, a credit is available when the item is returned to inventory for resale. Therefore, taxpayers need to not only monitor inventory withdrawals for potential use tax liabilities, but also watch for items returned to inventory that would result in a credit or reduction of future taxable withdrawals.

Items Consumed or Destroyed in the Manufacturing Process

In addition to machinery and equipment exemptions in some states, most states allow an exemption on purchases of tangible personal property that becomes an ingredient or component part of tangible personal property that is offered for sale by the manufacturer.

In some states, the material exemption is expanded to include property that is used and either consumed or destroyed in the manufacturing process. The criteria for exempting *consumed or destroyed* materials and supplies often differ from state to state.

Temporary Storage Exemption

Under a typical sales tax statute, all purchases of tangible personal property are deemed to be taxable, unless an exemption applies. Business-related exemptions would generally be for resale, for use in manufacturing, etc. Likewise for use tax purposes, the typical use tax statute imposes tax upon the storage, use, or other consumption of tangible personal property. As a consequence, taxpayers purchasing tangible personal property, which they wish to store and subsequently ship either to another state or within the same state, incur a taxable event for the mere act of storing the item in the state, unless some exemption applies, for example, inventory for resale, use in manufacturing, and so on.

For many businesses utilizing a centralized purchasing function, this can significantly increase their tax burden on purchases such as marketing materials, office supplies, computer equipment, and other items that are frequently purchased and shipped to a headquarters operation for storage before being distributed to regional or local offices around the country. For some businesses, this can be a substantial amount of tax for merely ware-housing the items in a convenient location.

To minimize this exposure for some taxpayers and to provide an inducement for locating such operations in their state, many states provide a temporary storage exemption for purchases of this nature. States that provide a temporary storage exemption allow tax-free storage of tangible personal property in the state. This exemption can be limited as to the type of items eligible for storage, such as advertising and marketing materials, or it can exempt all temporary storage of tangible personal property. Another common limitation that is imposed upon a temporary storage exemption is to restrict the materials to those that are to be processed, fabricated, or used in manufacturing, while in other states, doing anything more than mere storage of the item can defeat the exemption.

STUDY QUESTIONS

7. A use tax is always due on which of the following?

    a. Tangible personal property that becomes a component part of tangible personal property offered for sale by the manufacturer

    b. An exempt item that is consumed in the manufacturing process Some states allow an exemption for property that is used and either consumed or destroyed in the manufacturing process. The criteria for this exemption often differ from state to state.

    c. An exempt item that is purchased and then used by the purchaser in its business in a taxable manner

8. Many states allow a temporary storage exemption for purchases temporarily stored that will be subsequently shipped to other offices. *True or False?*

Printers

States offering production machinery exemptions often include printers in their definition of manufacturers qualifying for the exemption. However, the sales and use tax treatment of printers can be complicated by the varying services that printers provide.

Many printers perform a service when they use materials provided by their customers to produce their finished products. In this case, the printer is transformed from a manufacturer to a service provider, and this has a significant impact on the printer's tax obligations.

Printers function as *manufacturers* when they produce a printed document from raw materials. In such instances the printer is transforming tangible personal property from one form to another by a process that many states consider to be manufacturing.

In other instances, however, the customer may provide paper, ink, or other raw materials for the printer to use in producing the printed document. The customer may do that to coordinate color, texture, or appearance with some other document that will be displayed with the printed piece. In addition, the customer may be able to obtain a substantially discounted price for the supplies because of other commercial relationships with the vendor that may not be transferable to the printer.

In many states, when the printer produces a printed document using materials provided by its customer, the printer is viewed as performing a service. Performing this service can result in a loss of the sales tax exemption for machinery and equipment that is otherwise available to the printer, because the printer has stepped outside the role of a manufacturer. In addition, the tax treatment of the supplies provided may be impacted.

When the printer acts as a *manufacturer*, it is selling tangible personal property and is required to collect sales tax on the transaction. When the printer acts as a *service provider*, it may or may not have an obligation to collect the tax, depending on whether the state taxes the services performed by the printer.

State statutes often grant exemptions or reduced rates for manufacturing machinery and equipment as an incentive for manufacturers.

Generally, industrial machinery and equipment are exempt from tax if certain limitations or requirements are met. In addition, many sales and use tax statutes exempt sales of tangible personal property that become an ingredient or component part of tangible personal property that is resold.

CAUTION

Many companies have in-house print shops that create internal publications, advertising materials, and so on. In states allowing a manufacturing exemption, the printing equipment will usually qualify for the exemption. However, any supplies used in the production of materials that are given away will not qualify as tax exempt. Most states have an additional requirement that the item be resold for the materials consumed in order to qualify for the exemption.

Integrated Plant Doctrine

In states that offer a manufacturing exemption, the state has the option of viewing the manufacturing exemption narrowly or broadly. The narrower view of manufacturing requires that the manufacturing machinery and equipment come into direct contact with the product being manufactured and/or contribute to the transformation in some direct way.

The broader view of manufacturing, or the Integrated Plant Doctrine, does not view each manufacturing task separately, but rather looks to whether the equipment is part of a synchronized system that is engaged in manufacturing. For example, under the Integrated Plant Doctrine, a conveyer that moves raw materials and work-in-process from one workstation to another within the plant would be considered part of a synchronized system engaged in manufacturing.

Under the narrower view of manufacturing, the conveyor would likely *not* qualify for exemption, since it does not directly contribute to the change in the product being manufactured—it merely moves the product and raw materials from one point in the process to another point in the process. This distinction can be crucial when evaluating whether a particular piece of equipment should be considered exempt as manufacturing machinery and equipment.

Utilities Used in Manufacturing

For many manufacturers, the cost of fuel and electricity used in the manufacturing process represents a substantial expense—particularly in recent years, as the cost of fuel and other energy commodities have increased dramatically.

To help reduce those costs and to level the competitive playing field, many states have enacted exemptions for fuel and electricity consumed in the manufacturing process. The exemption can cover virtually all forms of energy that might be purchased for use in manufacturing, or the exemption can be broad enough to cover virtually every type of fuel that might be used or consumed in the manufacturing process.

Freight and Shipping Charges

The growth of the mail-order and the electronic commerce purchase of tangible personal property has heightened taxpayer awareness of the sales and use tax treatment of freight and shipping charges. This growth in remote purchasing has led to greater confusion for vendors and customers alike, because of the conflicting treatment afforded freight and shipping charges by the states.

There are several issues that can impact the taxability of freight and shipping charges.

As a general rule, many states impose sales and use tax on all charges that are incurred prior to the passage of title from the vendor to the customer. Despite that general rule, many states do not include separately stated freight and shipping charges in the tax base.

In many states, the treatment of freight and shipping charges varies depending on whether the charges are billed by the vendor to the purchaser or by a freight carrier directly to the purchaser. In some states, even if the freight or shipping charge is separately billed by the seller, it is subject to tax.

Conversely, if the freight or shipping charge is billed by the freight company directly to the purchaser, it is *not* subject to tax in most states, even if it is incurred in connection with the delivery of tangible personal property and would be taxable if billed by the vendor. It can be viewed either as a cost incurred after the passage of title or as a charge for a nontaxable service, regardless of the tangible personal property aspect of the transaction.

The following questions are integral in making the determination of taxability of freight and shipping charges. Are the charges subject to tax:

- Even if separately billed?
- If included in the selling price?
- If billed directly by a carrier?

> **PLANNING POINTER**
>
> If possible, a transaction should be structured so that either the freight and shipping charges are billed separately or the freight company directly bills the purchaser for the cost of the freight and shipping charges.
>
> Many states exempt separately stated freight and shipping charges. Therefore, structuring the purchase in such a manner avoids the unnecessary payment of tax. Since the majority of states do not impose tax on freight and shipping charges billed directly by the freight company, handling the transaction in this manner can even further reduce exposure to additional taxes.

When the charges are for *shipping and handling,* most states require that tax be charged on the entire amount. If the shipping charges can be billed separately, then that portion of the charge should be nontaxable in those states that do not impose tax on shipping charges.

> **CAUTION**
>
> In states that impose tax on freight and shipping charges, even postage can be subject to tax when billed to the purchaser as a freight or shipping charge.

STUDY QUESTIONS

9. When a printer acts as a service provider, which of the following is **not** true?

   a. It may or may not have an obligation to collect sales tax.
   b. The tax treatment of supplies provided by the customer may be impacted.
   c. It is selling tangible personal property and is required to collect sales tax on the transaction.

10. Which of the following statements is **not** true?

    a. Many states do not include separately stated freight and shipping charges in the tax base.
    b. Under the narrower view of manufacturing, a conveyor that moves raw materials and work-in-process from one workstation to another within the plant would probably qualify for an exemption.
    c. Under the Integrated Plant Doctrine, if a conveyer moves raw materials and work-in-process from one workstation to another within the plant, that would be considered part of a synchronized system engaged in manufacturing.
    d. Many states have enacted exemptions for fuel and electricity consumed in the manufacturing process.

MODULE 2: SALES AND USE TAXES — CHAPTER 7

Sales and Use Tax Treatment of Services

This chapter explains the state sales and use tax treatment of various service transactions. It discusses the issues involved in determining the sales and use taxability of:

- Mixed transactions
- Maintenance contracts
- Temporary help
- Professional services, including:
  - Advertising
  - Architectural
  - Computer
  - Printing
  - Carrier

LEARNING OBJECTIVES

Upon completing this chapter, the student will be able to:

- Explain the elements used to determine the sales and use tax treatment of mixed transactions

- Describe the issues involved in determining the sales and use tax treatment of professional, advertising, architectural, printing, and carrier services

- Indicate the various issues involved in the determination of sales and use taxability of computer consulting and services

- Describe how states treat maintenance contracts for sales and use tax purposes

OVERVIEW

In recent years, sales and use taxes have been expanded to tax the service sector of the U.S. economy. When sales and use taxes began, services made up only a small portion of the economy. Over time, however, the manufacturing base in the United States has diminished and the service sector has expanded. To maintain revenue streams from the sales and use tax, the states have expanded the base by including more and more services in the measure of tax. Initially only services related to tangible personal property were taxed; however, over time, the base has been expanded in many states to include other services not necessarily related to the sale of tangible personal property.

As noted above, most states have responded to those increasing revenue needs by gradually increasing the services that are subject to tax. However, most states have been hesitant to impose a general tax on most services after the unsuccessful attempts by Florida in 1987 and Massachusetts in 1991. (Both states were forced to rescind the general sales and use taxes on services shortly after they were enacted.)

The first services to be taxed were those related to the sale of tangible personal property. So, for example, the maintenance or repair of tangible personal property might be taxable. The latest trend has been to expand the definition of *service* to include business services (e.g., data processing) or other services that are completely unrelated to any transfer or sale of tangible personal property.

Hawaii, New Mexico, and South Dakota impose a sales or excise tax on a broad range of services. Although those taxes generally are structured as excise taxes on the gross receipts and services rendered by persons engaged in business in the state, the nature and extent of the services covered by the taxes vary among the states. The other states imposing sales and use taxes apply the tax only to a limited number of specifically enumerated services. So in a state with that statutory construction, if a service is not specifically enumerated in the statute, it is considered to be nontaxable.

Mixed Transactions

From a sales and use tax perspective, transactions involving the sale of both tangible personal property and services (i.e., mixed transactions) can be problematic. If a *lump-sum charge* is provided on the invoice (one charge for labor and material), many states take the position that the entire invoice amount, including the otherwise nontaxable services, is subject to sales and use taxes. In a few states if even a small amount of tangible personal property accompanies a nontaxable service, the *entire* transaction becomes taxable.

True object test. Many states, however, are more moderate in their treatment of such transactions. To determine taxability, those states generally use a test commonly referred to as the *true object* test. Under that test, if the true object desired by the customer is the nontaxable service rather than the tangible personal property, the transaction is *not* taxable. If the true object desired by the customer is the tangible personal property, the entire transaction is taxable.

> ### EXAMPLE
>
> In the case of a contract drafted by an attorney, the true object desired by the client is the attorney's professional advice rather than the paper on which the contract is written. Therefore, the transaction would be treated as a sale of professional services rather than as a sale of tangible personal property. Of course, the attorney would be charged use tax on the items of tangible personal property consumed in rendering the service.

> **CAUTION**
>
> When evaluating mixed transactions, it is important to carefully consult the state's statutes, cases, and rulings because the distinctions involved with this issue often are very narrow.

PROFESSIONAL SERVICES

Most states impose sales and use taxes only on specifically enumerated services. Professional services, such as those performed by physicians, accountants, and lawyers, typically are *not* among those specifically enumerated. The laws of several states provide that professional services that include the sale or rental of tangible personal property as *inconsequential elements* for which no separate charge is made are exempt from sales and use taxes. Few state statutes provide any clarification as to what constitutes an *inconsequential element*. Accordingly, contracts that are intended to be exempt service contracts but that also include the sale or rental of tangible personal property may be vulnerable to state and local sales and use taxes, if it is determined that the sale or rental of tangible personal property is more than an inconsequential element of the contract.

> **EXAMPLE**
>
> Code of Virginia Annotated §58.1-609.5(1) provides an exemption for "[p]rofessional, insurance, or personal service transactions which involve sales as inconsequential elements for which no separate charges are made."

Generally, charges for services are exempt from sales and use tax *unless* the service is provided in connection with the sale, maintenance, or repair of tangible personal property.

ADVERTISING SERVICES

Overview

An advertising agency's sales tax treatment can vary greatly, depending on:

- The nature of what is provided
- Whether it is selling tangible personal property or performing a service
- The means of delivery

In addition, because the nature of work performed by most advertising agencies ranges from the creative (such as developing advertising themes, writing copy, writing commercials, etc.) to the production of finished art (such as audio and video tapes, artwork used in advertising or promotion, etc.), further complexities can be introduced into the sales tax applicability to certain transactions. To further complicate matters, the use of computers and the delivery capabilities of the Internet give advertising agencies the ability to deliver many formerly tangible products in a digital form, thereby casting further doubt on the appropriate application of sales tax and creating new challenges for a sales tax that is deeply rooted in the transfer of tangible personal property as the basis for imposition. To address this issue, many states are adopting digital equivalent statutes. This means that if the item is taxable in its tangible form, it is also taxable when sold as a digital product.

> **EXAMPLE**
>
> Most states impose sales tax on sales of music CDs. So, when music is downloaded as a digital equivalent, most states take the position that the digital equivalent or download is taxable as well.

Scope of Advertising Agency Services

Before beginning a discussion of advertising agencies and the work they perform, some definitions may assist in understanding the scope of their activities.

Preliminary art. This term is used to describe the sketches, drawings, and other renderings that are frequently created in the *preliminary* planning of an advertising campaign or creation of a poster or other promotional piece. Usually, the preliminary art is created to help the client envision how the final piece will look.

Finished art. This term is used to describe the *final* rendering of the object, such as a logo, picture, or other promotional item. In most states, the creation of preliminary art is *not* taxed unless finished art is also created, because the rendering of preliminary art does not automatically result in the transfer of tangible personal property.

The advertising agency generally retains the preliminary art unless another company is coordinating the manufacture of the final piece.

> **NOTE**
>
> In some states, if finished art is created, the preliminary art that was created (and, in some cases, rejected to select other designs or themes) may also become subject to tax.

> **EXAMPLE**
>
> Assume that four pieces of *preliminary art* were created. From those, one was selected for production of the finished art. In some states, the taxable base for the finished art would include the cost of all the preliminary art that was created, even three of the preliminary designs that were rejected.

In addition to the creation of promotional items, advertising agencies perform a variety of services that are generally not subject to sales tax. These nontaxable services include the:

- Development of advertising campaigns
- Writing of advertising copy
- Creation of commercial jingles and songs
- Placement of advertising

When advertising agencies perform these services, they generally are treated as the consumers of the tangible personal property used in performing these services. Thus, their receipts for these services are generally not subject to sales or use tax.

Most states do not tax services of this nature. However, an exception to these rules could occur in cases where an advertising agency creates either audio or video tapes for airing commercials.

Commercials. When commercials are created, the advertising agency typically manages the entire process for the client, which entails:

- Writing the scripts
- Assembling a production staff
- Hiring the actors
- Producing and directing the commercial
- Editing and producing a final master copy of the commercial
- Delivering or distributing the commercial to local and national broadcast outlets
- Purchasing airtime for its showing during appropriate events or programs

Most states take the position that the cost of the commercial includes all the costs outlined here, with the exception of airtime charges, in the taxable measure for the commercial. A state would then tax its *pro rata* share of these costs, based on the number of showings, number of copies distributed in the state, or some other appropriate measure to allocate costs to a state.

Internet delivery. The growth of the Internet as a delivery tool for certain digital products and the increased use of personal computers in the creation of advertising media have further complicated the taxation of many advertising agency transactions. In the traditional model for the creation of artwork, the client received the finished art as tangible personal property at the conclusion of the manufacturing process—that is, the item itself was shipped or delivered to the client. With increased computer use in the design and manufacturing process, many clients now have the option of receiving their finished art in digital form. Many have questioned whether the transfer of a *digital* product constitutes the delivery of tangible personal property. However, many states have responded by enacting digital equivalent statutes (as noted earlier) and imposing tax on the cost of the digital product as if it was being sold as tangible personal property.

In addition, the increased use of the Internet as a delivery vehicle has afforded additional flexibility, allowing advertising agencies to e-mail models and finished products to their clients for approval, review, and final delivery. Although most states do not distinguish between the sale of a digital product, frequently referred to as a *digital equivalent*, and the sale of an item of tangible personal property, the question of whether in some cases a digital equivalent is selling tangible personal property or performing a service could be an area of increased controversy as the use of the Internet for delivery of such items continues to expand.

In the past, digital products were taxed in some states *only* if they were delivered through some tangible medium, such as a disk, CD, or tape. Presumably, digital products not delivered through a tangible means would not be subject to tax in those states. So, for example, a digital image delivered on a CD would be taxable, whereas a digital image e-mailed to the customer would not be subject to tax. In general this treatment has been dropped in favor of the digital equivalent treatment discussed above. So, for example, whether a book is purchased as tangible personal property, a digital download, or a CD, virtually all the states would impose tax upon the purchase.

ARCHITECTURAL SERVICES

Overview

Most states do not impose sales or use tax on architectural services, because they are professional service that the states typically do not tax. The architectural firm, however, is generally treated as a *consumer* of any equipment or materials used in performing the services.

EXAMPLE

If architects are hired to construct a model of a new building, they would not charge their client tax on the gross receipts billed to that client to create the model. However, they would be required to pay tax on the tangible personal property used to construct the model.

CAUTION

Complications can arise when architects sell tangible personal property or render architectural services for other than real property construction.

Taxing Architectural Services

Most state statutes do not impose tax on architectural services when those services are rendered in connection with real property improvements or construction. However, differing treatment may arise when the architect performs design services related to interior spaces or the layout or placement of equipment.

A number of states treat architects' performance of design services relating to the placement of moveable partitions or equipment as a taxable sale (Hawaii, New Mexico, South Dakota, and District of Columbia). Other states, South Carolina and Utah for example, impose tax on these services *only* if they are rendered in conjunction with a sale of the partitions and equipment. The other states (District of Columbia, Hawaii, New Mexico, and South Dakota) all generally impose tax on general service sales by architects. Overall, the majority of states do *not* impose any tax on architectural services. In addition, most states require that architectural firms pay tax on the supplies and equipment used in rendering their services.

Creation of Blueprints

It is common for architects to provide blueprints as part of their design services. In most states, blueprints provided as part of the design service are not a taxable item. In such instances, the architect would owe tax on the cost of the materials used to create the blueprints, but charges to the clients would not be subject to tax.

However, architects often provide additional copies or reproduce copies of blueprints for their clients. When additional copies are created and sold separately or for an additional charge, the charges are subject to tax in most states. Alabama, Hawaii, Indiana, Mississippi, New Mexico, Pennsylvania, South Dakota, Virginia, and the District of Columbia impose tax on the creation of blueprints.

STUDY QUESTIONS

> **1.** Which of the following is generally *not* taxable for sales and use tax purposes?
>
> **a.** Sales of tangible personal property
> **b.** Sales of services related to the sale of tangible personal property and included in a lump-sum with the tangible personal property on the invoice
> **c.** Sales of professional services

2. Which of the following is generally **not** part of the taxable measure of a commercial for sales and use tax purposes?

   a. The hiring of actors

   b. Airtime charges

   c. Production costs

3. Which of the following statements is true?

   a. Most states impose sales tax on architectural services when performed in connection with construction.

   b. Most states impose sales tax on blueprints supplied as part of a design service.

   c. Some states impose sales tax on design services performed by architects that relate to the placement of equipment.

COMPUTER CONSULTING AND SERVICES

Overview

When the sale of software is combined with computer consulting, does the sale constitute a sale of services, of the software, of both, or of neither subject to sales and use tax? Does the answer change depending on whether the sale consists of a package of consulting services and software or whether the charges for each are combined or stated separately? Is software taxable when it is first integrated with hardware and then sold? Answers to these questions can affect whether a transaction is subject to sales tax.

Most states exempt consulting-type services from sales and use tax. However, some states either impose a tax on a broad range of services or specifically tax computer hardware or software consulting.

When computer consulting involves taxable software sales, the *entire* sale is generally taxable—unless the consulting is separately stated on the invoice or in the contract. Computer consulting without the sale of software is usually *exempt* from sales and use tax (with the exception of the states mentioned previously). *Computer consulting* can include systems design or evaluation, programming, and training. Canned software combined with significant modifications will often *not* be taxable if the consulting services provided are in excess of half of the total sales price and over half of the underlying code is changed.

Several states impose a tax on data processing services, which may be defined as the compilation of information or the furnishing of a report. [See, e.g., Tex. Tax Code Ann. §151.0035.] In *Community Mutual Insurance Co. v. Tracy* [73 Ohio St. 3d 371 (1995)], however, the Ohio Supreme Court held that the coding of documents performed by an outside firm that was hired under attorney supervision was not subject to tax because the true object of the service was exempt professional services rather than taxable data processing services.

In most states that do not impose a broad-based tax on services, data processing and time-sharing services are simply not included in the enumerated services subject to sales/use tax.

Applying each state's sales and use taxes to transactions involving computer hardware, software, and related services raises a myriad of issues, many of which revolve around the question of whether the company is selling property, services, or a combination thereof.

In *mixed transactions*, which comprise the transfer of *both* property and services, some states look to the *true object* of the transaction to determine whether the buyer's underlying motivation is to obtain a service or property. This raises some important questions:

- If the object of the transaction is to obtain property, does the taxability of the transaction change when the property is transferred by intangible means?
- If the object of the transaction is to obtain a service, is the service subject to tax?
- Which state has authority to tax the service: the state in which the service is rendered, or the state in which the consumer obtains the benefit of the service?

Many states impose sales and use tax on the purchase by the service provider of property consumed or transferred incident to rendering a nontaxable service. As a general rule, the service provider is considered the *consumer* of any taxable property or services used in rendering the nontaxable service.

Therefore, the service provider is liable for sales and use taxes on the cost of any tangible personal property used or transferred as an incident or inconsequential element of providing a service that is not subject to tax.

EXAMPLE

If a vendor's charges for providing computer software consulting services are not subject to a state's sales and use taxes, but the finished product includes an explanatory report or manual to complement the package, the vendor must pay sales and use taxes based on its cost of the paper and other materials used to transmit the report.

If, however, the state imposes a sales and use tax on the consulting services rendered, the vendor's purchases of the paper used to prepare the report may be exempt as a purchase for resale.

In most of the states that do not impose a tax on computer-related services, charges for nontaxable services must be separately stated to preserve their nontaxable status when the charges are in conjunction with retail sales of taxable hardware or software. Failure of the vendor to itemize the taxable and nontaxable items separately will usually render the entire charge taxable.

Software Maintenance Contracts

Many computer and software consultants provide maintenance contracts as a complement to prewritten software platforms. Such contracts often entitle the user to automatically receive any upgrades or improvements made to the software or to receive services that maintain the software so that it operates properly and meets the needs of a specific user. The contracts may also include additional performance assistance through access to a *help desk* or other support services.

A majority of states now impose sales and use taxes on certain computer software maintenance contracts, particularly software maintenance contracts associated with the sale of prewritten software. For example, states often distinguish between maintenance contracts that are *required* with the purchase of prewritten software (which are often considered a component charge of the taxable software sale) and *optional* maintenance contracts for consultation, support, and training services. Alternatively, some states may tax computer software maintenance contracts, regardless of whether they are required as part of the software purchase. Still other states continue to embrace the canned versus custom software distinction and tax maintenance agreements pertaining to canned software only. States that otherwise tax maintenance contracts may exempt separately stated charges for telephone support services.

Many states impose tax on charges for software maintenance contracts that provide updates and future releases. When the maintenance contract provides for both support services *and* upgrades or improvements, most states will impose tax on the *entire* charge for the contract if the charge is not separately stated for each type of maintenance contract. If the maintenance agreement differentiates between maintenance agreement *support services* and *upgrades*, then generally only the portion of the charge attributable to the upgrades is taxable.

Invariably, the inclusion of software updates in a computer software maintenance contract increases the likelihood that a greater number of states will impose a tax on the contract price. That is probably because the maintenance contract includes a tangible personal property transfer component. If the software updates are not transferred via a tangible medium (e.g., discs or tapes), some states provide that the updates are not subject to sales and use tax.

Training

Many software vendors provide training services as a component of an integrated systems contract, particularly if the software is custom software designed specifically for the taxpayer at issue. Although personal and professional services, such as training, typically do not constitute taxable transactions in most states, software training may nevertheless be subject to sales and use tax. Whether such training is subject to sales and use tax may depend on whether the acquired software is custom or canned. If the state does not impose a sales and use tax on custom software, the training associated with such software generally is also not subject to tax. In contrast, training associated with taxable canned software usually is subject to sales and use tax unless it is separately itemized on the invoice, or purchased in a separate transaction.

The majority of states require a separate itemization of taxable and non-taxable items, or the entire charge will be considered taxable. Accordingly, the *total* charge for taxable services or for tangible personal property that includes services such as consulting or training provided in connection with the sale of taxable services or tangible personal property is subject to sales and use tax when the otherwise nontaxable services are included in the price of the taxable services or tangible personal property sold or leased.

User Manuals

Although sales of tangible personal property, including books and manuals, are typically subject to sales and use tax, exceptions may exist for software user manuals. In many instances, the imposition of tax on such manuals depends on whether the software that accompanies a manual is custom or canned.

For states that do not impose sales tax on custom software, user manuals that are *not* separately invoiced by the vendor are generally exempt from sales and use tax under the *incidental* or *inconsequential theory*. In such a case the vendor typically is liable for tax on the cost of any tangible personal property consumed in providing the manual. If the state imposes sales and use tax on canned software, user manuals for such software generally are subject to such tax if they are billed. Extra user manuals that are purchased and invoiced separately from the initial software sale are subject to sales and use tax in almost all the states, regardless of whether the software is custom or canned.

Electronic Computer Downloads and Online Services

Several states impose sales or use tax on one or more elements of electronic commerce. In general, the states that have traditionally taxed many categories of services are the states that are taxing electronic commerce. The extent of tax imposed differs greatly among the states. Some states tax electronic downloads (e.g., information) but exempt Internet access.

For states imposing tax on Internet-related services, the arguments under which online services or transactions are taxed vary. Some states impose their tax as an extension of the sales and use tax imposed on *tangible personal property*—particularly when the object of the transaction is traditionally sold in tangible format, such as information contained in publications. Other states will categorize such transactions as a separate category of *taxable services*.

Other states tax information services involving the furnishing of any news or current information, including financial information, whether transferred by printed or electronic means. A few states treat the electronic transmission of information as a taxable computer service.

The Internet Tax Freedom Act (ITFA). The IFTA became law on October 21, 1998. The Act provided a three-year state and local tax moratorium on certain Internet-related services and activities. The law provided that from October 1, 1998, to October 21, 2001 (subsequently extended to November 1, 2007), no state or political subdivision could impose a tax upon Internet access charges or discriminatory taxes on electronic commerce—except for certain grandfather provisions for states that had already imposed a tax upon access charges. Then, President Bush signed H.R. 3678, the Internet Tax Freedom Act Amendment Acts of 2007, into law. The law prohibits multiple and discriminatory taxes on electronic commerce until November 1, 2014.

Despite the restrictions imposed by the ITFA, the assessment and collection of sales or use tax for sales via the Internet are treated by state and local taxing jurisdictions in the same manner as any other transaction subject to sales or use tax. In other words, purchases over the Internet of otherwise taxable tangible products or services continue to be subject to sales and use tax. If the vendor does not have sufficient nexus with the state to collect the tax, the purchaser is obligated to file a report and remit the applicable use tax to the state.

Web Design and Hosting Charges

With the increased importance of the Internet in commerce, more and more businesses are using it as a means to reach customers who might otherwise not be aware of their services. The demand for this new method of advertising has increased demand for a new form of advertising, generically referred to as Web design.

Web design basically involves the creation of a site on the World Wide Web that is accessible either by directly entering its address or by entering certain key search terms that are referenced to the site. Like other forms of media advertising, it is designed to be attractive and eye-catching and, if done correctly, will drive customers to the business represented by the posting. While the majority of states do not impose tax on Web design charges, there are a handful of states, primarily those states imposing tax on broad-based services, that do impose tax on Web design charges.

Closely related to Web design charges are Web hosting charges. In Web hosting, a business will post its Web site, making it available to anyone on the World Wide Web on a server that could be located anywhere in the world. Internet users entering the Internet address for the Web site or the correct search term would be directed to the site for their review and use. Web hosts generally charge a fee to make the site available on the Internet. In a few states, the provision of that service is a taxable event for sales tax purposes.

As states become more aggressive in seeking new transactions to tax because of shrinking revenues, it will be interesting to see the extent to which these 21st-century charges become part of a tax system that some claim has not kept pace with the changes in modern commerce.

STUDY QUESTIONS

4. Even if a maintenance agreement distinguishes between *support services* and *upgrades*, only the portion of the charge attributable to *support services* is taxable. **True or False?**

5. Which one of the following statements is true regarding canned software?
   a. Canned software is generally treated as the performance of a service.
   b. Canned software is taxed like a sale of a book or CD.
   c. Canned software combined with significant modifications will often *not* be taxable if the consulting services provided are less than half of the total sales price.

6. Which of the following statements is *not* true?
   a. The extent of sales and use tax imposed on electronic commerce differs significantly among states.
   b. Extra user manuals that are purchased and invoiced separately from an initial software sale are subject to sales and use tax in most states.
   c. Purchases over the Internet of otherwise taxable tangible products or services are *not* subject to state sales and use tax.

MAINTENANCE CONTRACTS

Overview

The taxation of maintenance contracts varies widely from state to state. Although increasingly states search for ways to expand their revenue base, they often expand traditional definitions of *repair* and *tangible personal property* to include maintenance contracts. In fact, many states have amended their sales and use tax statutes to *specifically* include maintenance contracts in the tax base.

In addition to the varying statutory treatment, the fact that there are many different types of contracts complicates the taxation of maintenance contracts. In states that do not tax the gross receipts from the sale of maintenance contracts, the *repairer* is frequently taxed as the consumer of any parts provided under the contract.

Computer Software

Computer software maintenance contracts are typically sold in one of two ways. One type provides services to ensure that software is maintained so that it operates properly and meets the needs of a specific user. The other type of software maintenance contract not only provides the purchaser with maintenance services, but also provides the purchaser with software updates that will improve the software's performance or usefulness.

A majority of states now impose sales and use taxes on computer software maintenance contracts. Many of the states impose tax on computer software maintenance agreements only if certain conditions are met. Other states continue to embrace the *canned* versus *custom* software distinction and tax maintenance agreements pertaining to canned software only.

If the computer software maintenance contracts include software updates, an even larger number of states impose a tax on the *contract price*—probably because the maintenance contract includes a property transfer component.

Computer Hardware

Many computer users purchase maintenance contracts to preserve their investment in computer hardware and to ensure that the hardware continues to function properly. Typical contracts provide for inspection and maintenance of the hardware and are usually billed on an annual basis.

Most states impose sales and use taxes on computer hardware maintenance contracts. This is due largely to the fact that, although computer software was often treated as intangible property and therefore was not within the tax base, computer hardware falls squarely within the definition of *tangible personal property*. Thus, the taxation of hardware maintenance contracts usually depends on whether the repair or maintenance of tangible personal property is taxable in the state.

Fees for Computer Software Help Lines

Purchasers of computer software *help line* services can communicate with computer consultants who will assist the purchasers with computer software problems. Typically, such services are billed on an annual basis.

Compared with the taxation of software and hardware maintenance contracts, significantly fewer states impose sales and use taxes on annual fees for computer software help lines. That is probably attributable to the fact that such fees do not involve transfers of any property, tangible or intangible. Help lines are pure consulting services and, therefore, are outside of the traditional sales and use tax base. Nevertheless, those services are taxable in some states. As states continue to search for new areas of taxation, it is likely that more states will expand their sales and use tax base to include computer services such as help lines.

An additional complicating factor in the taxation of such types of consulting services is that the purchaser of help line services often is not located in the same state as the seller of those services. Sourcing the services can be problematic because the rules vary widely from state to state.

Production and Nonproduction Machinery

A purchaser of production machinery maintenance contracts typically pays an annual fee to a service provider to maintain production equipment. The maintenance can include inspection and regularly scheduled procedures to keep the equipment operating properly. Most states do *not* impose sales and use taxes on production machinery maintenance contracts. The nontaxable nature of such contracts can be explained under one of two theories:

1. States with exemptions for production, manufacturing, or processing equipment often extend the exemption to services performed on the equipment.
2. Maintenance contracts usually do not involve the transfer of tangible personal property. Therefore, the purchase of maintenance contracts is not taxable in states that have a sales and use tax structure that relies heavily on transfers of tangible personal property.

Fewer states exempt *nonproduction* machinery maintenance contracts than exempt production machinery maintenance contracts. The difference is probably attributable to the preferred status that states give to tangible personal property used in production activities.

Types of Equipment Maintenance Contracts

Equipment maintenance contracts can be divided into three broad categories:

1. Those involving labor only
2. Those involving both parts and labor
3. Those involving parts only

Labor only. With a labor-only contract, the customer will generally pay the repairperson a monthly or annual charge under a service agreement that entitles the customer to receive certain services on the equipment without an additional charge. Those might include, for example, a specified number of inspections or a limited or unlimited number of repair service calls. Any parts or materials required to make the equipment operational or to maintain it in an operational state, other than incidental items such as lubricant or cleaners, would necessitate *additional* charges.

Parts and labor. In the case of a parts and labor contract, the monthly service charge may cover all or a portion of the labor and material required to maintain the equipment.

Parts only. Parts-only contracts would only cover the parts required to maintain the equipment. Contracts that involve only parts replacement coverage and no labor follow the general rules for sales of tangible personal property.

If the repairperson is billing a *labor-only* contract, then the treatment of the billing for sales tax purposes will be governed by the state's treatment of repair labor incurred in connection with the repair of *tangible personal property*. If the repairperson is billing for a *parts and service* contract with each component separately billed as labor and parts, the correct treatment would follow the state's treatment of each of those components. In the case of parts-only contracts, virtually all states would impose tax upon the maintenance contract charge.

> **EXAMPLE**
>
> If the labor is exempt in the state, the correct billing is to tax the parts portion and to exempt the labor portion.

An element of complexity is introduced when the repairperson chooses to bill the customer for both parts and labor with a lump-sum charge. In that instance, it must be determined whether the state treats the repairperson as the *consumer* of the parts provided under the contract. If the state does so, then tax would *not* apply to the billing. The repairperson would, however, be taxed on the cost of any parts furnished under the contract. Conversely, if the repairperson is not considered the consumer, the entire billing would be taxable to the customer and the repairperson would not be taxed on the usage of the parts.

> **PLANNING POINTER**
>
> Care should be exercised when dealing in a multistate sales tax environment so that an estimate of any tax to be absorbed by the repairperson as a consumer is factored into the overall contract price.
>
> In addition, repairpersons need to have procedures in place to track parts consumption by location so that the appropriate taxes can be paid on their cost.

STUDY QUESTIONS

7. The *majority* of states impose sales and use tax on which of the following?

  a. Production machinery maintenance contracts
  b. Computer software maintenance contracts
  c. Computer software help lines

8. If a repairperson bills a customer for parts and labor under a maintenance contract with a lump-sum charge, the entire transaction is *always* nontaxable. **True or False?**

PRINTERS

Overview

States offering production machinery exemptions frequently include printers in their definition of manufacturers qualifying for the exemption. However, the sales and use tax treatment of printers can be complicated by the varying services that printers provide. Many printers perform a service when they use materials provided by their customers to produce a finished product. In such an instance, the printer is transformed from a *manufacturer* to a *service provider*, and this has a significant impact on the printer's tax obligations. State statutes often grant exemptions or reduced rates for manufacturing machinery and equipment as an incentive for manufacturers.

Manufacturers or Service Providers?

Printers function as *manufacturers* when they produce a printed document from raw materials. However, the customer may provide paper, ink, or other raw materials for the printer to use in producing the printed document. The customer may do that to coordinate color, texture, or appearance with some other document that will be displayed with the printed piece. In addition, the customer may be able to obtain a substantially discounted price for the supplies because of other commercial relationships with the vendor that may not be transferable to the printer.

In many states, when the printer produces a printed document using materials provided by its customer, the printer is viewed as performing a *service*. Performing this service can result in a loss of the sales tax exemption for machinery and equipment that is otherwise available to the printer because the printer has stepped outside the role of a manufacturer. In addition, the tax treatment of the supplies provided may also be impacted.

When the printer acts as a *manufacturer*, it is selling tangible personal property and is required to collect sales tax on the transaction. When the printer acts as a *service provider*, it may or may not have an obligation to collect the tax, depending on whether the state taxes the services performed by the printer.

> **CAUTION**
>
> Many companies have in-house print shops that create internal publications, advertising materials, and so forth. In states allowing a manufacturing exemption, the printing equipment will usually qualify for the exemption.
>
> Most states have an additional requirement that the item be *resold* for the materials consumed to qualify for the exemption, so any supplies used in the self-production of materials that are given away will *not* qualify as tax exempt.

COMMON AND CONTRACT CARRIERS

A *common* or *contract carrier* is a company that provides the for-hire service of transporting property or goods for a fee via a motor vehicle. In most cases, the motor vehicle is a semi-truck or a tractor-trailer. Many states provide an exemption from sales and use tax for common and/or contract carriers. The exemption is typically limited to the semi-truck itself and any attachments to the tractor or trailer.

In recent years, one common planning technique has been to create a limited liability company (LLC) that houses the trucking assets formerly held by a manufacturer and used to transport the manufacturer's products to its customers. In many states, this has resulted in converting previously taxable assets in the manufacturer's hands into tax-exempt assets in the hands of the limited liability company.

In many states the carrier must meet one or both of the following requirements to qualify for the exemption:

- The carrier must offer services to the general public.
- The carrier must have its own drivers, hire temporary drivers, or lease drivers from a related company.

Carriers meeting these requirements are generally exempt on the following purchases for use in providing this service:

- Tractor and trailer
- Repair and replacement parts for the tractor and trailer

> **CAUTION**
>
> Although not all states require that the common carrier offer its services to the general public, one common reason for failing to qualify for the exemption is not meeting that requirement when the state imposes it.
>
> Therefore, companies wishing to create a qualifying trucking company should carefully review the applicable state's requirements for the exemption.
>
> In most states, it is not necessary for the trucking company to actually transport goods for an unrelated party in order to qualify for the exemption; however, it may be necessary to offer that service as a prerequisite to qualifying for the exemption.

TEMPORARY HELP

Although imposing tax on temporary help is not fundamentally different from imposing tax on any other service, a state's imposition of tax only on temporary help associated with certain or a limited number of services introduces additional complexities and recordkeeping requirements into the tax determination.

Providers and purchasers of temporary help can relatively easily determine whether tax is due on the transaction if a state imposes tax on *all* sales of temporary help, regardless of the type of service performed, or on certain *categories* of services provided (such as office workers' services).

Therefore, if a state opts to tax all sales of temporary help, then providers and purchasers should know that the tax applies to any services performed in that state. However, additional complexities are introduced into the determination when tax is imposed only on temporary help that is provided for *certain* services or a narrow range of services.

For example, a state may impose tax on the repair of tangible personal property. In a typical transaction, such services would be purchased from a vendor that provided services such as the repair of automobiles, computers, manufacturing machinery, and so on.

However, it is also feasible to lease an employee who performs repair work on, among other things, tangible personal property. In such instances, some states are asserting that temporary help is taxable when otherwise taxable services are performed. Therefore, if temporary help were used to repair taxable equipment, tax would apply to the temporary help charge just as it would to a taxable repair labor charge.

Presumably, in such a scenario, the temporary help provider would be required to track the actual work performed by the employee to make that determination. This would require an additional level of detail and recordkeeping that currently does not exist and may not be readily available, given the nature of most temporary help assignments.

For example, purchasers of temporary help would be required to track the activities of individual workers to determine whether and when they were performing any taxable services. This information would then have to be reported to the temporary help provider so that it could determine whether tax should be imposed.

This level of detail reporting is fraught with problems and would likely result in additional tax, and potentially penalties, upon audit for most temporary help providers and purchasers. In addition, some states are not limiting the treatment of *temporary help* charges to traditional temporary help providers.

EXAMPLE

In many industrial settings, it is commonplace for various contractors, such as electrical and plumbing, to provide leased employees on a fill-in basis. These employees then work with company employees on whatever tasks have to be performed, much like an in-house maintenance staff would function. Presumably, some states would require tax collection on taxable work performed by these leased employees.

STUDY QUESTIONS

9. In which of the following situations might a printer be considered a *service provider*?

   a. When it creates a printed document from materials provided by a customer

   b. When it creates a printed document from materials that it purchases

   c. When it creates a printed document from materials that it purchases, but at exact specifications of the customer.

10. Which of the following statements is true regarding the sales and use tax exemption for carriers?

   a. Most states extend the exemption to equipment used to maintain the tractor and trailer.

   b. Most states do *not* require the carrier to transport goods for an unrelated party in order to qualify for the exemption.

   c. Most states do *not* extend the exemption to repair or replacement parts for the tractor and trailer.

MODULE 2: SALES AND USE TAXES — CHAPTER 8

Electronic Sales Tax Issues

This chapter discusses the problems encountered in determining sales and use tax liability when using prepaid phone cards and procurement cards and the possible solutions for these problems. It also covers the sales and use tax issues involved with electronic data transmission, telecommunications services, cloud computing, and computer software.

LEARNING OBJECTIVES

Upon completing this chapter, the student will be able to:

- Describe the problems that may be encountered in determining sales and use tax liability when using prepaid phone cards and procurement cards
- Explain the sales and use tax issues involved with electronic data transmission and telecommunications services
- Describe the state taxability of canned and custom software
- Explain how computer software and software licenses are treated for sales and use tax purposes
- Understand the sales and use tax issues posed by cloud computing

PREPAID PHONE CARDS

Overview

Prepaid phone cards (PPCs) may be sold in *units* or *dollars* (i.e., $10 of long-distance service). A unit typically equals one minute of domestic phone service. With respect to international service, one minute of phone service may cost the user several units.

Consumers typically redeem the phone cards through use of an 800 number and a validation code to access the service provider's telecommunications equipment through which the call is routed and rated, and the call details are recorded.

There are three types of PPCs:

1. **Standard.** The standard PPC generally is the type that is purchased from the local convenience store.
2. **Promotional.** Promotional PPCs are customized and are typically given to the purchaser's customers or are otherwise used for the purchasing entity's own use.

> **EXAMPLE**
>
> Jack's Hardware Store may have its name printed on PPCs that include $5 of domestic long-distance service and give the cards to customers who purchase more than $100 of merchandise.

3. **Collector.** Collector cards typically have a limited issuance, are made of plastic rather than paper, and include a color picture of an item or person (i.e., an Elvis PPC). The charge for these cards generally is greater than the face value of the future phone service included on the card; the value of a collector card is substantially reduced if it is removed from the sealed wrapping (i.e., if it is used).

The use of most PPCs is subject to certain restrictions, such as they:
- May not be used to make 900 calls
- Are nonrefundable
- Expire if not used within a predetermined period of time

Many PPCs may be recharged—that is, additional units may be ordered from the sponsor or wholesaler by calling an 800 number and charging the additional units to a credit card.

PPCs raise a number of significant sales and use tax issues, including the following:
- Is the sale of PPCs taxed at the point of sale as a sale of tangible personal property (the card itself), taxed as the telecommunications services are used by the consumer, or taxed both at the sale of the card and the use of the service?
- If the sale of the card is taxable as a telecommunications service:
  - Is it taxable for calls originating in the customer's state, calls terminating in the customer's state, or calls that both originate and terminate in the customer's state?
  - Or does the answer depend on where the card is purchased?
- If the sale of the card is taxable as a telecommunications service, who is liable for remitting the tax:
  - Retailer?
  - Sponsor/wholesaler?
  - Telecommunications services provider?
- If the sale of the card is taxable as a telecommunications service, is the tax base on which the sales or use tax is computed the monetary value of the services represented on the card or the retail cost of the card?
- What local sales tax rates apply to the sale of the cards or taxable telecommunications services?

With respect to the issue of whether it is the sale of the PPC or the use of the service that is taxable, without legislation to carve out PPCs from the imposition of the telecommunications excise tax and then include PPCs in the sales and use tax definition of tangible personal property, most state laws would provide that sales and use tax is *not* imposed on the sale of the PPC. This is because the *true object* of what is being sold is the future long-distance service, rather than the card itself.

From a state's perspective, the *advantages* of taxing the PPC at the *point of sale*, rather than on *use*, include:

- Ease of administration by the states and retailers
- Avoidance of multiple taxes
- Imposition of the tax on the full sales price of the card, regardless of use (i.e., if taxed as the service is being used, unused portions of the PPCs are not subject to tax)

Disadvantages of the taxation at the *point of sale* include:

- The creation of mail-order PPC companies located in Delaware or other states that do not impose sales and use tax could result in a significant loss of tax revenues for all states.
- Sales of PPCs outside the United States would not be subject to tax. Note that most foreign travel agencies recommend that travelers visiting the United States purchase PPCs to reduce the complexity and confusion when making calls from the United States.
- A significant problem could be created if the PPC is taxable on its purchase but then may be used to purchase both taxable and nontaxable goods.
- Many telecommunications service providers have already spent significant amounts of money on the development of elaborate systems to track and compute the telecommunications taxes on the use of PPCs.

Over the past several years, a number of states have changed their laws to provide that PPCs are taxable at the point of sale rather than as the telecommunications services are being used.

CAUTION

Sellers of PPCs should exercise great care when dealing in a multistate environment because of the variation of treatment of these transactions from state to state. Some states treat the sale of a PPC as a sale of *tangible personal property* and assess tax at the *point of sale*. Other states assess tax on the *use* of the PPC, when the call is placed using the card.

In recent years, a new dimension has been added to sales of PPCs. PPCs may now be sold through automated teller machines (ATMs). By inserting a PPC into the machine, the supply of available time can be replenished by an ATM charge to the customer's bank account or credit card. This eliminates the need to repurchase a physical card when the time available on the PPC has expired, and provides the customer with more options and greater flexibility for recharging and using the PPC. Essentially rather than purchasing a replacement card, the customer is purchasing a new personal identification number (PIN) that allows reuse of the card. This further complicates the sales tax treatment of PPCs and raises new questions about the taxability of such transactions.

STUDY QUESTION

> 1. Which of the following is an advantage to states of taxing PPCs at the point of sale?
>   a. Sales of PPCs outside the United States would be subject to tax.
>   b. Sales tax would be imposed on the total sales price of the card, regardless of use.
>   c. The smart card concept would work well with the point-of-sale approach when it extends to PPCs.

PROCUREMENT CARDS

Overview

In an effort to reengineer the purchasing function for high-volume, low-cost goods and services, some companies use procurement cards. Generally, *procurement cards* are similar to credit cards issued to a designated corporate cardholder who is authorized to make specified purchases from a specific vendor or vendors.

No purchase order is produced in a normal procurement card transaction. In addition, rather than receiving an invoice for each purchase, the cardholder receives a monthly statement with summary information about transactions that occurred during the monthly billing cycle. Only one check is drawn to cover all of the purchases included on the monthly statement. The simplification of the purchase and payment processes significantly reduces accounts payable processing costs.

Although procurement cards streamline the purchasing and payment processes and, therefore, reduce costs, they may also create sales and use tax exposure issues because the paper trail is virtually eliminated. Specific transaction information, such as a description of items purchased and whether sales and use tax was charged at the time of purchase, is typically not reviewed by company personnel to determine whether sales and use tax was paid or should be accrued on the purchases.

According to the procurement card white paper issued by the Steering Committee Task Force on Electronic Data Interchange (EDI) Audit and Legal Issues for Tax Administration in June 1997, the key issue for taxpayers and state tax administrators is:

[w]hether the information provided to card users on the periodic statements from the card issuer regarding purchases made with procurement cards is sufficient to document that the correct amount of state and local sales or use tax was collected on the transaction at the time of sale.

Reducing Exposure Risk

To reduce potential audit exposure, a company may decide to do one or more of the following:

- **Limit procurement card transactions to purchases of certain goods or purchases from certain vendors.** For example, the company could limit all purchases to either tax-exempt or taxable items to facilitate the decision to accrue use tax or to determine the measure on which such tax should be computed (or both). If the purchases are limited to a specific vendor, the vendor can be instructed to (or not to) collect tax on purchases made on the procurement card or by a specific purchaser.

- **Set up a liability account to accrue use tax on all procurement card purchases from out-of-state vendors.** Although such action could result in an overpayment of tax, the extent of the overpayment may be less than the costs associated with more accurately determining the amount of tax that is due.

- **Maintain supporting documentation.** Supporting documentation could be a simple logbook that includes detailed descriptions of items purchased, their "shipped to" locations, and sales tax amounts. Unfortunately, such a procedure creates some of the same paperwork that the use of the procurement card was intended to eliminate.

- **Negotiate, and get in writing, an up-front compliance methodology with state authorities.** If a taxpayer is concerned about the magnitude of a potential sales and use tax assessment that may result when a state aggregates the procurement card purchases with other purchases and associated compliance ratios, the taxpayer should consider discussing with state officials, before an audit, the right to audit the two types of purchases separately.

- **Work out an arrangement with the card service to provide the necessary detail.** Many card services have been working with their larger clients to minimize exposure in this area. In most instances, the information is available; it is just a matter of redesigning the statements to show the expanded information.

For some taxpayers, remitting use tax on all purchases may be the safest option, but it could result in an overpayment of tax.

Some procurement card issuers are developing the technology to capture documentation about sales tax collected on procurement card purchases, but it would require accurate data collection by vendors at the point of sale.

Determining When the Sale Occurs

Another issue that arises in procurement card transactions is the point at which the transaction is deemed to have occurred. In the typical procurement card transaction, an order will be placed and the card charged on one day, the goods will be delivered at a later date, and the statement from the card issuer will be received anywhere from several days to more than 30 days after the order was placed and fulfilled.

In general, taxpayers that will owe more than a nominal amount of sales or use tax are required to file sales and use tax returns on a *monthly* basis.

> **EXAMPLE**
>
> For purchases made in January, the taxpayer must remit the applicable sales or use tax during February.

In the case of a normal 30-day procurement card billing cycle, the taxpayer may not receive the statement of its purchases until the sales and use tax on the purchase is due. If the procurement card billing cycle is January 15 to February 13, the taxpayer will not receive the statement that includes purchases made on January 15 until after approximately February 16, yet the sales and use tax on purchases made during January may be due on February 20.

If the state takes the position that the date the card is charged with the purchase is the date to be used in accruing the tax, the taxpayer most likely will not be in a position to timely pay the tax on such purchases.

> **PLANNING POINTER**
>
> Taxpayers involved in percentage or managed compliance agreements should carefully evaluate the nature and use of any procurement card purchases. For many taxpayers, special handling of these purchases may be required to attain more accurate reporting.

> **PLANNING POINTER**
>
> Taxpayers entering into agreements to utilize procurement cards should discuss the card service company's ability to provide sufficient detail to resolve any questions in the event of a sales and use tax audit. If the card service company is unable to provide the required level of detail, other procurement card vendors should be evaluated, or transactions for the procurement card should be confined to tax-exempt purchases.

> **CAUTION**
>
> In an effort to reduce the cost of the procurement function by using procurement cards, companies should not overlook the potential sales and use tax liabilities that such cards may create. The savings on the front end may be overshadowed by the possible compliance deficiencies.

STUDY QUESTION

2. To reduce potential audit exposure related to sales and use tax on procurement card purchases, companies should do all of the following *except:*
   a. Destroy documentation
   b. Limit transactions to particular purchases
   c. Arrange with the card service to provide needed detail

ELECTRONIC DATA TRANSMISSION AND MISCELLANEOUS TELECOMMUNICATIONS SERVICES

Although the majority of states impose a sales and use tax or excise tax on the sale of certain telecommunications services, the proliferation of new and emerging services has made the distinction between taxable telecommunications services and nontelecommunications services unclear.

State Definitions

Telecommunication services. The definition of *telecommunications services* varies substantially among the states.

For example, for Wisconsin sales and use tax purposes (Wisconsin Rule §Tax 11.66; Telecommunication & CATV Services), it is defined as:

> …electronically transmitting, conveying, or routing voice, data, audio, video, or other information or signals to a point or between or among points. Telecommunications services includes the transmission, conveyance, or routing of such information or signals in which computer processing applications are used to act on the content's form, code, or protocol for transmission, conveyance, or routing purposes, regardless of whether the service is referred to as a voice over Internet protocol service or classified by the federal communications commissions as an enhanced or value-added nonvoice data service.

Telecommunications services does not include any of the following:
- Data processing and information services that allow data to be generated, acquired, stored, processed, or retrieved and delivered to a purchaser by

an electronic transmission, if the purchaser's primary purpose for the underlying transaction is the processed data
- Installing or maintaining wiring or equipment on a customer's premises
- Tangible personal property
- Advertising, including directory advertising
- Billing and collection services provided to third parties
- Internet access services
- Radio and television audio and video programming services, regardless of the medium in which the services are provided, including cable service, as defined in 47 USC 522(6), audio and video programming services delivered by commercial mobile radio service providers, as defined in 47 CFR 20.3, and the transmitting, conveying, or routing of such services by the programming service provider
- Ancillary services
- Digital products delivered electronically, including software, music, video, reading materials, or ringtones

However, the following services are *not* subject to sales and use tax [Wisconsin Rule §Tax 11.66; Telecommunication & CATV Services]:
- Interstate or international telecommunications service if the service is sourced to a location outside Wisconsin
- Revenues collected under Wis. Stat. Sec. 256.35(3), the surcharge established by the public service commission under Wis. Stat. Sec. 256.35(3m)(f), for customers of wireless providers as defined in Wis. Stat. Sec. 256.35(3m)(a)6., and the police and fire protection fees under Wis. Stat. Sec. 196.025(6)
- Transfers of telecommunications services to resellers who purchase, repackage, and resell the services to customers (The reseller is liable for sales tax on its final retail sales of those services.)
- Interstate 800 services
- Transfers of services, commonly called access services, to an interexchange carrier that permit the origination or termination of telephone messages between a customer in Wisconsin and one or more points in another telephone exchange, and that are resold by the interexchange carrier. The interexchange carrier is liable for sales tax on its final retail sales of those services.
- Detailed telecommunications billing services

Although the components of taxable telecommunications services vary among the states, many states do exempt specific telecommunications services such as access services to 800 numbers and private line services.

Internet Tax Freedom Act. The Internet Tax Freedom Act (ITFA) became law on October 21, 1998. The Act provided a three-year state and local tax moratorium on certain Internet-related services and activities from October 1, 1998, to October 21, 2001 (subsequent legislation extended the moratorium to November 1, 2007).

On October 31, 2007, President Bush signed the Internet Tax Freedom Act Amendments Act of 2007, extending the ban on Internet access and discriminatory taxes yet again to November 1, 2014 [Pub. L. No. 110-108 (H.R. 3678), Laws 2007, effective Nov. 1, 2007].

The 2007 Act added several provisions regarding grandfathering, backbone service, and the definition of *Internet access*. The grandfather clause was extended but only to jurisdictions that have continued to tax Internet access without interruption.

The 2007 Act also added clarifying language regarding the taxation of *backbone* service. Several states, including Alabama, Florida, Illinois, Minnesota, Missouri, New Hampshire, Pennsylvania, and Washington, had been taxing such service claiming that it was not covered by the ITFA. The new language should prohibit this practice.

The definition of *Internet access* was expanded to include incidental services such as instant messaging, electronic mail, and personal electronic storage. The 2007 Act made it clear that it did *not* prohibit the inclusion of Internet access in the tax base of gross receipts taxes such as Washington's business and occupation tax, the Texas margin tax, and the Ohio commercial activity tax. It also did not prohibit sales tax in states that imposed tax on Internet access charges before the IFTA became law.

The ITFA also created an Advisory Commission that studied the federal, state and local, and international taxation and tariff treatment of transactions involving electronic commerce and Internet-related transactions. Although the Commission held several meetings and public hearings during its review period, it was unable to reach the required supermajority opinion on the substantive tax treatment of Internet sales.

Streamlined Sales Tax. The Streamlined Sales Tax (SST) may provide a more permanent solution to this vexing issue. The SST, which became operational on October 1, 2005, was developed by several states and state tax professional organizations with input from the private sector.

It addresses the complexity in state sales taxation, which has often been cited as a hindrance to federal legislation requiring mail order, Internet, and other remote sellers to collect the tax on their sales. The SST provides detailed definitions in Section 314 of the Agreement for sourcing telecommunication and related services. The SST Agreement provides for the following sourcing of telecommunications and related services in member states:

Section 314: TELECOMMUNICATION AND RELATED SERVICES SOURCING RULE 22

A. Except for the defined telecommunication services in subsection (C), the sale of telecommunication service sold on a call-by-call basis shall be sourced to (i) each level of taxing jurisdiction where the call originates and terminates in that jurisdiction or (ii) each level of taxing jurisdiction where the call either originates or terminates and in which the service address is also located.

B. Except for the defined telecommunication services in subsection (C), a sale of telecommunications services sold on a basis other than a call-by-call basis, is sourced to the customer's place of primary use.

C. The sale of the following telecommunication services shall be sourced to each level of taxing jurisdiction as follows:

1. A sale of mobile telecommunications services other than air-to-ground radio-telephone service and prepaid calling service, is sourced to the customer's place of primary use as required by the Mobile Telecommunications Sourcing Act.

2. A sale of post-paid calling service is sourced to the origination point of the telecommunications signal as first identified by either (i) the seller's telecommunications system, or (ii) information received by the seller from its service provider, where the system used to transport such signals is not that of the seller.

3. A sale of prepaid calling service or a sale of a prepaid wireless calling service is sourced in accordance with Section 310. Provided however, in the case of a sale of prepaid wireless calling service, the rule provided in Section 310, subsection (A) (5) shall include as an option the location associated with the mobile telephone number.

4. A sale of a private communication service is sourced as follows:

a. Service for a separate charge related to a customer channel termination point is sourced to each level of jurisdiction in which such customer channel termination point is located.

b. Service where all customer termination points are located entirely within one jurisdiction or levels of jurisdiction is sourced in such jurisdiction in which the customer channel termination points are located.

c. Service for segments of a channel between two customer channel termination points located in different jurisdictions and which segment of channel are separately charged is sourced 50 percent in each level of jurisdiction in which the customer channel termination points are located

d. Service for segments of a channel located in more than one jurisdiction or levels of jurisdiction and which segments are not separately billed is sourced in each jurisdiction based on the percentage determined by dividing the number of customer channel termination points in such jurisdiction by the total number of customer channel termination points.

D. The sale of Internet access service is sourced to the customer's place of primary use. E. The sale of an ancillary service is sourced to the customer's place of primary use.

When Sales of Telecommunications Services Are Subject to Tax

The fact that a service is included in a state's definition of telecommunications services does not mean that the service automatically is subject to sales and use tax. Although several states impose sales and use tax on intrastate, interstate, and international telecommunications services, many states impose tax only on intrastate services (i.e., services originating and terminating within the state).

To determine the taxability of a telecommunications service:

- Ascertain whether the service involves an intrastate, interstate, or international service.
- Review the state's statutes to determine the factors necessary for the state to impose sales and use tax on the service. Such factors generally include the locations (states) where the service originates and terminates, and the billing or service address to which the service is charged.

CAUTION

Because of the growth of Internet and wireless communications, the sales and use tax treatment of telecommunications services is likely to be a controversial issue in most states. Providers of telecommunications services should carefully monitor developments in this area.

CELL PHONES

As the use of cell phones continues to expand, the providers of cell phone service continue to offer new features and services to distinguish their service from that of other providers in hopes of gaining a competitive edge with consumers.

While much of the competitive pressures are exerted through enhanced basic features (such as additional minutes of talk time, expanded coverage areas, and free minutes of talk time), an increasing number of cell phone service providers are offering new, add-on features to broaden their appeal.

In addition to voice communications, many cell phone providers now offer Internet access and provide customers with the ability to download games and other features to their phones. This expansion of offerings provides more options for consumers, but it also increases the complexity of the taxation of cell phone usage and related charges.

STUDY QUESTION

> **3.** Which of the following is true based on SST Agreement Section 314?
>
> **a.** A sale of post-paid calling service is sourced to the destination point of the telecommunications signal.
>
> **b.** Private communication service for segments of a channel between two customer channel termination points located in different jurisdictions and that are separately charged is sourced 50 percent in each level of these jurisdictions.
>
> **c.** Internet access service is sourced to each jurisdiction in which the customer uses the service based on percentage of usage.

COMPUTER SOFTWARE

Overview

Initially, software costs were not differentiated from computer hardware costs at the point of sale. Because the purchase price was for *bundled* property, these software sales received the same sales tax treatment as that associated with tangible property.

In 1969 IBM segregated the costs of software from the costs of hardware, allowing for the separate tax treatment of software. In the same year, the Internal Revenue Service issued Revenue Procedure 69-21 [1969-2 C.B. 303 1], which provided for software sold in an *unbundled* form to be regarded as an intangible, thus denying the taxpayer the benefits of the investment tax credit or accelerated depreciation.

These developments opened a veritable Pandora's box for taxpayers and taxing jurisdictions alike, who found themselves forced to decide whether to classify computer software as tangible personal property subject to state sales and use tax or intangible intellectual property historically outside the scope of such taxes.

In today's state tax scheme, transactions involving computer software raise a variety of sales and use tax questions regarding the continuing dilemma of whether to impose tax on such transactions. Some of these questions include:

- What exactly is being purchased or sold?
- Is it an intangible right, or is it a service?
- Is the software canned or custom? Why does it matter?
- What if the software is not sold, but rather is licensed to a customer?
- What is the difference if the software is transmitted to a user electronically instead of by means of a disc?

Canned vs. Custom Software

Most of the states that have statutes or regulations on the taxability of software treat canned and custom software differently. Generally, canned software is taxable and custom software is *not* taxable. However, definitions of the two types of software vary greatly among the states.

Canned software. Canned software is generally defined as computer programs or other prewritten applications offered for general or repeated sale or lease. It is not created to the specifications of any particular user, but rather is designed for a wide range of users.

The most pervasive example of canned software is the off-the-shelf or shrink-wrapped software created and standardized for multiple users. Absent extenuating circumstances provided for in certain states, canned software that is transferred via a disc or other tangible medium is subject to tax in every state imposing a sales or use tax.

Custom software. Most states provide an exemption from sales and use taxes for some level of custom software. By definition, custom software generally embodies programs designed to the specification of a single user.

Some states may further expand the definition of custom software to include computer programs that are modified to a particular user's specifications, provided certain criteria or thresholds are met. Most states consider the purchase of *true* custom software to be the purchase of a service or intangible and, therefore, outside the imposition of sales and use tax in those states that do not tax services.

In many instances, the taxability of software that is somewhere between canned and custom will turn on the distinction of how the state at issue defines custom software.

Wisconsin Department of Revenue v. Menasha Corp. In a case that drew national attention, an integrated business application software system that had to be significantly modified before it could be used by the purchaser,

Menasha Corp., was ruled *exempt* from Wisconsin sales and use tax as custom software by the Wisconsin Supreme Court [Wis. 754 N.W.2d 95, July 11, 2008].

Custom programs. A Wisconsin rule defines *custom programs* as utility and application software that accommodates the special processing needs of the customer. At one time, the State of Wisconsin applied the following factors to the determination of whether a software program is a custom program. (While the factors are no longer formally used, they nevertheless provide an excellent guideline to utilize in making canned or prewritten versus custom software distinctions.)

1. The extent to which the vendor or independent consultant engages in significant presale consultation and analysis of the user's requirements and system
2. Whether the program is loaded into the customer's computer by the vendor and the extent to which the installed program must be tested against the program's specifications
3. The extent to which the use of the software requires substantial written documentation and training of the customer's personnel
4. The extent to which the enhancement and maintenance support by the vendor are needed for continued usefulness
5. The rebuttable presumption that any program with a cost of $10,000 or less is not a custom program
6. Custom programs do not include basic operational programs.
7. If an existing program is selected for modification, there must be a significant modification of that program by the vendor so that it may be used in the customer's specific hardware and software environment.

Prewritten programs. Wisconsin also defines *prewritten programs* as programs prepared, held, or existing for general use normally for more than one customer, including programs developed for in-house use or custom program use that are subsequently held or offered for sale or lease.

In *Menasha*, the purchaser bought a modular software system made up of standard software modules. The seller mass marketed this system to thousands of different businesses, and the system always had to be modified to fit a client's particular business needs.

The seller and various consultants made over 3,000 modifications to the purchaser's software before the purchaser could use it as intended. The system was delivered to the purchaser on multiple CD-ROM disks.

Implementation of the system on a subsidiary-by-subsidiary basis took almost seven years to complete. The core software system cost $5.2 million, but, with installation and modifications, the total cost of the system was more than $23 million.

The Wisconsin Supreme Court held that the Wisconsin Tax Appeals Commission's decision that the software was a custom program was reasonable. The commission had determined that it was custom software because the purchaser made significant investments in presale:

- Consultation and analysis
- Testing
- Training
- Written documentation
- Enhancement
- Maintenance support

The significant cost of the system also weighed in favor of a finding that the software was custom software. The commission also determined, and the Supreme Court agreed, that the software system was *not* a prewritten program. The Supreme Court stated that a *prewritten program* is one that is ready to be used right off the shelf and does not require significant modifications in order for the purchaser to use the program. In this case, the software system was useless until it was modified. The modifications performed to make the software usable were time-consuming and expensive, and thus significant.

The commission also determined, and the Supreme Court agreed, that the software system was not available for general use and, therefore, could not be considered prewritten software.

Cloud computing. Cloud computing is one of the hottest topics in the information technology (IT) world and likely to become an equally hot topic in tax circles as well. Cloud computing has been defined as the offering of applications and services over the Internet. All that is needed to access the application or service is an Internet connection.

Chances are you have visited a cloud computing site without even realizing it. For example, if you periodically visit a social networking site, you are using a cloud computing application. An online computer backup service is another common cloud computing service. But from a business perspective, cloud computing is much more than an opportunity to exchange pictures or catch up with old friends. Cloud computing offers the business community an opportunity to streamline its IT function and reduce costs without sacrificing service. To do that, cloud computing providers offer a wide variety to services over the Internet.

The following are three of the more commonly used cloud computing services by businesses:

- Infrastructure-as-a-service—This is a service providing virtual servers with unique IP addresses and blocks of storage on demand.
- Platform-as-a-service—A set of software and product development tools are hosted on the provider's infrastructure.

- Software-as-a-service—Vendors supply hardware infrastructure, software, and a front-end portal by which the user interacts with the provider.

Acquiring these services over the Internet as opposed to investing in the hardware and software for in-house systems provides the user with the necessary hardware, software, and technical tools without having to make the huge investment in equipment, software, and personnel to maintain them. However, in terms of the sales tax system, the question becomes whether the transaction has been sufficiently recharacterized to avoid tax imposition on otherwise taxable items, such as hardware and canned software.

So, for businesses and individuals alike, cloud computing affords an opportunity to maintain their IT capabilities at a fraction of the cost. Businesses wishing to leverage their IT expenditures through cloud computing need to weigh these savings against the loss of control, data security issues, and so on, before making a final decision to source these services from a "cloud."

The tax issues associated with cloud computing are just starting to emerge. The key issue associated with cloud computing is whether the customer is purchasing tangible personal property or a service. If the customer is purchasing a service, then it depends upon whether the service is determined to be a taxable service or not. At present, many states appear to be taking the position that cloud computing is a service and therefore taxed only if it is enumerated in the statute. As the use of cloud computing expands and the offerings become broader in scope, it remains to be seen whether the states will continue this treatment.

Of course, if cloud computing is deemed to be a taxable service, it opens up a number of issues for consideration, including:

- Where is the service performed—the customer's location, service provider's location, or server location where programs actually run?
- Is that service considered taxable in the state? Is it specifically enumerated in the statute or otherwise defined as taxable?
- Does the service provider have nexus in the customer's state for other taxes beyond sales and use tax if it is in fact subject to sales and use taxes on the sale of these services?

Streamlined Sales Tax. It should also be noted that the SST contains uniform definitions for software and other common computer-related purchases. States opting to be part of SST would be required to adopt these definitions in lieu of their current statutes. Once adopted, however, a state could choose whether to tax or exempt any category adopted.

Under the SST, *prewritten computer software* means computer software, including prewritten upgrades, that is not designed and developed by the author or other creator to the specifications of a specific purchaser. The combining of two or more prewritten computer software programs or prewritten portions thereof does not cause the combination to be other than prewritten computer software. Prewritten computer software includes software designed and developed by the author or other creator to the specifications of a specific purchaser when it is sold to a person other than the specific purchaser.

Where a person modifies or enhances computer software of which the person is not the author or creator, the person shall be deemed to be the author or creator only of such person's modifications or enhancements. Prewritten computer software or a prewritten portion thereof that is modified or enhanced to any degree, where such modification or enhancement is designed and developed to the specifications of a specific purchaser, remains prewritten computer software if there is a reasonable, separately stated charge or an invoice or other statement of the price given to the purchaser for such modification or enhancement. Otherwise, such modification or enhancement shall not constitute prewritten computer software.

STUDY QUESTION

---

4. Most states *exempt* the sale of canned software from sales and use tax. **True or False?**

Licensing Agreements

The legal form of a software transaction may ultimately affect how the transaction is taxed in many states, irrespective of its similarity in substance to a transaction form that has a different sales tax consequence. A sale of software, where title passes to the purchaser, is generally subject to tax— unless the sale involves custom software, as noted above.

Generally, a *software licensing agreement* is defined as the contractual right to use software written by another party. Under such an agreement, the title to the software does not pass to the licensee, and the licensee is typically subject to restrictions on the use or reproduction of the licensed software. Software licensing agreements are generally treated as taxable sales of tangible personal property, unless the licensed software is custom software.

> **EXAMPLE**
>
> Virginia has ruled that a distributor of computer products must pay use tax on a computer software license agreement under which the distributor is conveyed the right to use master copies of the licenser's software.

Intangible Transmission

One of the arguments advanced by states for the taxation of computer software is the method of conveyance has traditionally been through tangible means, such as CDs, DVDs, discs, and magnetic tapes. As such, the transfer of the underlying software, transferred via CD, DVD, and so on, constitutes the sale of tangible personal property subject to tax.

In the past, the taxability of the transaction could be impacted by eliminating the transfer of any tangible personal property. So, for example, downloading otherwise taxable software by electronic means in some states was *not* considered the transfer of tangible personal property and therefore was not subject to sales and use taxes. As the use of downloads has expanded in recent years with the growth of Internet commerce, many states have adopted the so-called digital equivalent doctrine. The digital equivalent doctrine says that any downloaded item or transaction should be treated like its equivalent tangible item for sales tax application. So, for example, the purchasing of an e-book over the Internet should fundamentally be treated no differently than the sale of a hard-copy book at a shopping mall. However, not all states are necessarily adopting that policy.

New York State recently ruled in TSB-M-11(5)S (NYS Dept of Taxation & Finance, April 7, 2011) that e-books meeting all the following conditions are nontaxable:

- The purchase cannot entitle the customer to additional goods and services from the vendor, and any revisions to the e-book are made solely to correct errors.
- The e-book must be provided as a single download.
- The product must be advertised or marketed as an e-book.
- If the intended use of the product requires that it be updated or revised, any updates or new editions cannot be issued more frequently than annually.
- The product must be designated only to work with software necessary to make the e-book readable.

Other Exemptions

Taxing jurisdictions may provide exemptions for otherwise taxable software under other exempt criteria. Several states, recognizing the emerging importance of software in managing manufacturing machinery and equipment, have specifically enumerated certain types of software used in manufacturing production as exempt manufacturing machinery and equipment.

Even in states where software is not specifically enumerated as *manufacturing equipment*, an argument to expand the exemption for manufacturing machinery and equipment to software involved in manufacturing may be available.

Other states have provided specific exemptions for software used in research and development or in the production of additional software or related operating systems for resale. In any event, it is evident that otherwise taxable software used in special applications may well be exempt in certain jurisdictions. Accordingly, even canned software may not be subject to tax when used in specific applications, or by otherwise exempt entities.

PLANNING POINTER

While the distinction between canned or prewritten and custom software can be crucial in determining the incidence of sales and use taxation, many states provide scant guidelines to taxpayers seeking to make such a determination. Because of the variety of software and the diverse uses to which it can be put, consistently segregating it between canned and custom can be a daunting task. Although most states do not provide definitive guidelines, the following factors are generally applied in varying degrees to make the determination:

- Degree of presale consultation and defining of user needs
- Amount of new base code language written for a specific program
- The relative cost and selling price of the program
- Degree of modification to existing program
- Availability of software to other users through licensing or purchase agreements
- General business activity of software provider
- Degree of support for installation, training, and maintenance of software

Using these factors as a guideline, taxpayers should be in a better position to evaluate the taxation of their software purchases.

Master Copies

It has become commonplace for a business to purchase a master copy of computer software, retain possession of it, and then distribute copies of it to offices around the country. The following questions then arise:

- Does this distribution create a taxable event and if so, in which state?
- Is the distribution taxable in the state where the copy is initiated, or is it taxable in the state where the copy is distributed, or both?
- Does the storage of the software before the distribution of the copies constitute a taxable event in the state of storage?
- If the software is determined to be taxable, at what value should the tax be imposed?
- Should it be taxed based on the pro rata value of the software distributed in the state, or is the entire purchase price of the master copy of the software subject to tax in the state?

Depending upon the answer to these questions, there could be a significantly different tax liability on the transaction.

STUDY QUESTION

5. Which one of the following statements is true?
   a. Many states have adopted the so-called digital equivalent doctrine.
   b. There are a number of states where licensing software electronically for use over a limited period of time is *not* taxable if delivered by a tangible means.
   c. The SST takes the position that electronic purchases are *not* the same as purchasing a tangible item.

CPE NOTE: When you have completed your study and review of chapters 5-8, which comprise Module 2, you may wish to take the Quizzer for this Module.

For your convenience, you can also take this Quizzer online at **www.CCHGroup.com/TestingCenter**.

Answers to Study Questions

MODULE 1 — CHAPTER 1

1. a. *Incorrect*. Most states, including Alabama, impose a corporate income tax.
b. *Incorrect*. The California corporate franchise tax is computed essentially in the same manner as an income tax.
c. *Incorrect*. Although Florida does not levy a personal income tax, it does impose a corporate income tax.
d. *Correct*. South Dakota is one of only a handful of states that do not levy a corporate income tax.

2. a. *Incorrect*. This is a limitation of Public Law 86-272. For example, Public Law 86-272 provides no protection against the imposition of a sales tax collection obligation.
b. *Correct*. This is not a limitation of Public Law 86-272. Public Law 86-272 protects only sales of *tangible* personal property. It *does not* protect activities such as leasing tangible personal property, selling services, selling or leasing real estate, or selling or licensing intangibles.
c. *Incorrect*. This is a limitation of Public Law 86-272. If a salesperson exercises authority to approve orders within a state, or performs nonsolicitation activities, such as repairs, customer training, or technical assistance, the company does not qualify for protection under Public Law 86-272.

3. a. *Correct*. Conformity with federal provisions simplifies tax compliance for multistate corporations. Using the federal tax base as the starting point for calculating state taxable income is known as "piggybacking."
b. *Incorrect*. This is a disadvantage of state conformity to federal tax provisions. Changes to the federal tax law can significantly affect state tax revenues if there is conformity to federal tax provisions.
c. *Incorrect*. This is a disadvantage of state conformity to federal tax provisions. Complete conformity would allow the federal government to control a state's tax policy.

4. a. *Incorrect*. This is a true statement. All or some of UDITPA principles have been adopted by most states.
b. *Incorrect*. This is a true statement. Under UDITPA, business income is income from transactions and activity in the regular course of the taxpayer's trade or business. It includes income from tangible and intangible property

if the acquisition, management, and disposition of the property are integral parts of the taxpayer's regular trade or business operations. Nonbusiness income is all income that is not business income.

c. Correct. This is not a true statement. Under UDITPA, a taxpayer must apportion a percentage of its business income to each state in which it has nexus, but must allocate the entire amount of any nonbusiness income to a single state.

5. True. Incorrect. Assigning more weight to the sales factor than to the property or payroll factor tends to *increase* the percentage of an out-of-state corporation's income that is subject to tax, because the out-of-state corporation's principal activity in the state is likely its sales, and it may have little or no property or payroll in the state.

False. Correct. Assigning more weight to the sales factor tends to reduce the tax on *in-state* corporations that have significant amounts of property and payroll in the state but have sales throughout the country.

6. a. Incorrect. This only applies to sales to the U.S. government and so-called throwback sales, both of which are assigned to the state from which the goods are shipped.

b. Correct. This is known as the destination test.

c. Incorrect. Certain types of nonbusiness income, such as nonbusiness interest and dividend income, is assigned to the state of commercial domicile, but this is not where sales of tangible personal property are generally assigned.

7. a. Correct. Arizona generally requires a taxpayer member of a unitary business group to compute its taxable income on a combined unitary basis.

b. Incorrect. Delaware is one of a handful of states that requires separate-company returns under all circumstances.

c. Incorrect. Maryland requires separate-company reporting. In contrast, most states require or permit some type of consolidated or combined reporting.

8. True. Incorrect. Inclusion in a combined unitary report generally requires more than 50 percent ownership; however, inclusion in a state consolidated return generally requires 80 percent or more ownership.

False. Correct. Inclusion in a state consolidated return generally requires 80 percent or more ownership, which piggybacks on the ownership threshold for inclusion in a federal consolidated return.

9. a. *Correct.* **Nonsolicitation activities are not protected by Public Law 86-272, and generally create income tax nexus.**
b. *Incorrect.* Solicitation activities are protected by Public Law 86-272, and generally do not create income tax nexus.
c. *Incorrect.* Providing a sales representative with a company car that is used only in solicitation activities is protected by Public Law 86-272, and generally does not create income tax nexus.

10. True. *Incorrect.* Although filing a consolidated return can be beneficial, such as when one affiliate has losses that can be offset against the income generated by other affiliates, there can also be disadvantages that should be considered before making that election.
False. *Correct.* **There are advantages to filing a consolidated return, but there are also disadvantages. One disadvantage is that filing a consolidated return can limit a taxpayer's ability to use intercompany transactions to shift income from affiliates based in high-tax states to affiliates based in low-tax states.**

11. a. *Incorrect.* In *Geoffrey,* the South Carolina Supreme Court held that a trademark holding company that licensed its intangibles for use in South Carolina had nexus for income tax purposes despite the lack of any physical presence in South Carolina.
b. *Incorrect.* In *Lanco,* the New Jersey Supreme Court ruled that the Delaware trademark holding company of Lane Bryant had income tax nexus in New Jersey, even though it had no physical presence there.
c. *Incorrect.* In *MBNA,* the West Virginia Supreme Court of Appeals found that the physical presence test does not apply to state corporate income taxes, and that MBNA had "a significant economic presence sufficient to meet the substantial nexus" test under the Commerce Clause.
d. *Correct.* **In *Quill,* the U.S. Supreme Court ruled that the taxpayer did not have constitutional nexus for sales and use tax purposes because it lacked a physical presence in the state.**

12. a. *Incorrect.* The Ohio Supreme Court determined in *SFA Folio* that common ownership alone does not create nexus for an out-of-state affiliate. Other state courts have generally agreed.
b. *Correct.* **State courts in Illinois, Michigan, and New York have adopted the "more than a slightest presence" test, under which a company's in-state physical presence need not be substantial to satisfy the *Quill* "substantial nexus" requirement. Instead, it must be "demonstrably more than a slightest presence."**

c. Incorrect. State supreme courts in Massachusetts and Virginia have determined that deliveries in company-owned trucks constitute a protected activity under Public Law 86-272.

13. a. Incorrect. This result assumes that the sale is allocated pro-rata based on the percentage of actual performance in each state, which is not how the UDITPA cost-of-performance rule works.

b. Incorrect. This result assumes that the sale is evenly distributed to all states in which costs were incurred, which is not how the UDITPA cost-of-performance rule works.

c. Correct. The UDITPA cost-of-performance rule attributes the entire sale to the state in which the greater proportion of the costs of performance is incurred.

14. True. Correct. Under the market-based approach, receipts from services are generally attributed to the state in which the benefit of the service is received. This approach provides a more accurate measure of the taxpayer's customer base, and has the political appeal of reducing the tax burden on service providers that have in-state facilities but provide services primarily to out-of-state customers.

False. Incorrect. Under the market-based approach, receipts from services are generally attributed to the state in which the benefit of the service is received. Examples of states that have adopted this approach for sales of services include Georgia, Illinois, Iowa, Maine, Maryland, Michigan, Minnesota, Utah, and Wisconsin.

15. a. Correct. Separate-company reporting can provide taxpayers with opportunities to shift income through intercompany royalty and interest payments. For this reason, combined reporting, as opposed to separate-company reporting, is used as a mechanism by the states to limit tax base erosion.

b. Incorrect. This mechanism is used by states because combined reporting eliminates the tax benefits of intercompany transactions, such as royalty and interest payments.

c. Incorrect. The highest courts in several states have ruled that an economic presence, such as the licensing of trademarks for use within the state by affiliated companies, is sufficient to create constitutional nexus for income tax purposes. This mechanism limits the ability of taxpayers to shift income to out-of-state intangible property holding companies.

MODULE 1 — CHAPTER 2

1. a. *Correct.* Federal law permits a two-year carryback. A federal-state NOL difference may arise if the *state* has no provision for NOL carrybacks.

b. *Incorrect.* The federal government allows a 20-year carryforward. Some states have shorter carryforward periods, which can result in a federal-state NOL deduction difference.

c. *Incorrect.* If there are differences in federal and state group filing methods, this can create an NOL deduction difference. Other reasons for NOL deduction differences between federal and state returns include state statutory limitations on the amount of carryover permitted, and the effect state apportionment may have on the state NOL deduction.

2. True. *Correct.* Under the pre-apportionment method, the full amount of the loss year's NOL is offset against income in the carryforward year, and then the carryforward year apportionment percentage is applied to the net amount of apportionable income. Thus, if the apportionment percentage is higher in the carryforward year than in the loss year, the benefit of the NOL carryforward deduction is greater if the state uses the pre-apportionment method.

False. *Incorrect.* The value of the NOL deduction is based on the carryforward year apportionment percentage if the *pre-apportionment* method is used, and the loss year apportionment percentage if the *post-apportionment* method is used. Thus, if the apportionment percentage is higher in the carryforward year, the NOL deduction is more valuable if the state uses the *pre-apportionment* method.

3. a. *Correct.* Code Sec. 269 is the IRS's broadest and oldest weapon used to counter NOL trafficking. It permits the IRS to disallow a carryforward NOL deduction if the principal purpose for one corporation to acquire another corporation is to claim the benefit of the deduction.

b. *Incorrect.* Code Sec. 382 limits the amount of the deduction to the hypothetical future income that would be generated by the loss corporation, but it is not the IRS's oldest weapon against NOL trafficking.

c. *Incorrect.* Code Sec. 383 extends restrictions similar to those found in Code Sec. 382 to other types of carryovers, but it is not the IRS's oldest weapon against NOL trafficking.

d. *Incorrect.* Code Sec. 384 prevents a corporation with unrealized built-in gains from acquiring a loss corporation for the purpose of using that corporation's pre-acquisition NOLs to offset its built-in gains, but Code Sec. 384 is not the IRS's oldest weapon against NOL trafficking.

4. a. Incorrect. The decision in *American Home Products Corp.* involved a state restriction that a surviving corporation may *not* claim an NOL deduction if the year in which the predecessor incurred the NOL was not a year in which the predecessor was an Ohio taxpayer.

b. Correct. In *BellSouth Telecommunications, Inc.*, the North Carolina Court of Appeals would *not* allow a corporation to deduct a pre-merger net economic loss of a former subsidiary, because the merged corporation was *not* a continuing business enterprise.

c. Incorrect. In *Richard's Auto City, Inc.*, NOLs generated by a corporation, which had merged into a surviving corporation, were *not* deductible by the surviving corporation because it was not the same corporation that originally incurred the loss.

5. a. Incorrect. Colorado does not allow *any* carryback NOL deductions.

b. Incorrect. Iowa has eliminated its previous two-year carryback, beginning with NOLs incurred in tax years starting on or after January 1, 2009.

c. Correct. California has enacted legislation that provides a two-year carryback of NOLs, starting in 2013.

MODULE 1 — CHAPTER 3

1. a. Incorrect. A primary goal of income tax treaties is to reduce or eliminate withholding taxes on investment-type income derived by residents of one treaty country from sources within the other treaty country.

b. Correct. A primary goal of income tax treaties is to lessen international double taxation through tax reductions or exemptions on certain types of income derived by residents of one treaty country from sources within the other treaty country.

c. Incorrect. Tax treaty benefits are offered only to a treaty country *resident*—generally defined as any person who, under the country's internal laws, is subject to taxation by reason of domicile, residence, citizenship, place of management, place of incorporation, or other criterion of a similar nature.

2. a. Correct. This is possible because, in contrast to the tax treaty standard that requires a permanent establishment, state income tax nexus standards generally require a physical presence within the state that is not protected by Public Law 86-272.

b. Incorrect. The Due Process Clause and Commerce Clause of the U.S. Constitution both limit a state's ability to impose a tax obligation on an out-of-state corporation.

c. Incorrect. In *Quill*, the Supreme Court determined that a physical presence is required for sales and use tax nexus, but did *not* address the issue of whether physical presence is required for income tax nexus.

3. True. *Incorrect.* Public Law 86-272 does not apply to gross receipts taxes such as the Ohio commercial activity tax or the Washington business and occupation tax.

False. *Correct.* Public Law 86-272 applies only to net income taxes and does not provide protection against the imposition of a sales and use tax collection obligation, gross receipts taxes, or corporate franchise taxes on net worth or capital.

4. a. *Incorrect.* State courts in numerous states, including Iowa, Massachusetts, New Jersey, South Carolina, and West Virginia, have ruled that an economic presence can be sufficient to create income tax nexus.

b. *Correct.* An example of a factor presence nexus standard is in-state sales that exceed the lesser of $500,000 or 25 percent of the out-of-state corporation's total sales.

c. *Incorrect.* Since the South Carolina Supreme Court's 1993 ruling in *Geoffrey*, numerous states have enacted economic nexus standards for income tax purposes.

5. a. *Correct.* In *Scripto,* the U.S. Supreme Court stated that "to permit such formal 'contractual shifts' to make a constitutional difference would open the gates to a stampede of tax avoidance."

b. *Incorrect.* In *Scripto,* the U.S. Supreme Court held that this is a critical test for determining nexus.

c. *Incorrect.* In *Scripto,* the U.S. Supreme Court ruled that the use of independent agents to perform in-state solicitation activities created constitutional nexus for an out-of-state principal.

MODULE 1 — CHAPTER 4

1. a. *Incorrect.* Due to fiscal constraints, many states do not conform to the Code Sec. 199 deduction.

b. *Incorrect.* Although conforming to the federal Code Sec. 199 deduction costs states money, they do not all reject conformity.

c. *Correct.* Many but not all states require corporations to add back the Code Sec. 199 deduction in computing state taxable income.

2. a. *Incorrect.* Although states are prohibited from imposing a direct income tax on interest earned from federal obligations, such interest is included in federal taxable income.

b. *Correct.* The federal government exempts interest on all municipal bonds, and most states exempt interest paid on the state's own bonds.

c. *Incorrect.* Although the federal government exempts interest on all municipal bonds, many states tax interest received on municipal bonds issued by other states.

3. True. *Incorrect.* States that impose a direct corporate income tax must exempt from tax any interest earned on federal obligations. However, states that impose a nondiscriminatory corporate franchise tax are *not* prohibited from taxing federal interest.

False. *Correct.* **States that impose a nondiscriminatory corporate franchise tax are *not* barred from taxing federal interest, even if the value of the franchise is measured by net income.**

4. a. *Incorrect.* This is a common addition modification. States generally do not allow taxpayers to deduct state income taxes, and an addback is required because those taxes are deducted in calculating federal taxable income.

b. *Correct.* **Interest income on federal debt obligations is included in federal taxable income and is not a common addition modification. However, it is a common subtraction modification.**

c. *Incorrect.* This is a common addition modification. Many states do not allow federal bonus depreciation, so it must be added back to federal taxable income.

5. a. *Incorrect.* Although most states use federal taxable income as the starting point for computing state taxable income, each state has its own unique list of modifications to federal taxable income.

b. *Incorrect.* If the state adjusted basis is higher than the federal adjusted basis and the asset is sold, a subtraction modification is required upon the sale of the asset.

c. *Correct.* **These expenses are generally added back to prevent an unwarranted net tax benefit that would otherwise arise because the related income is exempt.**

6. a. *Correct.* **To prevent a double federal tax benefit, a U.S. parent must gross up its foreign dividend income by the amount of the Code Sec. 902 deemed paid foreign taxes.**

b. *Incorrect.* To close potential loopholes created by deferral, the Subpart F provisions subject certain types of undistributed foreign earnings of a controlled foreign corporation to immediate U.S. taxation.

c. *Incorrect.* The DRD prevents the imposition of multiple layers of U.S. corporate-level tax on the same underlying earnings.

7. a. *Correct.* **In the case of an affiliated group of corporations filing a federal consolidated return, the computation of a state NOL deduction may be complicated by the use of different group filing methods (e.g., separate company returns or combined unitary reporting) for state tax purposes.**

b. Incorrect. This statement is true. The same addition and subtraction modifications used to determine state taxable income generally must be reflected in the NOL calculation.

c. Incorrect. This statement is true. A number of states have carryforward periods that are shorter than 20 years.

8. a. Incorrect. This is a reason why there may be a federal-state NOL deduction difference. The amount of the state NOL deduction can vary considerably with the methodology (pre- or post-apportionment) used by the state.

b. Incorrect. This is a reason why there may be a federal-state NOL deduction difference. Some states impose flat-dollar or percentage limitations on NOL carryover deductions.

c. Correct. A federal-state NOL deduction difference may arise because some *states* do not allow carrybacks. For federal tax purposes, however, Code Sec. 172 permits taxpayers to carry an NOL back two years.

9. a. Incorrect. A *member* of a controlled group of corporations, as defined under Code Sec. 1563, is generally included in the definition of a related member.

b. Incorrect. A member of an *affiliated group* of corporations, as defined under Code Sec. 1504, is generally included in the definition of a related member.

c. Correct. An entity that owns *less than* 50 percent of the taxpayer's stock is generally not a related member.

10. True. Correct. To close perceived loopholes, many states require a corporation to add back to federal taxable income any royalties or interest expense paid to related parties.

False. Incorrect. This statement is true. Related party expense addback provisions are designed to close perceived loopholes associated with separate company returns and the use of intangible property holding companies.

MODULE 2 — CHAPTER 5

1. a. Incorrect. *National Bellas Hess* is a use tax case.

b. Incorrect. *Quill* is a case dealing with use taxes.

c. Correct. In *Wrigley,* the U.S. Supreme Court dealt with whether the taxpayer's activities in Wisconsin caused it to have income tax nexus with the state.

2. a. Correct. With respect to nexus, the Supreme Court has interpreted the Commerce Clause as prohibiting a state from taxing an out-of-state corporation unless that company has *substantial nexus* with the state.

b. _Incorrect._ With respect to nexus, the Supreme Court has interpreted the Due Process Clause as prohibiting a state from taxing an out-of-state corporation unless there is a _minimal connection_ between the company's interstate activities and the taxing state.

c. _Incorrect._ Public Law 86-272 allows taxpayers to engage in certain protected activities without triggering the imposition of income tax.

3. a. _Incorrect._ This activity was considered entirely ancillary to solicitation by the Court because it served no purpose, apart from facilitating requests for purchases.

b. _Incorrect._ The Supreme Court considered this activity as falling within its definition of solicitation, which encompassed "those activities that are entirely ancillary to requests for purchases—those that serve no independent business function apart from their connection to the soliciting of orders."

c. _Correct._ The Supreme Court found that storage of inventory (in this case, gum) within the state was _not_ ancillary to Wrigley's solicitation activities.

d. _Incorrect._ The use of hotels and homes in the state for sales-related meetings was considered by the Supreme Court to be an activity that was ancillary to the solicitation of sales.

4. a. _Incorrect._ Solicitation of orders is a _protected_ activity as is the passing on of orders, inquiries, and complaints to the home office.

b. _Correct._ Although solicitation of orders by a salesperson is considered a protected activity, order approval by a salesperson in the state is unprotected.

c. _Incorrect._ Furnishing and setting up display racks and advising customers on the display of the company's products without charge or other consideration is a protected activity under the MTC's policy statement, as is checking customers' inventories for reorder without charge.

5. a. _Correct._ Maintaining a sample or display room for two weeks or less at any one location within a state during a tax year is a protected activity under the MTC's policy statement.

b. _Incorrect._ Collecting payment on a current or delinquent account, whether directly or by third parties, is considered an unprotected activity.

c. _Incorrect._ Repossessing property as well as picking up or replacing returned property is considered an unprotected activity under the MTC's policy statement.

6. True. _Correct._ Court decisions indicate that the relative value of a company's in-state property, the number of in-state employees, or the relative amount of sales made in the state may not be determinative if

the company is otherwise found to have activities in the state that are more than *de minimis.*
False. *Incorrect.* The U.S. Supreme Court noted in *Quill* that the slightest presence in the state does not meet the substantial nexus requirements of the Commerce Clause, but did not define how much physical presence is necessary to establish substantial nexus.

7. True. *Correct.* However, many states provide targeted exemptions for selected activities that would otherwise create nexus.
False. *Incorrect.* The statement is true. However, states must provide the protections afforded taxpayers under the U.S. Constitution and Public Law 86-272.

8. a. *Incorrect.* The bulletin takes the position that this type of activity *does* create nexus.
b. *Incorrect.* Only a handful of states, including California, have taken a position contrary to that in Nexus Bulletin 95-1.
c. *Incorrect.* The position taken in the bulletin is not based on *Quill.* In *Quill,* the Supreme Court upheld the bright-line physical presence test.
d. *Correct.* The position taken in the bulletin is based on the Supreme Court's decisions in *Scripto* and *Tyler Pipe,* both of which dealt with the use of independent sales representatives, as opposed to independent service providers.

9. a. *Incorrect.* In *Borders Online,* the California Court of Appeals ruled that an out-of-state online retailer *had substantial nexus* in California for sales tax purposes because an affiliated corporation, which sold similar products in stores in California, performed return and exchange activities for the online retailer.
b. *Incorrect.* In *Reader's Digest Association,* the California Court of Appeals held that Reader's Digest *had* income tax nexus with California because of solicitation activities performed by its wholly owned in-state subsidiary.
c. *Incorrect.* In *Dillard National Bank,* the Tennessee Chancery Court ruled that an out-of-state subsidiary corporation that issued proprietary credit cards for use in a chain of in-state department stores that were operated by the parent corporation had income tax nexus in Tennessee.
d. *Correct.* In *J.C. Penney National Bank,* the Tennessee Court of Appeals rejected the affiliate nexus argument because the in-state retail stores did not conduct any activities that assisted the affiliated out-of-state bank in maintaining its credit card business in Tennessee.

10. a. *Correct.* The Supreme Court also noted in the *Scripto* decision that "to permit such formal 'contractual shifts' to make a constitutional difference would open the gates to a stampede of tax avoidance."

b. Incorrect. *Reader's Digest Association* is a California case in which the Court of Appeals held that an out-of-state parent corporation had nexus as a result of solicitation activities performed by its wholly owned in-state subsidiary.

c. Incorrect. *Kmart Properties, Inc.* is a New Mexico intangible holding company case.

d. Incorrect. *Share International, Inc.* is a Florida case in which the state Supreme Court upheld a district court's *insufficient nexus* decision.

11. a. Incorrect. This is also known as back-hauling and is likely *not* protected under Public Law 86-272.

b. Incorrect. A delivery truck driver collecting payments is likely *not* a protected activity under Public Law 86-272 because it exceeds solicitation of sales.

c. Correct. Also, the Texas Comptroller of Public Accounts has held that a taxpayer could claim immunity from the earned surplus portion of the Texas franchise tax under Public Law 86-272 even though the taxpayer delivered tangible personal property into Texas using company-owned trucks.

12. a. Incorrect. In this case, the South Carolina Supreme Court held that a trademark holding company that licensed its intangibles for use in South Carolina had nexus for income tax purposes despite the lack of any tangible property or employees in South Carolina.

b. Incorrect. In this case, the North Carolina Court of Appeals held that licensing intangibles for use in North Carolina was sufficient to establish income tax nexus for an out-of-state trademark holding company.

c. Incorrect. In this case, the Oklahoma Court of Civil Appeals ruled that licensing intangibles for use in Oklahoma was sufficient to establish income tax nexus for a Delaware trademark holding company, even though the holding company had no physical presence in Oklahoma.

d. Correct. In this case, the Missouri Supreme Court ruled that two trademark holding companies were not subject to the Missouri corporate income tax because they did not have any payroll, property, or sales in Missouri.

13. a. Incorrect. In addition to the presence of property, another factor that helps to *support* nexus is the negotiation or execution of the lease agreement in the state.

b. Incorrect. Nexus may be established for the lessor because of the in-state presence of owned business property. Another factor that helps to support nexus is the receipt of the rental payments in the state.

c. *Correct.* **For leased mobile property (e.g., airplanes and other transportation vehicles), many states provide that an isolated landing or trip through the state will not create nexus.**
d. *Incorrect.* In the case of leased property that is immobile, the creation of nexus generally is easy to identify because the lessor is informed of the state in which the property is expected to be located during the rental period.

14. a. *Correct.* **In *Bandag Licensing Corp. v. Rylander,* the Texas appeals court determined that under *Quill,* a state may *not* constitutionally impose its corporate franchise tax on an out-of-state corporation that lacks a physical presence in the state.**
b. *Incorrect.* In *Kelly-Springfield Tire Co.* (1993), the *Connecticut* Supreme Court also ruled that the authority to do business does *not* deny a corporation the protections afforded by Public Law 86-272.
c. *Incorrect.* In *Kelly-Springfield Tire Co.* (1994), the *Massachusetts* Supreme Judicial Court ruled that the authority to do business in a state is *not* a separate business activity that creates nexus.
d. *Incorrect.* In *LSDHC Corp.,* the Ohio Board of Tax Appeals ruled that registration to do business alone was *not* sufficient to create nexus for Ohio's corporate franchise tax on net income.

15. a. *Incorrect.* This statement is true. Treaty permanent establishment provisions are *not* binding for state nexus purposes because income tax treaties generally do not apply to state taxes.
b. *Correct.* **The Internet Tax Freedom Act imposed a three-year moratorium on any "new" state or local taxes on Internet access. Subsequent legislation extended the moratorium.**
c. *Incorrect.* This statement is true. Another potential solution is more uniform and simplified state and local tax systems.

MODULE 2 — CHAPTER 6

1. a. *Incorrect.* Contractors are treated as *consumers* of incorporated materials when they install tangible personal property. Since they are consumers of the materials, they are subject to tax on the cost of those materials.
b. *Incorrect.* Whether a contractor is treated as a *subcontractor* is irrelevant.
c. *Correct.* **Contractors frequently act as retailers when they resell tangible personal property but do not install it, or when they install it in a way so that it retains its character as tangible personal property. When contactors act as retailers, they are required to collect tax from any taxable purchasers.**

2. True. *Incorrect.* If the machine is independent of the real estate in function, it tends to retain its character as tangible personal property, and would not be considered part of the real estate even after installation.

False. *Correct.* A machine may be attached to a building but, if it performs functions independently from the real estate, it is not considered part of the real estate.

3. a. *Correct.* Industrial machinery and equipment are usually exempt from tax as long as specific requirements are met. An example of some state requirements is that the machinery and equipment be used directly in the manufacturing operation.

b. *Incorrect.* Most states insist that industrial machinery be used directly in the manufacturing process in order to obtain an exemption. Indirect use usually does *not* qualify.

c. *Incorrect.* Most states require that machinery and equipment be used primarily, predominantly or exclusively in the manufacturing process to be exempt from sales tax. Primary or predominant use ordinarily means greater than 50 percent utilization in the production process. Exclusive use is usually considered to be 100 percent utilization in the manufacturing process, but a *de minimis* nonmanufacturing use is often allowed.

d. *Incorrect.* The opposite is true. Many states require sales tax on returnable shipping containers but not on nonreturnable shipping containers.

4. a. *Correct.* Many states do have special provisions allowing a sales and use tax exemption on the sale of equipment and materials to taxpayers engaged in farming, agriculture, horticulture, and floriculture. However, there may be direct-use and exclusive- or predominant-use requirements.

b. *Incorrect.* In states that exempt shipping containers and packaging materials, shipping aids must usually be incorporated into the packaging such that the shipping aid becomes a part of the product sold. This means the item must be within the product packaging or attached to the packaging such that it is an integral part of the product.

c. *Incorrect.* Whether the cost of materials and labor for the repair and maintenance of taxable shipping containers, packaging materials, and shipping aids is subject to tax depends on how the state treats labor for the repair of tangible personal property.

5. a. *Incorrect.* As a prerequisite for exempting pollution control equipment and facilities, some states require that the equipment or facility used in pollution control be certified by the state department of natural resources or similar agency in order for it to be eligible for the exemption.

b. Incorrect. States with certification requirements provide a form for taxpayers to file with the state department of natural resources or similar agency that describes the equipment or facility.

c. Incorrect. States with certification requirements provide a form for taxpayers to file with the state department of natural resources or similar agency that describes the intended use of the equipment or facility.

d. Correct. Once the pollution control equipment or facility has been certified, future purchases are exempt as provided under that particular state's statutes. Taxpayers in states with these requirements must retain their certification documents for future audit use.

6. a. Correct. If machinery is purchased and then modified for another use, some states tax only the materials used in the construction of the machinery, or the allocated costs from the accounting records. Most of those states include component parts used in the construction in the tax base as the cost of those components, rather than using their retail value.

b. Incorrect. Even if the taxpayer's employees are used in construction, allocated labor costs are usually not included in the value for use tax purposes.

c. Incorrect. Applied overhead charges are usually not included in the tax base. Therefore, it is usually not a good idea to rely only on the asset or accounting records to calculate the taxable value of self-constructed machinery.

7. a. Incorrect. Tangible personal property that becomes an ingredient or component part of tangible personal property that the manufacturer will offer for sale is usually exempt.

b. Incorrect. Some states allow an exemption for property that is used and either consumed or destroyed in the manufacturing process. The criteria for this exemption often differ from state to state.

c. Correct. A use tax is due when an item is purchased from a vendor that is not registered to collect sales tax, and the item is later used in a taxable manner.

8. True. Correct. Many states _do_ allow an exemption for temporarily stored purchases, but the exemption may be limited as to the type of items eligible, such as advertising materials or inventory.

False. Incorrect. Because there can be a substantial amount of tax involved for merely warehousing items in a convenient location temporarily, many states do allow an exemption for temporarily stored purchases.

9. a. Incorrect. When the printer is performing a service, it may or may not have to collect sales tax, depending on whether the state taxes the services the printer performs.

b. Incorrect. In many states, when the printer produces a printed document using materials provided by its customer, the printer is viewed as a service provider. This can cause a loss of the sales tax exemption for machinery and equipment and may affect the tax treatment of the supplies provided by the customer.

c. Correct. **When the printer performs a manufacturing function, it is selling tangible personal property and is required to collect sales tax on the transaction.**

10. a. Incorrect. Although many states impose sales and use tax on all charges prior to the passage of title from the vendor to the customer, many states do not require that separately stated freight and shipping charges be included in the tax base.

b. Correct. **Under this view of manufacturing, the conveyor would probably not qualify for exemption because it does not directly contribute to the change in the product being manufactured, but simply moves the product and raw materials from one point in the process to another.**

c. Incorrect. The broader view of manufacturing, known as the Integrated Plant Doctrine, does not view each manufacturing task separately but instead looks at whether the equipment is part of a synchronized system that is engaged in manufacturing.

d. Incorrect. To help reduce fuel and electricity costs and to even out the competition, many states have enacted exemptions for fuel and electricity consumed in during manufacturing.

MODULE 2 — CHAPTER 7

1. a. Incorrect. Sales of tangible personal property are generally subject to sales and use tax. However, the taxability of sales of services varies.

b. Incorrect. The first services to be taxed are those related to the sale of tangible personal property and, if a lump-sum charge is shown on the invoice, many states tax the entire amount.

c. Correct. **Professional services performed by doctors, accountants, and attorneys are generally not among specifically enumerated taxable services, and most states impose sales and use taxes only on specifically enumerated services.**

2. a. *Incorrect.* Most states consider the hiring of actors, as well as writing scripts and other costs incurred to create a commercial, as taxable for sales and use tax purposes.

b. *Correct.* Although most states take the position that costs associated with making a commercial are taxable for sales and use tax purposes, airtime charges generally are not taxed.

c. *Incorrect.* Most states include production and directing costs in the taxable measure of commercials.

3. a. *Incorrect.* Most state statutes do *not* impose sales tax on architectural services performed in connection with construction or improvements to real property.

b. *Incorrect.* Most states do *not* impose tax on blueprints provided as part of a design service. However, if additional copies are separately sold, the charges for these additional copies are subject to sales tax in most states.

c. *Correct.* A number of states impose sales tax on design services that relate to the placement of moveable partitions or equipment.

4. True. *Incorrect.* When a maintenance agreement distinguishes between support services and upgrades, the amount attributable to support services is generally *not* subject to sales tax.

False. *Correct.* If a maintenance agreement distinguishes between support services and upgrades, only the portion of the charge attributable to *upgrades* is generally taxable.

5. a. *Incorrect.* Canned software is usually treated as the sale of *tangible personal property*, whereas *custom* software is usually considered the *performance of a service*.

b. *Correct.* Virtually all the states treat the sale of canned software like the sale of tangible personal property.

c. *Incorrect.* Canned software with significant modifications is often *not* taxable if the consulting services provided are *more* than half the total sales price.

6. a. *Incorrect.* This statement is true. Some states tax electronic downloads but exempt Internet access, while other states tax Internet service providers.

b. *Incorrect.* This statement is true, regardless of whether the initial software is custom or canned.

c. *Correct.* Purchases over the Internet that are otherwise taxable are still subject to sales and use tax. If the vendor does not have nexus with the state, the purchaser *must* file a report and remit the applicable use tax to the state where the purchaser is located.

7. a. *Incorrect.* Production machinery maintenance contracts are *not* taxable in most states; however, nonproduction machinery maintenance contracts may be taxable in these states.

b. *Correct.* Computer software maintenance contracts are taxable in most states, as are computer hardware maintenance contracts.

c. *Incorrect.* Some, but not most, states do impose tax on computer software help lines. Those that exempt these charges probably do so because the fees for the help lines do not involve the transfer of property.

8. True. *Incorrect.* Either the customer or the repairperson will be subject to tax, depending on whether the state considers the repairperson to be the consumer of the parts.

False. *Correct.* If the state treats the repairperson as the consumer of the parts, tax would be paid by the repairperson on the cost of any parts used. If the repairperson is not considered the consumer, the entire billing would be taxable to the customer.

9. a. *Correct.* Many states consider a printer to be a service provider when it produces a printed document from materials provided by its customer.

b. *Incorrect.* Printers function as *manufacturers* when they produce printed documents from their own raw materials.

c. *Incorrect.* Whether the customer provides exact specifications for the work does *not* impact whether the printer is considered a service provider or manufacturer.

10. a. *Incorrect.* Although some states may extend the exemption to equipment used to maintain the tractor and trailer, most states do *not*.

b. *Correct.* Although some states require the carrier to offer its services to the general public in order to qualify for the exemption, most states do not require the carrier to actually transport goods for an unrelated party.

c. *Incorrect.* Most states allow the exemption to apply to repair or replacement parts for the tractor and trailer as well as to the tractor and trailer itself.

MODULE 2 — CHAPTER 8

1. a. *Incorrect.* If PPCs are taxed at the point of sale and are purchased in foreign countries by travelers to the United States to be used in the United States, they would *not* be subject to tax in the United States. This would be a *disadvantage* to states.

b. *Correct.* **If PPCs are taxed at the point of sale, sales tax can be imposed on the entire price of the PPC. Whereas, if the sales tax were imposed as the service is being *used*, any part of the PPC that is not used would *not* be subject to sales tax.**

c. *Incorrect.* This could create a problem for states if the PPC is taxed when purchased but is then used to purchase taxable and nontaxable goods.

2. a. *Correct.* **Supporting documentation is needed to have effective audit management. Destroying documentation could lead to a worse audit outcome.**

b. *Incorrect.* This *would* reduce potential audit exposure. The company could limit all purchases to either tax-exempt or taxable items, or limit purchases to a specific vendor who could be instructed to collect, or to not collect, tax on purchases.

c. *Incorrect.* Statements can be redesigned to show the needed information. This *would* reduce potential audit exposure.

3. a. *Incorrect.* This service is sourced to the *origination* point of the telecommunications signal as first identified by either the seller's telecommunications system or, if using a service provider, information received by the seller from this service provider.

b. *Correct.* **This service is sourced 50 percent in each level of jurisdiction in which the customer channel termination points are located.**

c. *Incorrect.* Internet access service is sourced to the customer's place of primary use.

4. True. *Incorrect.* Most states *tax* canned software. However, the definitions of canned and custom software vary significantly among the states.

False. *Correct.* **Most states tax canned software but not custom software.**

5. a. *Correct.* **As the use of downloads has expanded, many states have adopted the digital equivalent doctrine, which says that any downloaded item or transaction should be treated like its equivalent tangible item for sales tax purposes.**

b. *Incorrect.* There are still a number of states where licensing software electronically for use over a limited period of time is not taxable, but licensing software for use over a limited period of time *and* having it delivered by a tangible means *is* subject to tax.

c. *Incorrect.* Numerous states and the SST have enacted regulations or statutes that indicate that purchasing anything electronically is *the same as* purchasing it as a tangible item.

Index

D

E

F

T

MULTISTATE CORPORATE TAX COURSE (2012 EDITION)

CPE Quizzer Instructions

The CPE Quizzer is divided into two Modules. There is a processing fee for each Quizzer Module submitted for grading. Successful completion of Module 1 is recommended for **7 CPE Credits.*** Successful completion of Module 2 is recommended for **8 CPE Credits.*** You can complete and submit one Module at a time or all Modules at once for a total of **15 CPE Credits.***

To obtain CPE credit, return your completed Answer Sheet for each Quizzer Module to **CCH Continuing Education Department, 4025 W. Peterson Ave., Chicago, IL 60646**, or fax it to (773) 866-3084. Each Quizzer Answer Sheet will be graded and a CPE Certificate of Completion awarded for achieving a grade of 70 percent or greater. The Quizzer Answer Sheets are located after the Quizzer questions for this Course.

Express Grading: Processing time for your Answer Sheet is generally 8-12 business days. If you are trying to meet a reporting deadline, our Express Grading Service is available for an additional $19 per Module. To use this service, please check the "Express Grading" box on your Answer Sheet and provide your CCH account or credit card number **and your fax number.** CCH will fax your results and a Certificate of Completion (upon achieving a passing grade) to you by 5:00 p.m. the business day following our receipt of your Answer Sheet. **If you mail your Answer Sheet for Express Grading, please write "ATTN: CPE OVERNIGHT" on the envelope.** NOTE: CCH will not Federal Express Quizzer results under any circumstances.

NEW ONLINE GRADING gives you immediate 24/7 grading with instant results and no Express Grading Fee.

The **CCH Testing Center** website gives you and others in your firm easy, free access to CCH print Courses and allows you to complete your CPE Quizzers online for immediate results. Plus, the **My Courses** feature provides convenient storage for your CPE Course Certificates and completed Quizzers.

Go to **www.CCHGroup.com/TestingCenter** to complete your Quizzer online.

---

* Recommended CPE credit is based on a 50-minute hour. Participants earning credits for states that require self-study to be based on a 100-minute hour will receive ½ the CPE credits for successful completion of this course. Because CPE requirements vary from state to state and among different licensing agencies, please contact your CPE governing body for information on your CPE requirements and the applicability of a particular course for your requirements.

Date of Completion: The date of completion on your Certificate will be the date that you put on your Answer Sheet. However, you must submit your Answer Sheet to CCH for grading within two weeks of completing it.

Expiration Date: December 31, 2012

Evaluation: To help us provide you with the best possible products, please take a moment to fill out the Course Evaluation located at the back of this Course and return it with your Quizzer Answer Sheets.

CCH is registered with the National Association of State Boards of Accountancy (NASBA) as a sponsor of continuing professional education on the National Registry of CPE Sponsors. State boards of accountancy have final authority on the acceptance of individual courses for CPE credit. Complaints regarding registered sponsors may be addressed to the National Registry of CPE Sponsors, 150 Fourth Avenue North, Suite 700, Nashville, TN 37219-2417. Web site: www. nasba.org.

CCH is registered with the National Association of State Boards of Accountancy (NASBA) as a Quality Assurance Service (QAS) sponsor of continuing professional education. State boards of accountancy have final authority on the acceptance of individual courses for CPE credit. Complaints regarding registered sponsors may be addressed to NASBA, 150 Fourth Avenue North, Suite 700, Nashville, TN 37219-2417. Web site: www.nasba.org.

CCH has been approved by the California Tax Education Council to offer courses that provide federal and state credit towards the annual "continuing education" requirement imposed by the State of California. A listing of additional requirements to register as a tax preparer may be obtained by contacting CTEC at P.O. Box 2890, Sacramento, CA, 95812-2890, toll-free by phone at (877) 850-2832, or on the Internet at www.ctec.org.

Processing Fee:
$84.00 for Module 1
$96.00 for Module 2
$180.00 for all Modules

Recommended CPE:
7 hours for Module 1
8 hours for Module 2
15 hours for all Modules

CTEC Course Number:
1075-CE-9814 for Module 1
1075-CE-9820 for Module 2

CTEC Federal Hours:
N/A hours for Module 1
N/A hours for Module 2
N/A hours for all Modules

CTEC California Hours:
3 hours for Module 1
4 hours for Module 2
7 hours for all Modules

One **complimentary copy** of this Course is provided with certain CCH publications. Additional copies of this Course may be ordered for $39.00 each by calling 1-800-248-3248 (ask for product **0-4459-500**).

MULTISTATE CORPORATE TAX COURSE (2012 EDITION)

Quizzer Questions: Module 1

1. Which of the following statements is true concerning Public Law 86-272?

    a. It is a federal law enacted in 1959.
    b. It applies to the imposition of any type of state tax.
    c. It applies to sales of services.
    d. None of the above

2. Which of the following is a limitation of Public Law 86-272?

    a. It does not apply to taxes on net income.
    b. It does not apply to sales of tangible personal property.
    c. It does not apply to solicitation of orders.
    d. It does not apply to sales and use taxes.

3. Income arising from transactions and activity in the regular course of the taxpayer's trade or business comprises the _____ test in determining whether an item of income is business or nonbusiness.

    a. classification
    b. functional
    c. transactional
    d. None of the above

4. Approximately how many states use a single-sales-factor apportionment formula?

    a. 0
    b. 12
    c. 30
    d. 47

5. Which of the following is **not** an advantage of filing a consolidated return?

   a. Ability to offset the losses of one affiliate against the profits of other affiliates
   b. Allows a taxpayer to create legal structures to shift income from affiliates in high-tax states to affiliates in low-tax states
   c. Deferral of gains on intercompany transactions
   d. Use of credits that would otherwise be denied because of a lack of income

6. Which judicial test for determining the existence of a unitary business specifically looks to functional integration, centralization of management, and economies of scale?

   a. Three-unities test
   b. Contribution or dependency test
   c. Flow-of-value test
   d. Factors-of-profitability test

7. To acquire the right to apportion its income, the corporation generally must have nexus in at least one state other than its state of domicile. For purposes of computing tax in the state of domicile, whether a corporation's activities or contacts in another state are considered adequate to justify apportionment is generally determined by:

   a. Reference to the tax laws of the domicile state
   b. Reference to the tax laws of states other than the domicile state
   c. Reference to the tax laws of all states
   d. None of the above

8. Creating nexus in another state would be detrimental in which of the following situations?

   a. The corporation wants to have the right to apportion its income.
   b. The corporation makes significant sales into that state and the state has a high tax rate.
   c. The corporation wants to avoid the application of a sales throwback rule.

9. Although there is diversity among the states' apportionment formulas, a corporation can **never** have more than 100 percent of its income subject to state taxation. **True or False?**

10. Most states that impose corporate income taxes tie the computation of taxable income directly to a corporation's federal tax return. **True or False?**

11. Nexus created by the licensing of trademarks for use within the state by out-of-state affiliated companies that have no property or payroll in the state is referred to as:

    a. Agency nexus
    b. Affiliate nexus
    c. Economic nexus
    d. Physical presence nexus

12. Which of the following states imposes a "margin tax" in lieu of a corporate net income tax?

    a. Pennsylvania
    b. Texas
    c. Utah
    d. West Virginia

13. A corporation sells a service. Ten percent of the income-producing activity is performed in State A, 15 percent in State B, and 75 percent in State C. Under the cost of performance rule in UDITPA §17(b), how is the sale allocated?

    a. 100 percent to State C
    b. 83 percent to State A and 17 percent to State B
    c. 10 percent to State A, 15 percent to State B, and 75 percent to State C
    d. 100 percent to the state in which the benefit of the service is received

14. A corporation sells a service. Ten percent of the income-producing activity is performed in State A, 15 percent in State B, and 75 percent in State C. Under the market-based approach, how is the sale allocated?

    a. 100 percent to State C
    b. 83 percent to State A and 17 percent to State B
    c. 10 percent to State A, 15 percent to State B, and 75 percent to State C
    d. 100 percent to the state in which the benefit of the service is received

15. All states conform to the federal tax treatment of a partnership as a pass-through entity which is **not** subject to any entity-level taxes. **True or False?**

16. Which of the following would be a reason for a difference between a state and federal NOL deduction?

    a. The state allows a carryback of two years.

    b. The state allows a carryforward of 20 years.

    c. The state requires the taxpayer to have nexus in the year the NOL is created.

    d. None of the above

17. Which of the following statements is **not** true?

    a. Every state with an income tax requires addition and subtraction modifications, and these modifications can cause a state NOL to differ from the federal NOL.

    b. Even if there is a major change in a corporation's state apportionment percentage between the year of the loss and the carryover year, the NOL deduction will be the same regardless of whether the state uses the pre-apportionment or post-apportionment method for determining the deduction.

    c. A corporation generally must be subject to tax and file a state tax return in the year of the loss to create a state NOL carryforward deduction.

    d. Some states impose percentage or flat dollar limitations on NOL carryovers.

18. Code Sec. 381 does **not** apply to which of the following transactions?

    a. Type A reorganizations

    b. Type B reorganizations

    c. Type C reorganizations

    d. Type F reorganizations

19. Which of the following statements is true?

    a. States that use Form 1120, Line 30, as the starting point in determining state taxable income allow the same NOL treatment for state and federal tax purposes, unless the state requires a modification for NOLs.

    b. Most states do not permit NOL deductions.

    c. The NOL deduction in a state consolidated return is always identical to the NOL deduction in a federal consolidated return.

    d. None of the above

20. Many states allow NOL carryforwards, but none allow NOL carrybacks, even though they are allowed for federal purposes. ***True or False?***

21. Which of the following is true concerning income tax treaties?

   a. The United States has bilateral income tax treaties with only two countries, Canada and Mexico.

   b. A U.S. permanent establishment exists only if the foreign corporation has at least 10 employees within the United States.

   c. Under a permanent establishment provision, the United States can tax the business profits of a foreign corporation that is a resident of the treaty country, even if the foreign corporation does not have a permanent establishment in the United States.

   d. Permanent establishment provisions generally are not binding for state tax purposes.

22. If a foreign corporation leases warehouse space in a state and uses it solely to store and deliver its merchandise to U.S. customers, this would generally be sufficient to create:

   a. A permanent establishment in the United States under an income tax treaty

   b. State tax nexus

   c. Both a permanent establishment and state tax nexus

   d. Neither a permanent establishment nor state tax nexus

23. Which of the following in-state activities would be protected from state income tax nexus by Public Law 86-272?

   a. An employee salesperson soliciting sales of tangible personal property

   b. An employee salesperson soliciting sales of services

   c. An employee salesperson soliciting sales of intangible property

   d. Both a and b

24. The ***Quill*** physical presence test for constitutional nexus definitely applies to which types of state taxes?

   a. Both sales and use taxes and income taxes

   b. Neither sales and use taxes nor income taxes

   c. Sales and use taxes

   d. Income taxes

25. Which of the following in-state activities conducted by an independent contractor is **not** protected from state income tax nexus by Public Law 86-272?

    a. Maintaining an office
    b. Making sales
    c. Performing repair services on the products it sells
    d. Soliciting sales

26. In many states, an addition modification is required for the excess of the federal Code Sec. 179 asset expensing amount over the maximum state amount. **True or False?**

27. Which of the following is a common state addition modification to federal taxable income?

    a. State dividends-received deduction
    b. Expenses related to federal credits
    c. Federal bonus depreciation
    d. None of the above

28. Which of the following is a common state subtraction modification to federal taxable income?

    a. Interest income on state debt obligations
    b. Related party interest expenses
    c. Interest income on federal debt obligations
    d. None of the above

29. A difference between a corporation's federal NOL deduction and state NOL deduction may arise due to all of the following reasons **except:**

    a. Differences in group filing methods
    b. State restrictions on the amount of NOL carryover allowed
    c. State disallowance of NOL carrybacks
    d. States having a 20-year NOL carryforward period

30. Which of the following statements regarding state treatment of dividends is **not** true?

    a. Most states allow some type of dividends received deduction.

    b. No state provides a subtraction modification for dividends received from a foreign corporation.

    c. Most states provide a subtraction modification for a Subpart F inclusion.

    d. If the starting point for computing state taxable income is Line 30 of the federal return, the state DRD conforms to the federal DRD unless an additional modification is required.

31. Which of the following is generally allowed in computing a corporation's state income tax liability?

    a. A deduction for state income taxes

    b. A credit for foreign income taxes

    c. A credit for federal income taxes

    d. None of the above

32. Which of the following are **not** expenses that are commonly targeted by state related party expense addback provisions?

    a. Interest expenses

    b. Royalty expenses

    c. Compensation expenses

    d. Licensing fees

33. Which of the following is a common exception to state related party expense addback provisions?

    a. The addback adjustment produces a reasonable result.

    b. The payee pays the amount to another related person.

    c. The payee's corresponding income is not subject to tax in another state or country.

    d. The state and the taxpayer agree to an alternative adjustment.

34. Because states do **not** permit a Code Sec. 902 deemed paid foreign tax credit, a subtraction modification is generally provided for:

    a. Code Sec. 179 asset expensing

    b. Code Sec. 78 gross-up income

    c. Federal bonus depreciation

    d. Code Sec. 199 domestic production activities deduction

35. Even if there is a major change in a corporation's state apportionment percentage between the year that an NOL is incurred and the year in which the corresponding NOL carryforward deduction is claimed, the NOL deduction is the same regardless of whether the state uses the pre-apportionment or post-apportionment method. **True or False?**

Quizzer Questions: Module 2

36. Which of the following is true?

    a. Public Law 86-272 applies only to a sales or use tax.

    b. Public Law 86-272 protects only sales of services.

    c. For businesses that send employees into other states to sell tangible personal property, Public Law 86-272 applies only if those employees limit their in-state activities to the solicitation of orders that are approved out-of-state and are filled by a shipment or delivery from a point outside the state.

    d. None of the above

37. Which of the following activities, if **not** *de minimis*, would create nexus with a state for income tax purposes?

    a. Installation

    b. Solicitation of orders

    c. Recruiting and training sales personnel

38. Which of the following activities is considered "protected" under a statement adopted by the MTC?

    a. Maintaining a display room for two weeks at a location in the state

    b. Providing maintenance in the state for previously sold property

    c. A salesperson in the state conducting order approval

39. Which of the following states have enacted affiliate nexus statutes?

    a. Alabama

    b. Arkansas

    c. Minnesota

    d. All of the above

40. In **Share International Inc.,** the Florida Supreme Court determined that the taxpayer's attendance at annual seminars in Florida, each lasting three days, was sufficient activity to create nexus for sales and use tax purposes. **True or False?**

41. In which case did a state Supreme Court rule that the activity of making deliveries in company-owned trucks is protected under Public Law 86-272?

    a. *National Private Truck Council*
    b. *Asher, Inc.*
    c. *Geoffrey, Inc.*
    d. *Bandag Licensing Corp.*

42. Which of the following is *not* a true statement?

    a. Texas has a statute that requires a corporation to file a franchise tax return and pay tax if the corporation has the authority to do business in the state.
    b. Treaty permanent establishment provisions are binding for state nexus purposes.
    c. California has a statute that provides a nexus exemption in certain situations where an employee attends an in-state trade show or convention.
    d. It is possible for a foreign corporation to have nexus for state tax purposes but not federal income tax purposes.

43. Which of the following statements is *not* true regarding leased property?

    a. A factor that helps to support nexus is the negotiation of the lease agreement in the state.
    b. In the case of immobile property, the lessor typically is considered to have established nexus with each state where the leased property is located.
    c. In the case of leased property that is immobile, the creation of nexus generally is difficult to identify.
    d. A factor that helps to support nexus is the receipt of the rental payment in the state.

44. In which case did the Massachusetts Supreme Judicial Court hold that various warranty claims activities performed in the state created nexus?

    a. *Tyson Foods*
    b. *Dell Catalog Sales*
    c. *Alcoa Building Products*
    d. *Amgen*

45. Which of the following activities is considered "unprotected" under a statement adopted by the MTC?

    a. Providing an automobile to a salesperson for use in conducting protected activities

    b. Providing a personal computer for use in conducting protected activities

    c. Maintaining a display room for two weeks at one location within the state

    d. Repossessing property

46. In which of the following situations would a lessor be most likely to have nexus with a state where the leased property is used?

    a. Lease of mobile property that landed in the state on one occasion

    b. Lease of mobile property that made a trip through the state

    c. Execution of the lease agreement in the state

47. Which of the following is a potential solution for the problems in the state tax arena because of electronic commerce?

    a. Federal legislation

    b. State legislation

    c. Local legislation

48. Which of the following is an in-state activity by independent contractors that is **not** protected by Public Law 86-272?

    a. Soliciting sales

    b. Replacing damaged property

    c. Making sales

    d. Maintaining an office

49. For nexus purposes, the U.S. Supreme Court has held that there is a critical distinction between the duties of an employee and an agent engaging in solicitation. **_True or False?_**

50. An economic nexus standard is broader than a physical presence standard. **_True or False?_**

51. In most jurisdictions, the key to understanding the treatment of a construction contractor is to understand:

   a. Whether the contractor is a retailer or consumer
   b. The distinction made between real and tangible personal property
   c. The treatment of labor associated with real and tangible personal property
   d. The type of contract involved

52. Which of the following would **not** be exempt from sales and use tax in most states?

   a. The cost of materials incorporated into a contractor's real estate repair project
   b. Labor performed by a contractor to repair real estate
   c. Parts consumed in the repair of tangible personal property by a contractor
   d. Labor performed by a contractor to repair tangible personal property for a tax-exempt customer

53. Which of the following is a requirement most states impose for production machinery equipment to be exempt from sales tax?

   a. It must be used indirectly in the manufacturing process.
   b. It must be used directly in the manufacturing process, but often with a *de minimis* exception.
   c. It must be used at least 40 percent in the manufacturing process.
   d. It must be used at least 25 percent in the manufacturing process.

54. Which of the following statements is **not** true?

   a. Many states have special provisions exempting from sales tax the sale of equipment and materials to taxpayers engaged in farming.
   b. Many states impose tax on returnable shipping containers but not nonreturnable shipping containers.
   c. Generally, production machinery and equipment are exempt from tax if certain requirements are met.
   d. Sales to manufacturers and processors are usually subject to sales tax if the property purchased becomes or is made a part of a product that is to be sold by the manufacturer.

55. Manufacturing activities that generally fall within a state's manufacturing or processing exemption and are *not* considered marginal activities include:

    a. Shipping and receiving
    b. Research and development
    c. Machine handling in the step-by-step process

56. In states that provide a manufacturing exemption, equipment and tools used to manufacture self-constructed production equipment:

    a. Are covered by the state's manufacturing exemption
    b. Are not covered by the state's manufacturing exemption
    c. May or may not be covered by the state's manufacturing exemption
    d. Are covered under the state's use-on-use exemption that is part of every state's manufacturing machinery and equipment exemption

57. In which of the following situations would most states most likely impose sales and use tax on freight and shipping charges?

    a. The billing is for shipping and handling.
    b. The freight and shipping charges are separately stated.
    c. The freight or shipping charge is billed by the freight company directly to the purchaser.

58. Which one of the following statements is *not* true?

    a. States offering production machinery exemptions often include printers in their definition of manufacturers qualifying for the exemption.
    b. When the printer acts as a manufacturer, it is selling tangible personal property and is never required to collect sales tax on the transaction.
    c. Printers function as manufacturers when they produce a printed document from raw materials.
    d. When the printer acts as a service provider, it may or may not have an obligation to collect the tax, depending on whether the state taxes the services performed by the printer.

59. Which of the following statements is true?

    a. Property that is used and either consumed or destroyed in the manufacturing process is never exempt.

    b. Applied overhead charges are ordinarily included in the tax base for machinery that is purchased and modified for another use.

    c. Whether the cost of materials for the repair and maintenance of taxable shipping containers is subject to tax is unrelated to the treatment of labor to repair tangible personal property.

    d. None of the above

60. Which of the following is true concerning the Integrated Plant Doctrine?

    a. Under the doctrine, a conveyer that moves work-in-process from one workstation to another within the plant would probably not qualify for an exemption.

    b. It requires that manufacturing machinery come into direct contact with the product being manufactured and/or contribute to the transformation in some direct way to qualify for any exemption.

    c. Each manufacturing task is considered part of a synchronized system engaged in manufacturing.

    d. It is considered a narrow view of manufacturing.

61. According to the *true object* test, which of the following would be considered a sale of *tangible personal property*?

    a. A will prepared by an attorney

    b. Canned computer software with training included

    c. Custom software

    d. None of the above

62. When determining whether a *mixed transaction* is subject to sales and use tax, which of the following generally should **not** be a consideration?

    a. Whether the vendor is registered to collect sales tax

    b. Whether there are inconsequential elements

    c. What the true object is

    d. The state's cases and rulings

63. Which of the following statements is true?

    a. Professional services are usually specifically enumerated services.

    b. Most states impose sales tax on architectural services.

    c. Most states distinguish between the sale of a digital product and the sale of other tangible personal property.

    d. Most states do *not* impose sales tax on advertising services such as writing copy and creating jingles.

64. Which of the following is *not* helpful in making a distinction between canned software and custom software?

    a. The total cost of the software

    b. The extent of pre-sale consultation

    c. How much support is provided for the installation and maintenance of the software

    d. None of the above

65. Which one of the following statements is true regarding sales and use taxability?

    a. Training associated with taxable canned software is *always* taxable, even if it is separately stated on the invoice.

    b. Software training is *never* taxable.

    c. Training associated with custom software is generally *not* taxable if custom software is *not* taxable.

    d. None of the above

66. When a repairperson bills a customer for parts and labor under a maintenance contract with a *lump-sum* charge, which of the following is true?

    a. No sales or use tax is due.

    b. If the state treats the *customer* as consumer of the parts, the *repairperson* is taxed on the cost of the parts.

    c. If the state treats the *repairperson* as consumer of the parts, the *repairperson* is taxed on the cost of the parts.

    d. If the state treats the *repairperson* as consumer of the parts, the *customer* is taxed on the cost of the parts.

67. Most states that allow a sales and use tax exemption to carriers extend the exemption to which of the following purchases?

    a. Equipment used to repair the tractor and trailer
    b. Replacement parts for the tractor and trailer
    c. Office equipment

68. Which of the following statements is true?

    a. Printers function as *service providers* when they produce a printed document from their own raw materials.
    b. When printers function as *manufacturers*, they are not required to collect sales tax on the transaction.
    c. Printers are *always* considered manufacturers and *not* service providers.
    d. None of the above

69. Which of the following statements is true concerning software consulting services?

    a. If a vendor's charges for providing computer software consulting services are not subject to a state's sales and use taxes and the vendor provides an explanatory report with the package, the vendor is also not required to pay sales and use taxes on its cost of materials used to transmit the report.
    b. If a state imposes a sales and use tax on consulting services rendered, and the services include an explanatory report with the package, the vendor's purchases of the paper used to prepare the report may be exempt as a purchase for resale.
    c. In most of the states that do *not* impose a tax on computer-related services, charges for nontaxable services do not have to be separately stated to protect their nontaxable status when the charges are concurrent with retail sales of taxable hardware or software.
    d. None of the above

70. The majority of states do **not** impose sales and use taxes on which of the following?

    a. Computer hardware maintenance contracts
    b. Computer software maintenance contracts
    c. Production machinery maintenance contracts
    d. Nonproduction machinery maintenance contracts

71. Which one of the following statements is **not** true?

    a. A disadvantage of taxing PPCs at the point of sale is the difficulty of administration for retailers and states.

    b. More than a dozen states have recently changed their laws to tax prepaid phone cards at the point of sale.

    c. Absent specific state legislation, most state laws would *not* impose sales and use tax on the sale of prepaid phone cards because the *true object* of the sale is future long-distance service.

    d. A disadvantage of taxing PPCs at the point of sale is the possible difficulties encountered when using smart cards.

72. Possible *problems* related to the use of procurement cards include all of the following **except:**

    a. Difficulty in determining when a sale occurs

    b. Receiving documentation too late to timely pay tax

    c. Overpaying use tax to avoid underpayments

    d. Increased administrative costs

73. Which of the following statements is true?

    a. The definition of *telecommunications services* is uniform among the states.

    b. The Internet Tax Freedom Act does *not* forbid sales tax in states that imposed tax on Internet access charges before the Act became law.

    c. The Streamlined Sales Tax agreement does not include definitions for sourcing telecommunication services.

    d. None of the above

74. According to the **Menasha Corp.** decision, which of the following is true in determining whether software is *canned* or *custom*?

    a. Programs requiring significant presale consultation and analysis of the user's needs are custom programs.

    b. Custom programs include basic operational programs.

    c. Any program costing $20,000 or less is a canned program.

    d. None of the above

75. Which of the following is true concerning cloud computing?

    a. If it is taxable as a service, it is easier to determine taxability issues than if it is taxed as tangible personal property.

    b. It has many benefits but increases costs for businesses.

    c. Most states have determined that it should be taxed as tangible personal property for sales tax purposes.

    d. None of the above

MULTISTATE CORPORATE TAX COURSE (2012 EDITION)   (0764-3)

Module 1: Answer Sheet

NAME _____

COMPANY NAME _____

STREET _____

CITY, STATE, & ZIP CODE _____

BUSINESS PHONE NUMBER _____

E-MAIL ADDRESS _____

DATE OF COMPLETION _____

CRTP ID (for CTEC Credit only) _____ (CTEC Course # 1075-CE-9814)

On the next page, please answer the Multiple Choice questions by indicating the appropriate letter next to the corresponding number. Please answer the True/False questions by marking "T" or "F" next to the corresponding number.

A $84.00 processing fee will be charged for each user submitting Module 1 for grading.

Please remove both pages of the Answer Sheet from this book and return them with your completed Evaluation Form to CCH at the address below. You may also fax your Answer Sheet to CCH at 773-866-3084.

You may also go to **www.CCHGroup.com/TestingCenter** to complete your Quizzer online.

METHOD OF PAYMENT:

☐ Check Enclosed ☐ Visa ☐ Master Card ☐ AmEx

☐ Discover ☐ CCH Account* _____

Card No. _____ Exp. Date _____

Signature _____

* Must provide CCH account number for this payment option

EXPRESS GRADING: Please fax my Course results to me by 5:00 p.m. the business day following your receipt of this Answer Sheet. By checking this box I authorize CCH to charge $19.00 for this service.

☐ Express Grading $19.00   Fax No. _____

Mail or fax to:
CCH Continuing Education Department
4025 W. Peterson Ave.
Chicago, IL 60646-6085
1-800-248-3248
Fax: 773-866-3084

PAGE 1 OF 2

MULTISTATE CORPORATE TAX COURSE (2012 EDITION)   (0764-3)

Module 1: Answer Sheet

Please answer the Multiple Choice questions by indicating the appropriate letter next to the corresponding number. Please answer the True/False questions by marking "T" or "F" next to the corresponding number.

1. ___	10. ___	19. ___	28. ___
2. ___	11. ___	20. ___	29. ___
3. ___	12. ___	21. ___	30. ___
4. ___	13. ___	22. ___	31. ___
5. ___	14. ___	23. ___	32. ___
6. ___	15. ___	24. ___	33. ___
7. ___	16. ___	25. ___	34. ___
8. ___	17. ___	26. ___	35. ___
9. ___	18. ___	27. ___	

Please complete the Evaluation Form (located after the Module 2 Answer Sheet) and return it with this Quizzer Answer Sheet to CCH at the address on the previous page. Thank you.

MULTISTATE CORPORATE TAX COURSE (2012 EDITION)   (0765-3)

Module 2: Answer Sheet

NAME _____

COMPANY NAME _____

STREET _____

CITY, STATE, & ZIP CODE _____

BUSINESS PHONE NUMBER _____

E-MAIL ADDRESS _____

DATE OF COMPLETION _____

CRTP ID (for CTEC Credit only) _____ (CTEC Course # 1075-CE-9820)

On the next page, please answer the Multiple Choice questions by indicating the appropriate letter next to the corresponding number. Please answer the True/False questions by marking "T" or "F" next to the corresponding number.

A $96.00 processing fee will be charged for each user submitting Module 2 for grading.

Please remove both pages of the Answer Sheet from this book and return them with your completed Evaluation Form to CCH at the address below. You may also fax your Answer Sheet to CCH at 773-866-3084.

You may also go to **www.CCHGroup.com/TestingCenter** to complete your exam online.

METHOD OF PAYMENT:

☐ Check Enclosed   ☐ Visa   ☐ Master Card   ☐ AmEx

☐ Discover   ☐ CCH Account* _____

Card No. _____ Exp. Date _____

Signature _____

* Must provide CCH account number for this payment option

EXPRESS GRADING: Please fax my Course results to me by 5:00 p.m. the business day following your receipt of this Answer Sheet. By checking this box I authorize CCH to charge $19.00 for this service.

☐ Express Grading $19.00   Fax No. _____

Mail or fax to:
CCH Continuing Education Department
4025 W. Peterson Ave.
Chicago, IL 60646-6085
1-800-248-3248
Fax: 773-866-3084

CCH
a Wolters Kluwer business

PAGE 1 OF 2

MULTISTATE CORPORATE TAX COURSE (2012 EDITION)   (0765-3)

Module 2: Answer Sheet

Please answer the Multiple Choice questions by indicating the appropriate letter next to the corresponding number. Please answer the True/False questions by marking "T" or "F" next to the corresponding number.

36. ____	46. ____	56. ____	66. ____
37. ____	47. ____	57. ____	67. ____
38. ____	48. ____	58. ____	68. ____
39. ____	49. ____	59. ____	69. ____
40. ____	50. ____	60. ____	70. ____
41. ____	51. ____	61. ____	71. ____
42. ____	52. ____	62. ____	72. ____
43. ____	53. ____	63. ____	73. ____
44. ____	54. ____	64. ____	74. ____
45. ____	55. ____	65. ____	75. ____

Please complete the Evaluation Form (located after the Module 2 Answer Sheet) and return it with this Quizzer Answer Sheet to CCH at the address on the previous page. Thank you.

MULTISTATE CORPORATE TAX COURSE (2012 EDITION)   (4459-5)

Evaluation Form

Please take a few moments to fill out and mail or fax this evaluation to CCH so that we can better provide you with the type of self-study programs you want and need. Thank you.

About This Program

1. Please circle the number that best reflects the extent of your agreement with the following statements:

	Strongly Agree			Strongly Disagree
a. The Course objectives were met.	5	4	3	2	1
b. This Course was comprehensive and organized.	5	4	3	2	1
c. The content was current and technically accurate.	5	4	3	2	1
d. This Course was timely and relevant.	5	4	3	2	1
e. The prerequisite requirements were appropriate.	5	4	3	2	1
f. This Course was a valuable learning experience.	5	4	3	2	1
g. The Course completion time was appropriate.	5	4	3	2	1

2. This Course was most valuable to me because of:

    ____ Continuing Education credit   ____ Convenience of format
    ____ Relevance to my practice/   ____ Timeliness of subject matter
    employment   ____ Reputation of author
    ____ Price
    ____ Other (please specify) _____

3. How long did it take to complete this Course? (Please include the total time spent reading or studying reference materials and completing CPE Quizzer).

    Module 1 ____   Module 2 ____

4. What do you consider to be the strong points of this Course?

5. What improvements can we make to this Course?

MULTISTATE CORPORATE TAX COURSE (2012 EDITION)   (4459-5)

Evaluation Form *cont'd*

General Interests

1. Preferred method of self-study instruction:
    _____ Text   _____ Audio   _____ Computer-based/Multimedia   _____ Video

2. What specific topics would you like CCH to develop as self-study CPE programs? _____

    _____

    _____

    _____

3. Please list other topics of interest to you _____

    _____

    _____

About You

1. Your profession:

    _____ CPA   _____ Enrolled Agent
    _____ Attorney   _____ Tax Preparer
    _____ Financial Planner   _____ Other (please specify)

    _____

2. Your employment:

    _____ Self-employed   _____ Public Accounting Firm
    _____ Service Industry   _____ Non-Service Industry
    _____ Banking/Finance   _____ Government
    _____ Education   _____ Other _____

3. Size of firm/corporation:

    _____ 1   _____ 2-5   _____ 6-10   _____ 11-20   _____ 21-50   _____ 51+

4. Your Name_____

    Firm/Company Name _____

    Address _____

    City, State, Zip Code _____

    E-mail Address _____

THANK YOU FOR TAKING THE TIME TO COMPLETE THIS SURVEY!

NOTES

NOTES

NOTES

NOTES

NOTES

NOTES

NOTES

NOTES